T0315132

IT'S NOT COMPLICATED

RICK NASON

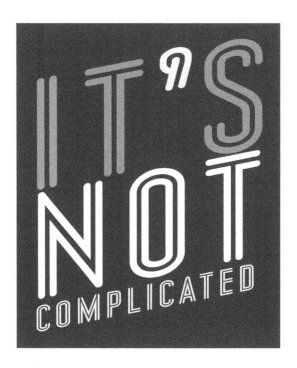

The Art and Science of
Complexity in Business

UNIVERSITY OF TORONTO PRESS
Toronto Buffalo London

© University of Toronto Press 2017
Rotman-UTP Publishing
Toronto Buffalo London
www.utppublishing.com

ISBN 978-1-4426-4487-8

_____

Library and Archives Canada Cataloguing in Publication

Nason, Rick, 1962–, author
It's not complicated: the art and science of complexity in business /
Rick Nason.

Includes bibliographical references and index.
ISBN 978-1-4426-4487-8 (cloth)

1. Industrial management.   2. Problem solving.   I. Title.

HD30.29.N37 2017   658.4'03   C2017-901247-9

_____

University of Toronto Press acknowledges the financial assistance to its
publishing program of the Canada Council for the Arts and the Ontario
Arts Council, an agency of the Government of Ontario.

Canada Council   Conseil des Arts
for the Arts   du Canada

ONTARIO ARTS COUNCIL
CONSEIL DES ARTS DE L'ONTARIO
an Ontario government agency
un organisme du gouvernement de l'Ontario

Funded by the   Financé par le
Government   gouvernement   **Canada**
of Canada   du Canada

To my wife, Lori, and my daughters, Sarah and Meaghan, who daily demonstrate to me the wonders of complexity

CONTENTS

PREFACE

Albert Einstein was once asked how he happened to develop relativity. His response was that he simply "questioned an axiom." An axiom is something that is considered to be so obviously true as to be unquestionable. I do not want to compare myself to Einstein, but I do want to question an axiom – the axiom that implicitly claims that "business is complicated."

This is a book that explains the difference between complicated and complex issues as a scientist would explain the difference between "complicated" and "complex." The difference is intuitive and easy to understand but also subtle and profound. It is a difference that needs to be consciously appreciated and understood by business managers.

Questioning the basic but never-stated axiom of "business is complicated" is the purpose of the book that you hold in your hands (or your electronic reader). You may not think of "business is complicated" as an axiom, much less an axiom worth writing a book about. However, I will argue that in our increasingly connected business world, understanding the difference between "complicated" and "complex" is an imperative for an engaged and enlightened manager.

In questioning the "business is complicated" axiom, this book develops a new way to think about business problems and issues. It provides a practical and common-sense introduction to the science of complexity and its application to business, and opens a conversation about this fascinating and paradigm-shifting way of thinking about managerial problems and how they might be better dealt with. This book is intended to be a practical manager's guide to complexity, including how complexity differs from the current paradigm of complicated thinking and how to deal effectively with complex issues.

This book does not go into the grand secrets of the universe, as Einstein's writings on relativity did. Also, this book most certainly does not require an understanding of any advanced mathematics, unlike Einstein's theories. Nor does it require a wild and overactive imagination or the leaps of creativity that Einstein's ideas brought to physics. All it requires is a purposeful curiosity and an open mind, both about business concepts and about how business leaders at all levels can make their organizations more efficient, agile, and better able to compete in an increasingly complex world.

In the current context of economic turmoil, financial institution risk, workplace stress, demographic change, and time pressures, why would anyone want to write a book about complexity? Isn't the whole goal of the business manager to reduce complexity? Before answering that question it is necessary to take a step back and briefly explain what complexity is. First off, "complex" and "complicated" are not the same, although in common usage the two words are generally considered to be synonyms. To a scientist – a biologist, for example – a complicated issue is one where the components can be separated and dealt with in a systematic and logical way that relies on a set of static rules or algorithms, such as the laws of physics. A complex issue is one where one cannot separate out the parts and for which there are no rules, algorithms, or natural laws such as are found in physics. A complicated situation is one where there is order, as well as cause-and-effect relationships that give one the ability to reproduce results. Things that are complex have no such degree of order, control, or predictability. An orientation that acknowledges complexity is one that recognizes that the whole is often much greater than and, more importantly, quite different from the sum of the parts. Complexity explicitly accounts for the interconnectedness of things and how that interconnectedness leads to fascinating characteristics such as adaptive behavior and leaderless emergence.

As this book explains, complexity, or more accurately complexity science, is a way of examining how people and events interact and evolve. That makes it sound like a very philosophical and abstract concept, but it is a practical framework that has allowed tremendous advances in a diverse number of fields that span ecology, medicine, and social engineering, to name only a few. Engineers, scientists, and ecologists have been thinking in terms of complexity for approximately fifty years, and it is time that the business community considered some of the valuable and interesting lessons the field has to offer.

In a modern business context, complexity appears in many places. Cyber-security, financial markets, economic turmoil, demographic shifts, social media activity, politics, and marketing are just a small sample of business-related areas where complexity plays a major role. Complexity is also present in the daily activities of managers as they manage their team, their clients, and even themselves.

Complexity thinking is the opposite of what I call complicated thinking. Complicated thinking implicitly assumes that everything works by some type of formula or grand design that can be manipulated if only enough brainpower and understanding are applied to uncovering the root mechanisms. It is a science-and-technology-centric view of the world. It assumes that there is an answer, and that the answer is absolute and unchanging. For fundamental science this way of thinking has proven to be for the most part appropriate, and indeed it has produced significant advances in our understanding of the natural and physical world. Complicated thinking also worked well during the Industrial Revolution, and during the years when the factory dominated. In the new globalized and connected "knowledge economy," however, complicated thinking is like a dinosaur – part of an obsolete past.

Conversely, complexity thinking has the power to explain diverse events, such as why certain products become seemingly instantly popular while other similar and perhaps superior products languish in obscurity. Complexity is a major explanation for why certain YouTube videos go viral. Complexity explains how economic crises, such as the 2008 financial meltdown or the European debt crisis of 2010, emerge, despite the best efforts of politicians, economists, and regulators using the sophisticated analytical tools of some of the most astute financial analysts and policy wonks. Complexity helps us to understand the success of companies such as Google and Facebook. It is the mechanism by which social media and the Internet are fundamentally changing the business landscape. It helps decision makers to comprehend global trends and how these trends might impact strategic planning. And it allows managers to understand how their companies function in the face of increasing diversity in the workplace and a changing work-force demographic. In short, complexity can help business leaders understand and make sense of a wide range of business phenomena. Complicated thinking can only explain pieces in isolation. Complexity, however, explains how intersecting and connected people and societies evolve in a holistic manner. Complexity also provides a guide for managing in these changed times. But all of these advantages and insights can only be realized by first understanding and appreciating the differences between complexity thinking and complicated thinking.

So, to continue to answer the question "Why write a book about complexity?," it is necessary to acknowledge seven key facts.

1 Complexity thinking is very different from complicated thinking. The two ways of thinking involve different mindsets, different expectations, and different tolerances of ambiguity. They involve different attributes and skills. They require dramatically different management techniques.

2 Complexity naturally exists in both the workplace and the economy as a whole, and there is nothing that any manager or any organization can do avoid or eliminate it. Of course, one can ignore it, but that does not make it go away. Ignoring complexity is also not a particularly effective way of dealing with it.

3 While complexity cannot be controlled, it can be managed. Furthermore, complexity is being managed by many different types of successful companies. Indeed, it is imperative that complexity management techniques be utilized in our increasingly globalized and knowledge-intensive economy. Whether intentionally or by accident, leading companies such as Google, Amazon, 3M, and Facebook are using the principles of complexity thinking to grow their businesses and gain competitive advantage. The Barack Obama campaign used complexity thinking and complexity tactics to great effect in winning elections in both 2008 and 2012. The United States military uses complexity to increase their battlefield effectiveness. Most successful entrepreneurs are implicitly, and probably

unknowingly, going against the conventions of complicated thinking and using complexity to develop new businesses. In fact, whole new industries are becoming important engines of economic growth through the power and use of complexity. In short, complexity thinking helps businesses succeed.

4 The predominant business mindset is that of a complicated thinker – the antithesis of complexity thinking. The distinction between complicated and complex systems is not well known or understood or even acknowledged in business and by managers. In fact, complexity as a field of knowledge is essentially an unknown amongst business leaders. Complicated thinking has its place, and at times it is necessary, but in reality it has limited practical value in the vast majority of critical managerial situations. Complicated thinking is generally not only inappropriate but inefficient. It leads to suboptimal results, wasted effort, and frustration and usually produces unintended consequences that have disastrous results. Complicated thinking is often the least effective operating mindset that a manager can employ. It frequently produces outcomes that are worse than doing nothing. Even more unfortunately, complicated thinking is the default mindset. It is time to change that.

5 Complexity thinking is not difficult. It is intuitive, simple, and only requires an open mind and basic common sense. However, for a variety of reasons that will be discussed, it is rarely, if ever, utilized. Even something as simple as taking the time to ask whether a given issue is complicated or complex can be incredibly helpful and valuable.

6 Managing people is a complex function. Managing an organization is not the same as constructing a watch. Constructing a watch is a complicated task. A watch runs by the physics of springs, gears, and levers. The myriad pieces of a fine watch have to be assembled in a very precise way. A watch is calibrated by the constant passing of time. Management, however, is about dealing with people. People do not function like springs or levers. People and, by association, organizations are complex entities. They are constantly in flux. Individually as well as collectively, they adapt and change. People cannot be put together and made to act in a precise and preordained manner like the gears and springs of a watch. To excel in

management, you need to excel in managing people and in managing groups of people. Doing so requires the ability to understand,
appreciate, leverage, and respect complexity.
7 The final concept to acknowledge is that complexity thinking requires a paradigm shift. Such a paradigm shift can accelerate your
career, your organization, and, indeed, the economy as a whole.
Perhaps never in the history of business management has such a
paradigm shift been as necessary as it is now.

Together, these facts provide a compelling argument that anyone
with an interest in better management techniques would be interested
in complexity. This is the rationale for writing a book about complexity.

How This Book Came About

Three seemingly unrelated events occurred within a short period of
time that made me realize that this book needed to be written. The three
events were (1) a student fainting in class, (2) a frustrating and embarrassing television interview, and (3) a professional association presentation that nearly ended in a fistfight amongst audience members.
You might be wondering what all three events have in common, and
the answer is not complicated – it's complex, or, more accurately, it's
complexity.

Jennifer,[1] a particularly bright student who had always received top
grades, was in one of my case classes – a business school class that, like
many others, is taught using real business cases. We were coming to
the end of the class, and Jennifer wanted to know what the answer to
the case that we were examining that day was. During the class we had
discussed several different ways that the business situation could have
been handled and the advantages and disadvantages of each approach.
As with all good cases, I stated that there was no absolute right answer;
some solutions might seem to be better than others, but there was no
clear-cut solution that was preferable to all of the others in all conceiv-
able situations. This response did not discourage Jennifer from pressing
for a more definitive and thus, in her mind, a more satisfactory answer. I
reiterated in several different ways my point that business situations do

not always provide us with clear-cut and distinct "answers" and that, unlike in physics, business academics cannot go to a controlled laboratory to test different ideas and hypotheses. Despite my explaining all of this, Jennifer became more and more agitated until she fainted. So much for my teaching evaluations, I thought.

Jennifer's reaction, while extreme, is not untypical of the degree to which students who set high goals for themselves and, by extension, business professionals want and indeed expect to know "the answer." This event dramatically shows that we have conditioned a whole generation of business school students – future managers – to think only in terms of very objective right and wrong answers. Furthermore, it is not just students who think this way. The Hollywood stereotype of the manager who states "Just give me the bottom line" rings true. Nuanced answers are not particularly appreciated, despite how appropriate or necessary they may be for the situation at hand.

As will be discussed at length later in this book, this is a natural consequence of what I call the Sputnik effect, where society has come to believe that through science and technology all answers are possible and everything is achievable if only enough intellectual resources are brought to bear on an issue. Of course this is an illusion, as many of the greatest problems in the world have messy – or perhaps only partial – solutions. Likewise, most of the greatest challenges in business do not have clear-cut solutions. Furthermore, if a solution seemingly exists, it is more than likely that it is constantly changing, in that what worked yesterday may not work today or tomorrow. Nevertheless, our education system, like the business world, likes to deal in measurable absolutes, and few things are as absolute as teaching and testing and subsequently rewarding students based on complicated thinking.

The second incident motivating the writing of this book was an interview I did for the six o'clock news hour on the local television station. The time was at the height of the 2008 financial crisis. The interview was going along quite well until the interviewer, an experienced news anchor who I was assured would not do anything to embarrass me, asked the wind-up question, "How do we solve the crisis?" For good measure, he also included the qualifier, "We only have twenty seconds left." I was dumbfounded. I thought I had clearly and concisely articulated a plethora of causes both direct and indirect that had led to the crisis, and now I was being asked in the wrap-up to take the pot full of cooked spaghetti and to put it neatly back into the box that the uncooked spaghetti had come from. I sputtered out something that was only barely intelligible as English and hoped the twenty seconds would stop seeming like hours as I fumbled for a coherent answer to put everything into the nice, neat little box that I knew the interviewer wanted.

My TV interview experience is a clear example of how the media, and by extension the general public, want and expect to receive simple, clear-cut answers, regardless of the depth and breadth of the problem or issue. For issues such as a financial crisis, there is no magic solution, much less a magic solution that can be clearly explained in twenty seconds or less. There are a variety of nuances to issues such as an economic crisis, but there is a lack of willingness to deal with the nuances, much less do the hard work of cutting through embedded layers of political and economic ideology in order to be able to recognize the complexity of the underlying factors. Furthermore, the demand for "the answer" makes the implicit assumption that the global economy works like a mechanical watch, and all that is needed when the watch is broken is to find the broken spring or cracked gear cog and replace it. It is a wishful view of the world, and one that is not only naive but harmful. When I was put on the spot in front of a TV camera, I began to realize just how inappropriate a techno-centric view of the world based on complicated thinking truly is.

The final incident that convinced me I needed to write this book was the response to a public presentation I gave to a professional audience composed of risk managers. The title of the talk was "Have We Lost the Plot?," and the theme was to suggest that finance and risk managers should look for more holistic solutions than simply the reductionist mathematical solutions that theory and the latest computer models provide. Although I thought my remarks were somewhat obvious and based on common sense, a veritable shouting match between audience members started about halfway through my presentation and continued to escalate out into the hallway after the talk concluded. The interesting thing I noticed was that there were two very distinct "camps" in terms of agreeing or disagreeing with my comments, and the difference between those two camps correlated to the age of the "discussants," with the older members of the audience agreeing with my points and the younger (and probably more academically qualified) members strongly disagreeing with my propositions. Although I possess the "proper" academic credentials, I realized that I was "old."

It is perhaps easy to see how journalists, without specific expertise in a field and with a constant need to move on to the next story, might take a simplistic view of complex problems and ask a naive question such as "Tell us in twenty seconds how to solve this." Likewise, it is also easy to see how students' youth and inexperience might lead them to assume that a clear-cut solution is possible. However, it has been my experience that such views are also common within the largest and most sophisticated organizations – organizations that employ some of the world's most experienced and well-trained business practitioners. The belief that concrete and definitive solutions can be found for all problems and issues is widespread, despite strong evidence to the contrary. Thus, the third impetus for writing this book, namely the reaction of an audience of risk-management experts, made me realize the true extent of the problem. We all want to believe that we can control and manage our world as we would a complicated problem, when many issues are complex and thus not resolvable by such an approach. This has profound implications for our command-and-control desires. Complicated thinking does not work for complex problems!

These three events had a profound influence on my thinking about how business managers think and the parallels between creative thinking in business and other disciplines such as science or medicine. I was struck by the irony that while business is considered a "soft and fuzzy" discipline and science and medicine are considered "hard and objective," it is business that demands and expects concrete and definitive answers to its issues, while science and medicine are much more comfortable with and accustomed to ambiguity, imperfection, and the fact that quite often a definitive answer is simply not available, forthcoming, or even conceptually possible.

The modern business community of consultants, experts, MBAs, and media-savvy business leaders has created an expectation and a belief that, if only enough brainpower and critical thinking are applied to any business or economic problem, a perfectly implementable solution will eventually be found. Not only is this belief unfounded, it is misleading. It leads directly not just to disappointment but also to actions that are counterproductive and potentially harmful.

The central theme of this book is that the world of business is usually complex rather than complicated. That may seem like word play, but the difference between "complicated thinking" and "complexity thinking" is profound. This important distinction is well accepted in the scientific community but is virtually unknown in business. Thus, the ultimate rationale for writing this book is to correct that oversight and get out the message that it's not complicated.

What This Book Is About

This book explains complexity in a nontechnical manner. It is specifically written in a manner relevant to a business manager. There are many excellent books and articles that explain complexity, but they are couched in the language of the biologist, the theoretical economist, the mathematician, or the computer scientist. However, complexity has a practical and important place in business as well, and thus business and business management are the focal points of this book.

The first step in being able to manage complexity is to recognize what is complex and what is complicated. Chapter 1, "Introduction to Systems and Complexity," explains the difference between complex and complicated systems and provides a framework for distinguishing between the two. Chapter 1 also introduces a third idea, namely that of simple systems, and simple problems. The ability to distinguish between situations that are simple, complicated, and complex can itself lead to significant insights and more effective decision making and management.

Chapter 2, "The False Axioms of Business," highlights some of the false axioms or myths of business that lead us to assume that things are complicated when in fact they are complex. Understanding and acknowledging these false axioms is important, since doing so will help to build a better appreciation of how complexity thinking is needed as a complement to the more prevalent complicated thinking.

Chapter 3, "It's Not Complicated," explores our natural tendency to automatically accept complicated thinking as the default and why this leads to inefficient decision making and problem solving. Rarely are important business problems complicated problems. The most interesting, challenging, and valuable problems are complex. Reversing the ingrained habits of complicated thinking is key for business success on both the personal level and the organizational level. Indeed complexity thinking is critical for regulators, politicians, and stakeholders at all levels. A better appreciation and understanding of complicated versus complex thinking will lead to better policy decisions, strategic decisions, and tactical decisions.

Chapter 4, "The Wonders of Complexity," explains in more detail the underlying characteristics and dynamics of complex systems and how they apply to the world of business. In particular, the fundamental elements of how complexity arises are discussed. By its nature, capitalism, as opposed to a planned economy, is a dynamic and complex system. Competition, one of the cornerstones of capitalism, is a perfect catalyst for complex dynamics. Additional factors, such as connectedness through technology and social media, accelerate and enhance the complex nature of business. By nature, humans are themselves complex. Thus the fact that businesses are run by people for the benefit of customers who are also people means that the traits that make us human manifest themselves as complexity in business.

Chapter 5, "Managing Complexity," presents four essential strategies for managing complexity. Managing complexity often requires counterintuitive thinking – or at least thinking that seems counterintuitive to someone with a complicated mindset. This chapter provides a series of explanations, illustrated with numerous examples, for why the counterintuitive approaches often work best. In particular, it discusses managing the key complexity elements of connectedness and emergence and explores their increasingly important role in the current business environment. The global information economy in particular provides many useful illustrations.

In chapter 6, "The Complexity of Strategic Planning," I discuss strategic analysis and planning, which are probably the areas of business where complicated thinking is most strongly rooted. However, they are also the areas of management where the negative consequences of using complicated thinking to manage complex situations are most prevalent. The chapter examines as a case study the professional career of Robert S. McNamara, one of the original "Whiz Kids" of the 1950s and the epitome of a complicated thinker who later came to appreciate the strategic value of complexity thinking. The second part of the chapter examines the related topic of forecasting and long-term planning. It is argued that the manager needs to be very clear about which aspects of the forecasting and planning process are complicated and which are complex in order to utilize the most appropriate forecasting techniques. The implications for strategic planning are thus made clearer.

Chapter 7, "The Complex Economy," is about the change in thinking that is slowly transforming economics from a reductionist field of study to the new way of thinking of complexity economics. While still controversial, complexity economics and the closely related field of econophysics are challenging the some of the sacred cows of economics, such as ideas of equilibrium and diminishing returns, and replacing them with concepts of connectedness and complexity. The chapter illustrates the changes in the economic environment by comparing traditional versus contemporary business media and companies exemplifying the age of conglomerates versus today's social media companies.

Chapter 8 discusses "Risk Management and Complexity." All managers are risk managers, whether or not their job title explicitly includes the term "risk." Risk management and the regulation that is usually associated with it have been particularly impacted by complicated thinking, with less than desirable results. As a specific example, the chapter explores the development of financial risk pricing models and how they fell apart during the 2008 financial crisis, as the complexity of the markets overwhelmed the complicated thinking that produced the risk models and the regulatory frameworks established to monitor them.

The concluding chapter, "The Complex Future," explains why the business environment will likely continue to become more complex, with a resulting decline in the relevance of complicated thinking, and presents ideas about how complexity thinking can become more of an accepted paradigm for business managers. I conclude the book by arguing that complexity thinking is challenging, dynamic, and profitable. Rather than being a concept to be feared, complexity is an idea whose time has come. Complexity should be enthusiastically embraced by all enlightened business managers and leaders.

The objective of this book is not to provide a definitive scientific guide to complexity. Although complexity has become a very active and exciting field of academic research, the field is still too undeveloped and unexplored to be tackled in a completely scientific manner in business situations – at this point. Thus, this book will not cover the various underlying theories of complexity or the various academic schools of thought, except as they are directly applicable to business. Likewise, it will not cover the mathematical developments of complexity.

It might be argued that complexity is nothing more than a metaphor for an element that business managers might want to consider in their decision making. However, I believe that a more emphatic case needs to be made for its importance. I believe that the evidence is very strong and clear that complexity is a factor to be reckoned with in business, in the markets, and in the economy in general. It is imperative that managers wake up to this reality and adjust their mindsets accordingly. The reigning paradigm that the world is complicated is increasingly being shown to be a naive illusion.

As you read this book, I trust that you will not faint, be flummoxed, or become infuriated. Instead, I hope that you will find this book to be full of useful concepts that enrich your thinking and help you generate business ideas and solutions that are realistic, effective, and profitable. It's not complicated.

ACKNOWLEDGMENTS

The list of people who have assisted me, encouraged me, taught me, influenced me, and prodded me to the completion of this book is very long. I really need to begin with some of the teachers and professors that I have been so incredibly lucky to have had play a role in my education. Mr. Mathews and Mr. Hill of Lorne Junior High School were more influential in my education than they could ever realize. They instilled in me a love of science and of trying to figure things out that continues to this day. Drs. Dulin, Sharp, and Harkleroad at McMurry College (now McMurry University) furthered that love of science in the context of a liberal arts education that was critical to my understanding of how we really need to appreciate C.P. Snow's Two Cultures in order to grow intellectually. Dr. Cohen at the University of Pittsburgh, and Dr. White at the University of Western Ontario sealed the curiosity with a critical education in academic rigor and research.

I also have been blessed with wonderful work colleagues, especially Stephen McPhie, who has been my long-suffering consulting partner. Stephen is the smartest person I know, and he is frustratingly quick at spotting the flaws in my thinking. Jenny Baechler and Scott Comber of Dalhousie University have helped me form several of the ideas in this book and gave many clues for further exploration while we constructively argued about the widest variety of issues possible over greasy-spoon breakfasts. The clients that I have worked with were in essence the experimental group as I developed many of the ideas presented here. I appreciate their trust in me. I am extremely fortunate to be an academic – it is the best career that one could imagine. The students in the Corporate Residency MBA program at Dalhousie University are some of the most diverse and creative students that one could be privileged to work with.

This book would never have seen the light of day without the limitless patience of Jennifer DiDomenico of the University of Toronto Press, who worked tirelessly to nurse it along and eventually make an author out of me. I cannot sufficiently express my appreciation for her not giving up on me. I also appreciate the anonymous reviewers who looked at several drafts of this book. Their insightful comments helped to make the book much better, and for that I am very grateful.

I would most of all like to thank my family. When I was growing up, my parents created an ideal set of circumstances in which my sister and I could let our curiosity run free. My sister, Nancy, has always been my hero and a constant source of encouragement as well as inspiration. Finally, I thank my wife and children for putting up with my weird work hours, my materials and papers spread throughout the house, and the random comments and thoughts that I run by them. Their support is beyond value, and I love them for that and so much more.

IT'S NOT COMPLICATED

ONE

INTRODUCTION TO SYSTEMS AND COMPLEXITY

Systems Thinking

If you look up the words "complicated" and "complex" in the dictionary you will find that the two words are synonyms. Indeed, in common usage the two words are frequently used interchangeably. However, if you ask a scientist at the Santa Fe Institute in New Mexico, a multidisciplinary research center that focuses on how the science of complexity impacts society, you will get a very different set of definitions. The multidisciplinary scientists at the Santa Fe Institute think in terms of systems. Systems thinking, which is simply a fancy way of classifying how things work or how tasks get done, has been applied with great success in biology, engineering, and the study of politics and is a major component of explaining how our interconnected digital world grows and functions. To a systems scientist, the words "complicated" and "complex" denote two very different and distinct types of systems. This book is about systems thinking, and more specifically the important distinction between simple, complicated, and complex systems as applied to common business problems.

Consider three different tasks that are performed in virtually every business, on every working day: making coffee, preparing accounting statements, and making sales presentations. There is nothing special about these tasks, and in fact they might be considered to be rather mundane. However, each of these tasks involves varying degrees of complication and complexity and requires differing levels of knowledge, skill, and expertise. A scientist thinks of each task as a type of system, while an engineer would likely draw a process flow map for each. A manager, however, goes about each of the tasks without consciously thinking about any of this. It is time for the manager to think a bit more consciously about the differences, as the scientist and the engineer do.

Consider first the task of brewing the coffee. This is an example of a simple system. It is simple in both the day-to-day sense of the word and also in the technical sense that is used in systems thinking. There are three main characteristics of a simple system or a simple task: (1) it is relatively easy to determine if a successful outcome has been achieved; (2) there is a set of steps or a recipe for producing an acceptable outcome; and (3) the steps for completing the task are robust, meaning that they do not have to be followed exactly to achieve an acceptable outcome.

Making coffee in the office coffee machine is something that virtually anyone can do. It requires little to no expertise, and the process is often done absentmindedly. It is likely that the only time people making coffee read the directions is the first time they try using the machine. Even then they might simply resort to trial and error or intuition learned from operating other coffee machines. If it is a typical office, there might be a list of instructions for setting up the coffee machine on the wall by the coffee maker. The one thing a novice coffee maker might not know is exactly how much ground coffee to place in the filter to get the optimal strength brew that most people in the office prefer. However, that too would be worked out after a couple of attempts.

The next task in our list, preparing financial accounting statements, is what a systems scientist would classify as complicated. There are four main characteristics of a complicated system or a complicated task: (1) there is generally a well-defined outcome or a set of criteria that signifies a successful outcome; (2) there is a rigid set of rules or regulations that need to be followed to achieve a successful outcome; (3) these rules are not robust, in that they must be followed exactly or a successful outcome will not be achieved; and (4) the process is completely reproducible in that if you repeat the exact same steps, you will achieve the exact same outcome.

In preparing a company's financial statements, an accountant or a similarly knowledgeable expert will rely on a knowledge of well-established accounting rules and regulations. Without knowledge of the specific accounting rules and regulations the company is subject to, an individual will not be able to prepare acceptable statements. However, every accountant, making the same assumptions, will produce the exact same outcome, barring a mathematical error.

The list of rules and procedures for preparing a company's financial statements is much longer than the instructions for using the coffee maker, but this is not what makes it complicated. Instead, a key distinction is that in making the coffee you can approximate the coffee to water ratio, while the same level of guessing or approximating is not suitable for preparing financial statements. Approximations will produce results that will not only be wrong but could also have legal and regulatory implications. To prepare coffee no special training or certification is required. The preparation of the accounting statements, however, might require a professional certification such as a Chartered Accounting designation, particularly if the statements are to be used for public reporting purposes or tax calculation. In addition everyone will make coffee slightly differently, with slightly different results in taste, but everyone will agree that the end product is still a cup of coffee, slight differences in outcome aside. However, all accountants, given the same data and the same accounting rules will produce the exact same set of financial statements. There is little to no latitude allowed with financial accounting.

The final example is a sales presentation to a potentially important client.[1] To a systems scientist this task is fundamentally different from the previous two tasks. It is not a simple task that can be completed with a list of a few simple rules like the preparing of the coffee. Nor is it a task where one can consult a handbook of rules or regulations. (This is despite the large number of best-selling sales skills books and sales training workshops.) In addition, there is generally no need to be certified or to have extensive training or any sort of advanced education. However, it is most certainly not a task that would be given to someone with limited training or experience, especially if the client is an important prospect. There is no regular pattern or routine to making a sales call, although there may be general themes that tend to get repeated with experience. Each sales meeting will be unique, with the same sales process leading to different results depending on the client or even depending on even more mundane factors such as the time of the day or the mood of the customer or even the salesperson. Repeating the exact same sales process is not likely to produce the same sales outcome. Finally, and paradoxically, the more important the client, the more different the sales call is likely to be from other sales calls that the manager might make.

The sales task is different, and the professional's mindset when making it is also likely to be fundamentally different. Unlike with making coffee, the salesperson will be actively engaged in the sales call rather than completing it absentmindedly. While preparing financial statements may not be considered to be an enjoyable task, it is not likely to stir up the feelings of trepidation that a sales call is likely to produce. A business person is not going to rehearse making the coffee or doing the accounting. Scenario plans are not needed for how those tasks might proceed. Finally, no one would be fretting and losing sleep over making coffee or doing accounting, while the sales meeting might be quite stressful. The sales call is different; the sales call is complex.

Each of these three common office functions requires a different set of abilities; a different type of training, possibly requiring certification; a different level of experience, knowledge, and intuition; and even a different mindset or personality.

Our short sample of tasks results in an ironic quandary. The least important task of the day – the coffee preparation – could be handled in an almost trivial manner by anyone in the office. The necessary but not very value adding task of the day – the preparation of the financial statements – is a complicated task but one that could be completed successfully by any suitably knowledgeable accountant. However, perhaps the most important and the most valuable task of the day – the sales call – essentially has to be done by trial and error and intuition. There is something very special and unique about the sales call. That specialness is complexity.

Simple, Complicated, and Complex Systems

Our short list of three tasks illustrates three specific types of processes or systems: simple, complicated, and complex. Classifying tasks into these three categories has proved to be a very useful way of studying and learning about a wide variety of natural processes. Scientists have identified and written about the differences between simple, complicated, and complex systems in the natural world for approximately fifty years.[2] It can also be shown to be productive to apply systems analysis to business situations.

There are three main reasons why it is imperative for the differences between types of tasks to be recognized. The first is that recognizing the differences leads to different strategies for analyzing, managing, and successfully completing them. It allows both managers and organizations to be more effective and profitable. Even simple tasks like making coffee can be made more efficient by appreciating the differences inherent in systems thinking. A second and perhaps even more important reason is the fact that the manager or the organization that best understands and manages the differences will have a distinct comparative and competitive advantage. Finally, in our ever increasingly connected world, the occurrence of complexity is becoming more common and important.

The aim of this book is to illustrate clearly and in a non-technical manner how systems thinking can be successfully applied to a wide range of business tasks. The various methods for dealing with each different type of system are also discussed. Dealing with complexity can appear to be counterintuitive. Managers seem to be hard-wired as business professionals to default to "complicated thinking" techniques, when in fact such techniques are inefficient at best, and frequently destructive.

All three types of systems and tasks exist in business. However, simple and complicated tasks are not generally the most important; nor are they the most value adding. For instance, a series of successful sales meetings is considerably more important to the ongoing success of an organization than the compiling of the quarterly financial statements, and much more important than the making of coffee. While there are simple and complicated tasks that are necessary, important, and valuable in operating a business, the reality is that successful completion of complex tasks is increasingly proving to be the deciding factor in creating competitive advantage.

What Is Complexity?

In chapter 3 the essentials of complexity will be examined in depth, but to begin our analysis, it is important to first realize that complex tasks cannot be completed by following a recipe or a set of instructions, or even an extensive list of rules and regulations. Nor does being extremely precise necessarily work. As discussed at length later, such attempts at precision may actually be quite harmful because of the unintended consequences they produce. Just think how disastrous a face-to-face sales meeting would be to an important prospect if a precise sales script were used verbatim. Call centers are an example of a type of sales call that uses sales scripts, but they do so solely because their calling is based on the law of large numbers. Each call is known to have a small probability of success, and thus a standardized script is sufficient. Also, the products they are promoting tend to be simple and of low value, such as magazine subscriptions or carpet-cleaning services. The call center approach to sales is a complicated approach to selling particular types of low-value products to a limited range of potential customers. It would be sheer foolishness to use such a standardized approach for an important prospect on a high-value sales item or for a business-to-business transaction. Imagine trying to sell a $300 million commercial aircraft using a canned sales pitch!

Thus, a key delineation point is that simple processes and complicated processes can be codified, while complex processes cannot. That is, simple and complicated processes can be set down in words as a set of instructions for successful completion of the task at hand. There is a finite set of steps to be taken, and each step is well defined – for example, as in the instructions for making coffee. Increasingly, the ability to codify simple and complicated tasks means that they are tasks that are being done more and more by a computer or a robot. The self-driving car or truck is one example, but there are so many other examples that we almost take the robotization of simple and complicated tasks for granted. For instance, many of us now get our coffee made by an automated coffee machine that only requires the pressing of a button to produce coffee on demand, and others of us have our personal accounting and taxes done by a low-cost computer program.[3] A complex task cannot be codified, however, and thus, not even conceptually, can a complex task be fully completed by a computer.

Complexity involves an unknown number of steps. More significantly, each of the steps in a complex system is generally unknown or even conceptually unknowable. For example, what are the exact steps for completing a successful sales call? Some sales calls are completed quite successfully in a short period and with little trouble, while other sales processes may start out optimistically but drag on for an extended period and even then ultimately end in failure. With a complex system you can never tell. There may be rules of thumb or guidelines, but they are at best guideposts, and these rules of thumb do not at all guarantee successful completion of the task at hand. This ambiguity means that complexity does not have a set of steps, procedures, or rules that can be written down or codified.

Another key differentiator is that with simple and complicated systems the outcomes are predictable and reproducible while complex outcomes are not. If the steps for making the coffee are followed, a pot of coffee will be produced. If the accounting rules are followed then a set of acceptable financial statements will be the outcome. With the sales call, however, there is no predictability. We do not know whether potential customers will buy or not, and if they do buy we have no way of accurately predicting how much they will buy or when they will buy. Before the sales call is made we do not know which sales tactics will work and which will not. In fact some of the salesperson's favorite sales tactics may actually backfire. The only thing that the salesperson can rely on is experience or intuition. Each sales call is unique. Experienced and successful salespeople intuitively know this and are flexible in their approach. They are willing and able to change tactics whenever necessary. This is an approach that most definitely would not work for a complicated task such as accounting.

Not only are the results of a complex process not predictable, they are also not reproducible. A sales pitch may be successful one day, but meeting a similar potential customer the next day, with the exact same sales procedure, will not necessarily lead to the same result. This gives complex systems a feeling of randomness and uncontrollability. Unfortunately, unpredictability and non-reproducibility are characteristics that no one feels comfortable dealing with. These traits make one want to believe the implicit myth that all business processes are complicated. In turn, this implicit belief gives us false hope that, if only enough research and development energy are put into understanding the consumer or market or competitive dynamic, the situation will become controllable and predictable. Unfortunately, this is patently not true.

Another distinguishing characteristic between systems lies in the ability to objectively define success. Success in making a pot of coffee can be easily defined and agreed upon by everyone: is there drinkable coffee in the coffee pot when the process is completed? Likewise, success can be easily and objectively defined for producing the division's financial statements. But now consider what success for the sales call to the prospect is. Is success going to be that the customer places an order for 5,000 units, or would 200 units be considered a success? What if, after the initial sales meeting, the prospective client wanted brochures sent, or perhaps even a follow-up meeting? Would that be considered a successful outcome for the call? Success is rarely unambiguously definable for a complex situation. With complexity there can be many different definitions or degrees of success. Success is also likely to be an ongoing process without a clearly defined end point. For instance, most sales relationships do not end with the sale but, it is hoped, will expand into further sales and an ongoing business relationship.

Another way in which the three types of systems differ is in our knowledge of the critical success factors. All of the factors and elements that go into a simple or a complicated system are known. For making coffee, you need ground coffee, some type of filter, boiling water, and some type of pot and brewing device. Accountants know the data they need, such as sales revenues and cost figures, to produce the financial statements. What are the factors of success for our sales manager? It helps to know something about the client, but exactly what information is needed is not clear-cut. It also helps to know about the product or service that is being sold, but which parts of that information will be helpful or relevant to the customer can only be guessed at. The effectiveness of the sales call can be affected by the time of day it is made, but again, the optimal time of day to call is rarely known with certainty, and is likely to change from day to day, and perhaps even moment to moment, depending on the mood of the prospect. Perhaps the normally preferred time to call happens to occur just after the manager comes out of a particularly stressful personnel meeting. If so, all of the sales manager's best-laid plans and tactics are likely to be unsuccessful. Experienced salespeople will tell you that the success of a sales call can depend on the tiniest of details. Successful salespeople develop an ongoing intuition for how a pitch is going and continually adjust as the sales process moves along. They know that the best they can do is try to create the conditions and context that they believe will lead to the highest probability of success. However, despite their best efforts, professional salespeople know that success with a client is not certain until the sale is completed.

Finally, when making coffee or preparing the financial statements, our manager's necessary actions are not going to be affected by the actions of competitors. The sales pitch, however, will likely take on an entirely new character based on whether or not the company's competitors have previously called on the client or if they can be expected to call. This leads us to what is ultimately the most important characteristic of complex systems, which is that they are adaptive or emergent, while simple or complicated systems are static. The quality of being adaptive means that the actions of all of the elements in a complex system affect one another, and in response each of the elements changes accordingly. Furthermore, change is continuous and ongoing. As one element in the economy changes, businesses change, and as each business changes its strategy, all of its competitors change their strategies. In turn the response of the customers will also be altered, and the process continually cycles and evolves. All of the players in a business setting – the company, its employees, the industry, its competitors, the customers, the regulators, the financial backers, the general public, and other players – are constantly adjusting their actions and opinions, based on the changes in actions, opinions, and perceptions of others. It is this never-ending and unpredictable dance that ultimately defines complexity. It is a phenomenon that scientists label emergence and that business calls competition.

Emergence

The most fundamental and important outcome of a complex system is a property called emergence. Emergence occurs when interconnected elements, such as a sector of consumers, or the actions of an industry, or even economic developments, evolve in ways that produce trends or patterns that look highly organized but in fact occur without any definable guiding hand. For instance, the ups and downs of the stock market exhibit emergence. There appear to be up trends and downtrends, but there is no mathematical model that can predict which way the market will go next, and there is no one individual, group, or organization dictating that the market should move in a certain direction. Analysts and investors form and state all kinds of opinions about the relative investment merits of one asset over another, but there is no central control agency or figurehead that sets prices or demand. The prices move in waves that are totally independent of any one investor or group of investors. However, collectively, certain patterns or trends can certainly be seen in asset prices, although not to the point where they can be predicted or exploited.

Fads and fashion trends, particularly among the high-school demographic, provide another case in point. No one person decides that a certain brand of jeans is the "must-have" pair to be cool and popular, but, seemingly like magic, a specific brand becomes wildly successful. In fact a given brand or product might become successful despite the marketing efforts of competing brands and perhaps even despite the lack of a marketing effort by the "popular" brand in question.

Whole economies show a similar behavior. For instance, during the late 1980s and the early 1990s, the Japanese economy was soaring. The prevailing assumption was that Japan would become the next dominant economic superpower. The subsequent reality was that the Japan economy crashed and remains stagnant even twenty years later. Currently, the Chinese economy is one of the world's fastest growing, and India's appears to be on the verge of breaking out. History, however, shows us that realistically no one can predict which economies will be leading ten years hence.

Emergence is not confined to large-scale effects such as economic trends. Emergence can and does occur on smaller scales as well. A common example of emergence is office politics. Who is in favor and who is out of favor is a constantly evolving drama. The culture and mood of an office also exhibits emergence. Despite all the books written about creating an organizational culture, the reality is that a corporation's culture dips, changes, evolves, and sometimes even dramatically flip-flops, and all of this occurs in spite of, rather than because of, the actions and best intentions of senior managers.

Emergence, along with its causes and implications, will be discussed at length in chapter 3. At this point, however, it is important to begin to grasp the significance of emergence and how it defines complex systems. With emergence, things happen and events unfold in unanticipated ways, almost as if by magic. Emergence occurs naturally and organically. Emergence unfolds in unpredictable ways, with the only constant being that things will change. How they change, and the direction of the change, and the catalyst for the change are all a priori unknowable. That is the fundamental reality of emergence and of complexity.[4]

Emergence is the business imperative the manager needs to recognize and appreciate. It is also what makes the manager who understands complexity so valuable, particularly in today's economy, which (for a variety of reasons to be discussed later) is becoming ever more complex, and in which understanding complexity is increasingly becoming the key to success.

Identifying Complexity

The following rudimentary decision framework is offered to help in identifying the type of process or task that one is faced with. The framework is based on the defining characteristics discussed and relies on three easy-to-answer questions: (1) Is a successful outcome for the process easily and objectively definable? (2) Are the factors and elements necessary for success known? (3) Is exactness in execution required or, equivalently, are the factors for success robust?

You will notice that some important traits of complexity have been left out of the framework. Traits such as unpredictability and emergence do not appear. That is because these traits, while playing a critical and important role in complex systems, are difficult to identify a priori. The objective of the framework is to be functionally useful for the business manager rather than scientifically accurate.

The framework is illustrated in figure 1.1 below.

We can illustrate the use of the framework by revisiting the three tasks that were discussed at the beginning of the chapter: (1) making coffee, (2) preparing financial statements, and (3) making a sales call to a prospective client. Table 1.1 summarizes the following discussion.

Starting with the first question, defining success for making coffee and preparing financial statements is obviously easy to do. You simply have to ask if drinkable coffee is available or if the financial statements are legally acceptable. While people may dispute whether the coffee is any good or not, all would agree on whether or not coffee has in fact been made. Likewise, while the results of the financial statements might not be considered to be encouraging based on the company's performance over the period in question, it is clear that all observers would agree that legally acceptable financial statements have been prepared.

The question of whether the sales call has been successful or not is generally ambiguous and subjective. There are degrees of success, and what the threshold of success is will be determined subjectively by each different observer. For a timid salesperson, a successful sales call might be one where the prospect did not rudely and abruptly end

Figure 1.1: Decision Framework for Classifying System Type

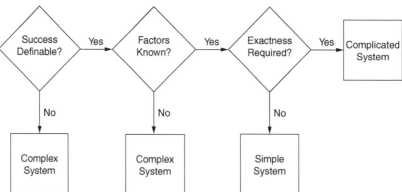

Table 1.1

Framework Question	Making Coffee	Accounting	Sales Call
Is success objectively definable?	Yes	Yes	No
Are success factors known?	Yes	Yes	No
Is exactness required?	No	Yes	Not applicable
Type of System	*Simple*	*Complicated*	*Complex*

the meeting. For others, the only definition of a successful sales meeting might be one in which a record commission is earned.

Turning to the second question: the success factors for making coffee are well known, and for accounting they are also well documented. Conversely, for a sales call, what makes one person a successful salesperson and another a flop is still a mystery, despite the fact that there is a plethora of books and training courses on how to be successful in sales. There will be some factors that are thought to be important, such as, perhaps, the prospect's mood when the call is made, or the prospect's known need for the product or service being offered. However, any list of factors for sales call success that you make is going to be incomplete and inadequate, and the elements are likely to be shaped by subjective factors and to be constantly changing or evolving. At this stage, therefore, we can conclude that making a sales call is a complex problem (although we will get further confirmation of this at the next step) and that further analysis is needed to determine the nature of making coffee and preparing financial statements.

The final step, determining whether or not exactness is required, is relevant for distinguishing between simple and complicated systems. Making coffee does not require exactness, while accounting is known for requiring attention to detail and exactitude. We thus classify making coffee as a simple process and preparing financial statements as a complicated process. The exactness question is not applicable to complex tasks, since the factors for success are not even known, much less measureable. As such, it does not make sense to ask if a particular procedure needs to be followed exactly or not.

Other criteria can be developed for classifying systems, but in the context of business, this proposed framework is not only easy to understand but also practical.

A Different Test for Complexity

There is a different test that we can use to determine if a system is complex, but it does involve some imagination to apply. Mentally construct a movie of a specific business process or issue. In other words, build a history of the events that have led up to the present situation, and describe a set of steps that will outline the future as the issue at hand plays out. The test then becomes whether you can run the movie forward and backward repeatedly and get replicable results. To restate the question: given the current state of a situation, can you explain what will happen next and, likewise, can you explain what came before, without any prior knowledge?

With a complicated system you can predict the steps that will unfold going forward. More importantly, with a complicated system you can reverse-engineer the steps that came before – the steps that led to the current set of conditions and circumstances.

As an example, assume that I know the height, speed, and direction of a cannonball flying through the air. A common physics problem is to calculate where the cannonball was fired from, with what speed or force, and at what angle. It is also an easy calculation to determine where the ball will land, at what angle, and at what speed. Now compare that classic physics textbook problem with trying to determine the path of a flock of starlings swarming through the sky.[5] You cannot tell in what direction the starlings will swoop next, nor can you tell what direction the starlings came from. The starlings will dart and dip through the sky as a highly organized flock. There is obviously a phenomenon at work, but little to nothing can be said about how the "movie" of the starling flock came into being or about how it will turn out. The cannonball's flight path is a complicated system; the starlings' flight path is a complex system.

As another trivial example, reconsider our example of making coffee. If the manager is enjoying a hot cup of coffee, and you know it came from the office coffee pot, you can quite easily retrace the steps that must have occurred. Namely, someone poured the coffee into the mug, and before that the coffee brewer dripped the coffee into the coffee pot. The step before that was someone turning the coffee brewer on after pouring water into the maker and measuring out the proper amount of coffee into the brewer's filter. The reverse movie can be constructed quite accurately, and everyone would construct the reverse movie in a similar way. For instance, no one in constructing the reverse movie would state that the coffee dripped upwards from the coffee pot into the coffee brewer.

Now consider the case of a sales call. Suppose you know that the client just ordered 500 units. Can you definitively tell it was because of the sales call? Perhaps they ordered the units from the website or catalog. Perhaps they were going to order 1,000 units but only ordered 500 units after talking to the salesperson. Assuming that the sale was made over the phone, can you tell who initiated the call? Was it the salesperson (probably)? But many times sales are initiated by a call from the customer. If the customer bought product A, can you with certainty state that that was what was initially discussed in the sales call? Perhaps the salesperson started by trying to sell the customer product C but, when that did not work, shifted to product B, and then to product A. There is no way to run the movie backward with any degree of reliability or accuracy.

Yet another way to look at this test is to ask if you could expect to arrive at the same starting point if you traced back the steps as they occurred. Is there the ability to replicate the process? With our cannonball example we will always be able to trace back to the same initial point. With the starling example it will be impossible to do that. Each cannonball will go in the exact same path given the same initial conditions, while each murmuration of starlings will take a different path each time.

With making coffee or preparing financial statements we can replicate the results, assuming that the inputs are the same. However, it is quite easy to imagine the same salesperson making the exact same sales call to a similar client (or even the same client) five minutes after the initial call and getting a very different result.

In some business situations, the path of outcomes resembles the flight of cannonballs more than the flight of starlings. For instance, given weather conditions and the time of day, we can fairly accurately calculate events such as the flow of consumers through a coffee shop or the usage of wireless data. Other business situations are more like the flight of starlings, such as the behavior of individuals in a business meeting, where it is never possible to tell with accuracy how someone will react to a given presentation or idea.

A Turing Test for Business Complexity

Alan Turing was a brilliant British mathematician who accomplished many things in his too-short life. Winston Churchill often credited Turing's work on breaking the German Enigma code as a key to the Allies' winning the Second World War, and this work has been dramatized in the movie *The Imitation Game*. Turing's work on computing devices helped to lay the groundwork for the modern computer. In addition, Turing made important advances in theoretical mathematics. However, perhaps what Alan Turing is most commonly remembered for is the thought experiment that bears his name.

A Turing Test involves a thought experiment about an individual who is engaging in a conversation with two different entities that are hidden behind curtains. Behind one curtain is a human being. Behind the other curtain is a computer. Turing's Test involves whether or not the individual can tell which responses are coming from a computer and which responses are coming from a human. While computer development has come a long way since Turing died in 1954, most of us would agree that being able to distinguish a human from a computer based on a conversation is still a relatively easy task. While a computer can deal with some complicated tasks extremely efficiently, computers cannot deal with the nuances of conversation. The reason is complexity.

The Turing Test was designed as a thought experiment for differentiating between machine intelligence and human intelligence. An understanding of the difference between systems and tasks that are complicated and those that are complex will make one realize that the Turing Test is ultimately a test for complexity.

A computer has high levels of machine intelligence. A machine is perfectly suited to following a set of concrete and unchanging instructions. A machine does not have to think or, perhaps more accurately, a machine does not have to imagine. A machine simply has to follow an unwavering and objective set of instructions. The instructions may include decisions, such as in the classification decision tree in Figure 1.1, but each decision will be well defined, objective, and consist of a discrete number of answers, such as yes or no. Computers, as well as computer-controlled robots, are ideally suited for such tasks. If a question or task is clearly defined, objective, and has a discrete number of answers or paths to follow, then a computer can function much quicker than a human can.

A computer, however, cannot create, imagine, have emotions, or deal effectively with ambiguity and randomness. These are the features that define humans and differentiate us from machines, including robots and computers. These are also elements that are consistent with complexity. Furthermore, and as will be discussed at length throughout this book, since most business activity is composed of the actions of humans interacting, it necessarily follows that business is complex.

From this we can adapt the Turing Test to test business complexity. Consider any task that a manager has to do in the course of a day. The task is to be done behind one of two curtains – as in the original Turing Test. Behind one curtain is a business professional. Behind another curtain is either a computer, a robot, or a temporary worker such as an outsourcer or an intern. The Turing Test for Business Complexity is whether or not the stakeholder of the task (customer, senior manager, or even staff) can tell whether the task was done by the business professional or not. If it makes a difference that the manager actually completed the task, then we can say with assurance that the task was complex. If it makes no difference if the task was done by a computer, a robot, or by someone who was employed at an outsourcing firm, then we can claim that the task was complicated or simple.

For example, the simple task of making coffee could have been done by an intern, or a coffee shop, or a coffee brewer that was programmed to grind beans and make coffee at a preset time each day. If a cup of coffee was produced, it would make no difference whether the task was performed by a machine or outsourced or made by the manager. Likewise, it would make no difference if the financial statements were produced by an accounting program, by an accountant working for an unrelated accounting firm, or by the manager. Thus, the making of coffee and the production of financial statements would not pass the Turing Test for Business Complexity.

Now consider the sales meeting. Everyone has experienced an automated sales call. These are obviously not generated by a live person. A more enhanced version is a sales call from someone calling from a call center – which would be an example of an outsourced sales call. Again, it is obvious that such a call is not coming from a manager of the company. However, when a true salesperson calls, it might still be an annoyance, but at least you can distinguish that the call was not automated, and you can usually ascertain whether or not it was outsourced to someone reading a script. The sales call thus passes the Turing Test for Business Complexity.

The original Turing Test was a thought experiment designed to start a discussion about whether or not computers could think and, ultimately, to ask if computers could replace humans. The Turing Test adapted for business complexity is asking if managers can be replaced. In the postwar economy large parts of the role of business workers have been replaced. Factories in developed economies have been shut down as manufacturing has been outsourced to lower-cost jurisdictions. Secretarial roles have all but disappeared as the rise of word-processing programs and scheduling programs has eliminated the need for secretaries. Many white-collar jobs have disappeared as consultants have been engaged to deal with specific complicated tasks such as accounting. Enterprise management systems have replaced business analysts. Explicitly, few businesses characterize tasks as simple, complicated, or complex, but the reality is that in the search for operational and cost efficiencies, tasks that are simple or complicated have gradually been eliminated or outsourced. Indeed, a simplified form of the Turing Test for business complexity just might be determining if a task can be outsourced, computer automated, or completed by a robot or computer.

The Complex Business World

Business is ultimately about human interactions. Someone develops and provides a product or service, and someone else buys that product or service. Business is not about machine interactions. This obvious and trivial distinction is critically important, as it is also what distinguishes complexity. Complexity generally occurs whenever and wherever there are human interactions. Where the presence of a human manager is necessary, there is complexity.

Examples of business complexity abound. The manufacture of a product may be complicated. The initial creative idea behind developing the product as well as the marketing of it, however, are almost always complex. Modern manufacturing is frequently not dependent upon human interactions, as the rise of the use of robots demonstrates. Marketing, however, is about appealing to human emotions, whether of individuals or of a "target market" group. The human element is the defining distinction between the complicated world of manufacturing and the complex world of marketing. Even more complex is the development of an original product or service idea.

Consider, for example, the iPhone. When the iPhone was first introduced it instantly became wildly popular. What made it popular were the design and the perceived "coolness" factor of the device. Few consumers cared about how it was manufactured or where it was manufactured. The manufacturing was complicated, as was the electronic design of the device. However, this was not the iPhone's competitive advantage. Similar devices had equivalent if not better internal electronic design and manufacturing, yet few of these other devices inspired the excitement of the iPhone. What consumers cared about was the way they interfaced with the iPhone. It was the small and almost imperceptible details, such as how the phone felt in their hand, that counted. As well, the larger-than-life persona of Apple's CEO, Steve Jobs, also played a huge role. It was Apple's command of the complexity of the smartphone market that gave them a competitive advantage and not the complicated task of the manufacturing and engineering. Very few laud Apple for its manufacturing prowess. In fact most of the company's manufacturing is outsourced. What makes Apple successful is its creativity in seeing a product need and its ability to create market hype around it. It can be argued that it was subjective and complex "people design" rather than objective and complicated "engineering design" that made the iPhone so popular.

The iPhone is just one example that illustrates the system dichotomy between manufacturing and marketing. Manufacturing and functional design, such as the internal design of the phone, are complicated tasks that a business must perform, and perform competently. However, the complex task of marketing and packaging the products is more likely to lead to competitive advantage. Marketing requires capturing and keeping the imagination of the consumer, which Apple was able to do spectacularly successfully with the iPhone. The imagination of the consumer and, perhaps more accurately, the imagination of a group of consumers, is a complex system. With the iPhone, Apple mastered the complexity.

There is an interesting counter-example to the iPhone that also involves Apple. The Lisa personal computer was developed by Apple in the early 1980s. It had many advanced features for the time, including being the first serious business computer to use a graphical user interface. In terms of technology and manufacturing it was clearly superior to most of what else was available in the market at the time. It was also a commercial failure. It did not capture the imagination of its target market, and it did not sell. With the Lisa computer, Apple did most things right in terms of the complicated tasks but failed at the complex task of engaging the consumer. Ironically, Apple was much more successful with the Mac computer, which was introduced after the Lisa. Although the initial Apple Mac computer was in many ways technically inferior to the Lisa, it was marketed to engage the imagination and emotions of the consumer. The Mac quickly became a status symbol for the "coolness" that Apple subsequently has been known for. The Lisa was marketed with "complicated thinking," while the Mac was marketed with "complexity thinking." The change in marketing mindset made all the difference.

Culture and Complexity

Consistent with the observation that complexity involves human interaction, it follows that developing a corporate culture is another complex business task. While payroll functions of the human resources department can be automated or outsourced, the creation and maintenance of the corporate culture cannot be outsourced; the managers of an organization must handle it themselves. Culture cannot be created through a set of rule books or guidelines. Neither can culture be created by edict. Culture is something that must be actively and dynamically managed. One cannot objectively define or label a company's culture, but culture is something that is recognized as distinct and important yet constantly changing and evolving. Corporate culture is emergent, which as previously discussed is one of the key characteristics of a complex system.

One of the key methods by which corporate culture is developed is through the hiring process. The recruitment and selection of strategically important employees is another task that cannot be outsourced and that exhibits clear signs of complexity. While résumés can be scanned by a computer for the applicant's functional traits and perhaps even personal tendencies, the hiring decision for all but the most low-level jobs is ultimately based on the interview. The interview plays the role of the original Turing Test. While machine filtering of résumés and social media activity can select candidates with the right experience, skills, and credentials, it is the interview that determines which candidates are the best "fit" for the organization. It is true that many companies follow a scripted set of interview questions, which may be thought of as a decision "recipe." However, anyone who has conducted hiring interviews knows that virtually every candidate brings a different set of strengths and weaknesses to the interview, and thus hiring decisions are almost always subjective. If the hiring decision is made by a committee, there is rarely a candidate who is universally favored by all of the panelists. This fact clearly illustrates the complexity inherent in hiring.

Office politics is another area rife with business complexity. Office politics plays a large part in the efficiency of the organization and helps, at least partially, to define the corporate culture as a dynamic complex system. The workplace culture is based on cliques of people who continually form and reform among themselves. These cliques are constantly changing. Relationships change based on individuals' opinions of others in an adaptive way that in large part is based on their perception of how they themselves are being perceived by others. Office politics – in a classic game-theory fashion – is shaped by considerations such as whether or not I want to go along with you depends on whether or not I think you want to go along with me. The resulting interplay demonstrates classic characteristics of complex system dynamics.

Product Development and Complexity

Research and development (R&D) is a critical business function in many industries. Pharmaceuticals, social media, telecommunications, automobiles, sporting goods, and agriculture are just a few of the industries where R&D separates the business winners from the losers. Success in research and development is based in large part on creativity and imagination, and also, in no small part, on luck. Creativity, imagination, and, yes, even luck are all complex in nature. R&D obviously requires highly trained and capable researchers to carry out the work, but skill alone accounts for a very small percentage of R&D success. Ironically, the greater the skill and talent of the researcher, the smaller the probability that the result of the research will be a truly path-breaking product. Paradigm-changing products tend to come from thinking differently, which, by definition, one cannot be trained to do. For this reason alone, breakthroughs in research frequently occur by accident.

Consider, for instance, the development of the Post-it Note, which has been a standout product for its developer, 3M. The original research behind the Post-it Note had the objective of producing a super-strong industrial adhesive. What resulted was the exact opposite; a super-weak adhesive that is used for office and stationery applications. A further irony with Post-it Notes is that when they were first test marketed under the name "Press'n Peel" the results came back extremely negative. The product testing showed that the notes would be a commercial flop. As a research project the Post-it Note was an abject failure, on both the scientific side and from the marketing research angle. Yet Post-it Notes have become one of the most popular and profitable products ever for 3M, and remain so to this day. If 3M management had stuck with complicated-style thinking, Post-it Notes never would have seen the light of day commercially. The complex nature of research and development combined with the complexity of marketing are what made the product such a success.

The dynamics of industry competition provide another prime example of complexity. While companies make plans and attempt to implement well-thought-out and meticulously researched strategies, the reality is that their competition is also doing the same. In addition there is the shifting landscape of the consumer market, which also reacts to the changing offerings provided by the various industry participants. Apple dominated the early personal computer market, while IBM ignored the market completely. Upstart competitors such as Commodore arose to become a force but then disappeared forever into the dustbin of history as personal computers developed into mainstream staples. In turn, Apple became a niche player in the computer market but then re-emerged as a leading-edge company with the introduction of the iPod and iTunes, which also fundamentally changed the music industry. The history of the personal-computing-devices industry has so many twists and turns, with participants falling in and out of favor with consumers, that it would be almost unbelievable if it were written up as a novel – a drama about the changing actions and activities of the players as they simultaneously tried to create sustainable market niches for themselves while the market was simultaneously developing unthought-of new uses for their products. All of this adaptive change and emergence is of course ongoing still, and the industry has much more evolving to do. The evolution from mainframes to desktops to laptops to tablets, to smartphones, to smart watches, and so on, is not complete. The future phases of computer development are as exciting to look forward to as they are ultimately unknown.

Complexity Matters

Complexity abounds in business. Arguably, most business functions can be considered to be complex to at least some degree. In fairness, most business functions also consist of components that are simple or complicated processes. Without an understanding and appreciation of the three types of systems, managers are working with an incomplete toolset. However, even a basic understanding of complexity can lead to a significant competitive advantage for an enlightened manager who is willing to try to acknowledge and embrace complexity.

Up until now, this chapter has focused on identifying and distinguishing between systems that are simple, complicated, or complex. This may seem to be an academic exercise that, while interesting, has few practical implications. Nothing could be further from the truth.

There are four major reasons why understanding complexity in a business context is not just an academic exercise. The first is that the ability to manage complexity is the key to competitive advantage. The second is that while complex systems need to be managed differently from complicated systems, it is likely that virtually all of a manager's formal training has been based on complicated thinking. The third reason is the fact that complex systems are being mistakenly managed with complicated thinking. This is a modus operandi that leads to not just suboptimal but potentially disastrous results as unintended consequences rise to the surface. Finally and perhaps most importantly in the current global business context, ideas and information matter more than muscle and technical know-how. For individual managers, this means their career-based competitive advantage is based on their understanding of complexity rather than their complicated thinking. In a complex environment, knowledge becomes a commodity, and thus the manager must learn new skills and develop a different mindset to be successful. Ultimately, business is complex, not complicated.

Knowledge and competencies can be easily replicated, outsourced, offshored, or delivered by a robot or a computer. The only competitive advantage of manager or of a business is the ability to create products with perceived value added and to respond better to the complex, ever-changing wants and needs of their clients. This requires skill not in complicated management but in complexity management.

Consider, for instance, the popular situation comedy *The Big Bang Theory*, which is centered on four geeky young scientists. The entire premise of the comedy is the hopelessness of the lead character, Dr Sheldon Cooper, to cope in modern society. Sheldon is a perfectly rational and fact-oriented individual. He views the world as a completely complicated system, where every action is to be solved by knowledge of the laws of science and by rational thought. This hyper-rationality, however, leads to absurd conclusions and actions on his part, particularly by comparison with Penny, the much less well-educated next-door neighbor, an aspiring actress who works as a restaurant waitress. Sheldon is living in what he falsely perceives to be a completely complicated world – and the results are both humorous and ridiculous. His personal management style is complicated but far less successful than Penny's less rigid and less intellectual approach to life. While *The Big Bang Theory* takes complicated thinking to the extreme, it clearly illustrates the folly of strictly complicated thinking in a complex world.

Managers today are frequently acting more like Sheldon than like the better adapted and more worldly Penny. Assuming that management issues can and should be solved through rational analysis and calculation is a form of complicated thinking. The only thing that prevents real managers from suffering the comical results achieved by Sheldon is that most managers are not as intelligent or as persistent as Sheldon. In the quest for perfection, however, there is a danger that professional managers will become more and more like Sheldon and thus less able to deal with the reality of complexity.

The more complex an issue is, the more valuable the role of the manager becomes. In addition, the more complex the system, the more differentiated the abilities and the actions of different managers will be. The fact that complex systems are not predictable or reproducible is a profound and, at first glance, a disturbing truth. If results cannot be predicted, and if results cannot be reproduced, then the task of managing complex systems seems to be hopeless. However, this does not mean that complex systems can or should be ignored by managers. In fact, the opposite is true. As will be argued at length in later chapters, the lack of predictability and reproducibility means that the role of the manager becomes ever more important and an understanding of the complexity-based tactics to be discussed throughout this book all the more essential for achieving a competitive advantage.

If one considers the variety of tasks that the business professional performs it becomes obvious that many of the most value-adding tasks are complex. Complexity is the dominant paradigm that both managers and organizations need to master to become successful. Knowledge of simple or complicated systems might provide a company with a patent and a short-term competitive advantage, but ultimately it is an appreciation of complexity that leads to long-term success.

Player Piano, published in 1952, was the first novel by Kurt Vonnegut, one of America's most critically acclaimed writers.[6] In this novel, Vonnegut explored what would happen in a world where the decisions and actions of workers are programmed into machines. This concept was taking the scientific-management ideas of Frederick Taylor and the then nascent fields of computers and robotics to a futuristic conclusion. The novel chronicles how the actions of skilled laborers could be digitized by closely examining their precise moves and then programming their moves into a computer. In turn the computers would control robots that would replicate the same moves and produce a similar level of craftsmanship, but only without labor. In Vonnegut's literary scenario, corporations and governments were run solely by those who had PhDs in various areas of specialization, to take advantage of their academic credentials and unique expertise.

In terms of systems thinking, the novel was an examination of what would happen to business if only complicated thinking was applied and complexity thinking was completely ignored. You don't have to read the novel to speculate that things ended up badly in Vonnegut's not-so-imaginary future. We all recognize that there are still roles for skilled craftsman and for ideas that emanate from places other than academia. Despite all of the advances in scientific management, robotics, and executive management training, the reality is that manufacturing and the management of manufacturing are still as much of an art as a science in virtually all sectors of the economy. While many formerly labor-intensive factory jobs have indeed been replaced by robots or outsourced to less costly foreign workers, the reality is that the nuances and actions of skilled laborers and the decision-making abilities of managers cannot and likely never will be totally replaced. The reason for this is that business is complex; it's not complicated.

Chaos and Wickedness

Before concluding this chapter, we need to quickly consider two other types of systems that are often considered to be related to complexity. These system types are chaos and wicked problems.

The meteorologist Edward Lorenz is generally credited with discovering chaos theory. Dr. Lorenz was building computer models of how weather patterns develop. The models took a long time to run on the computers, particularly with the computer technology that Lorenz was using in the 1960s. It was often necessary for Lorenz to pause the running of his models, and when he did so he would copy down the current state of the weather pattern he was studying so he could use it as the initial point to restart and thus continue his model. What Lorenz noticed, however, was that he achieved very different results with his models when he stopped at an intermediate point than when he let his models run continuously without stopping. This was despite the fact that there was no randomness in his models; all the equations were identical, and he started each model with the exact same inputs. What Lorenz concluded was that the small rounding errors made when he copied down the intermediate results to restart the model were the reason for the total change in the eventual outputs of his models.

Lorenz had a very concrete and very objective mathematical model. The terms and factors in his model were known – in fact, they were created by Lorenz and his research team. Moreover, there were no random variables in his models. The models were completely deterministic. However, if the conditions used to start the model were off by even the tiniest fraction, the outcome of the model would be totally different and totally unpredictable.

This effect became known as sensitivity to initial conditions or, more commonly, the Butterfly Effect. In essence it was as if the small perturbation of a butterfly flapping its wings on the west coast would in time totally change the weather on the east coast a few days later. The smallest change in initial conditions would produce complete unpredictability or chaos in the results – and thus the science of chaos theory was born.

Chaos, or chaos theory, has many elements in common with complexity. However, there are a couple of important differences as well. The primary similarity is that in both types of systems a small perturbation can produce a big change in results. The Butterfly Effect is exhibited in both chaos and complexity. Another common element that is related to the Butterfly Effect is that prediction is practically impossible in both types of systems. A key difference, however, is that a chaotic system is completely deterministic. That is, a set of equations can be written down for a chaotic system. This means that, if and only if one knows the exact starting conditions, then with a chaotic system one can predict how the system will evolve. In contrast, with complexity there is no set of equations that underlies the system, and thus one cannot, even conceptually, hope to predict accurately how events will evolve.

Chaos theory is in practice a very interesting branch of mathematics. Using relatively simple equations and a computer drawing program, one can produce beautiful "fractal" diagrams, such as Mandelbrot Sets, that evolve from a chaotic system.[7] Chaos patterns can also be seen in various places in nature, such as in the shape of the leaves of ferns or the growth and decline of animal populations. Chaos theory also has a practical use in cryptology for computer security. However, for most managerial purposes, chaos theory has limited practical applicability. This is because of the critical importance of initial conditions – which in business are rarely if ever quantifiable to the degree of precision necessary. In addition, it is generally not possible to determine an exact set of equations for how a practical business situation may evolve. However, researchers are constantly looking for business applications in areas such as financial market trading and economic patterns in which chaos theory might be applied.

Complexity does share a lot of traits with chaos. Scientist and author Scott Page calls complexity the "interesting in-between" between systems[8] that are complicated and those that are chaotic. While complex systems are not deterministic like chaotic systems, they do share the important and common trait of unpredictable outcomes.

While "chaos" can be well defined mathematically, "wicked problems" have no such clarity. As with complexity, there is no universally accepted definition of what a wicked problem is. The meaning of "wickedness," like that of "complexity," depends more on what it is not than on what it is. Generally, a wicked problem is one that has many interrelated parts such that changing one part affects every other part, making it seem impossible to come to a comprehensive solution. A wicked problem could be composed of simple, complicated, and even complex parts.

The concept of wicked problems rose to prominence in the field of social engineering and change. In dealing with issues of social change there are often competing interests between factions and constraints, with a variety of interrelated feedback loops or connections between them. An example of a wicked problem would be the issues surrounding the expansion of a city's garbage infrastructure. Everyone wants waste collection, but no one wants the garbage dump or the recycling plant in their neighborhood. Various lobbying groups, both formal and informal, will form to put forward their own issues but usually without solving the competing issues. The politics of climate change are often considered an example of a wicked problem, in that we all want readily available, convenient, and low-cost energy but do not want the associated harmful environmental effects that such energy often produces.

Complexity, as with chaos, shares a lot of traits with wickedness. For starters, both wicked problems and complex issues generally have no clearly defined way to measure success. Furthermore, both wicked and complex issues tend to have no well-defined end point: that is, they tend to be long-term or ongoing issues that change or evolve. The main difference between complex and wicked issues is that complexity exhibits the property of emergence. While wicked problems frequently change their characteristics, they do so in a way that is fundamentally different from that of the emergence exhibited by complexity.

Another practical difference between issues that are considered to be complex and those that are considered to be wicked is that wicked problems often have clear desired outcomes. Complexity, in contrast, has emergence, which frequently is characterized by unpredictable outcomes.

For practical purposes, wicked problems can be considered to be closely aligned with and similar to complex problems. Little can be gained from attempting at this stage of development of the fields to articulate the differences in what are imprecise categories to begin with. The main commonality is that wicked situations and complex situations are not complicated.

TWO

THE FALSE AXIOMS OF BUSINESS

There are many implicit axioms in business. You will recall from the preface that an axiom is something that everyone unquestioningly assumes to be true – something that is agreed upon as a universal fact. Axioms are often present in a complicated system. The axioms of business outlined below are implicit, rather than being explicitly stated like the axioms you may have learned in a university math class. They are also implicit in that no one really spells out business axioms as clearly as they do the axioms of mathematics. However, we know they exist because, consciously or unconsciously, managers act as if they believe them.

   Despite the fact that the overwhelming majority of managers act as if the axioms outlined below are true, I will argue that each of these supposed truths is indeed false, or at least a misconstrued myth. Collectively these axioms support the paradigm that business is complicated – perhaps the biggest false axiom of all. What follows is a critical examination and questioning of these axioms.

People Are Complicated

The first false axiom is that "People are complicated." In other words, it is assumed that people act according to a well-established set of laws and their actions are completely reproducible given the same set of conditions and inputs.

   The central underlying premise of this axiom is the concept of the rational economic man. The initial version of this concept assumes that individuals will act in such a way that their wealth is maximized. There are a couple of problems with this. First, it assumes that individuals are knowledgeable enough to know exactly what is and is not in their own economic best interests. Anyone who has tried to manage their own retirement portfolio, including the tax implications, knows that this assumption does not necessarily hold true.

A second and perhaps more conceptually important problem with belief in the concept of the rational economic man is that not everyone behaves in a way that is strictly wealth enhancing. Perhaps nothing is more central to wealth enhancement than a person's choice of career. However, many people choose careers or choose to live in certain locations where they know that their wealth will most likely not be maximized. Most people, and especially the younger generation of workers, tend to choose careers they are interested in or because they believe they will enjoy the work. The perceived lifestyle of a career, or an interest in working for a certain company, will often trump a more lucrative job offer. Organizations know this, of course, and many now offer corporate facilities such as a games room, assistance with child care, or even allowances for letting employees devote a certain percentage of their time to charitable activities or to their own business or professional development.

Many people still choose their careers by resorting to a default choice based on whatever job offer they receive from rather indiscriminately distributing their résumé to a variety of different employers. The reality is that most people fall into a career through luck or serendipity. They happen to make a chance contact that leads to a job that eventually develops into a career. Despite the availability and advice of career counselors, it seems that many young people exercise little or no conscious control over their career choices. The idea that a person's career is the result of a conscious decision appears to be a product of the rational man myth.

The widespread assumption that the choice of a career is usually governed by a desire to maximize one's wealth is just one example of a mistaken belief in the myth of "rational economic man." Even most economists agree that a strict adherence to the belief that "rational economic man" is primarily focused on maximizing wealth is flawed;

rather, "wealth maximizing" should instead be defined more broadly as "utility maximizing." From this perspective, "utility" can be loosely thought of as "happiness." Thus, a more realistic approach is to see rational economic man as someone who acts to increase his or her utility or personal happiness. The problem with this is that we are also bad at maximizing our happiness. Anyone who has watched children (or adults, for that matter) struggle to choose their favorite flavor at the ice-cream store knows how hard it can be to make up our minds about what makes us happy. As well, what makes us happy depends to a large extent on the context – something that retailers are knowledgeable enough to exploit with the design and the mood they create in their stores.

There is an inherent issue with optimization of utility functions of happiness. By definition, there is supposedly a choice or a decision that will maximize our utility for a given situation. There are also likely a large number of other choices that will give us almost but not quite maximum utility. Returning to the earlier example of choosing a flavor of ice cream, the optimal choice might be chocolate at a particular time. However, for most children (and adults), strawberry, maple swirl, or even vanilla might also be very satisfying, although not quite optimal. The difference between optimal and almost optimal will most likely be within measurement error and thus undetectable. However, in the quest to be optimal we may worry so much about making the correct and most rational choice that we actually lower the overall happiness or utility of buying ice cream because of the stress of believing we should, and can, pick optimally.

The analogy holds for business as well. It is safe to assume, by definition, that there is a mathematically optimal decision for a manager to make. However, other choices are likely to be almost as suitable. The difference between the choices is likely to be so small as to be undetectable. However, as in the ice-cream example, the time and energy expended in trying to make the most rational choice are likely to be much larger than the difference between the optimal decision and the many almost-optimal decisions.

Furthermore, not only do we have trouble deciding what makes us happy or maximizes our utility, but we also change our mind about our choices seemingly at random. Our choices appear to be inconsistent or irrational when studied by the unbiased eye of the academic researcher. Daniel Kahneman and Amos Tversky are two such academic researchers who studied the intersection between psychology, economics, and how people make decisions under uncertainty and risk.

One of Kahneman and Tversky's discoveries is what they called prospect theory.[1] In a series of cleverly designed experiments, they showed that people weigh the possibility of a gain differently than they weigh the possibility of a loss. They showed that the possibility of losing a dollar is considered by most people to be more harmful or painful than the benefit from the possibility of gaining a dollar. One implication of this is that most people will not take a fair bet. This, of course, is irrational according to classical economic decision making. If a bet is fair, one should, all else being equal, be indifferent to taking the bet or not taking the bet. For example, assume that a fair coin is about to be tossed. If it comes up heads, you win one dollar. If it comes up tails you lose one dollar. Even though the expected value of the gamble is zero, most people will not accept that bet.[2] Now contrast this outcome with the fact that millions of people play the lottery each week even though they know that the expected outcome of their lottery ticket is negative. As another example, consider the popularity of casinos, where again all but the most foolhardy gamblers know that the odds of winning are stacked against them. This is not only irrational decision making, it is also inconsistent. It also, especially in the case of the casino, shows that our decision making might be highly dependent on context.

In finance, an entire field of study called behavioral finance has arisen to study the known irrationality in the way people deal with financial matters. There are many behavioral finance effects besides prospect theory. For instance, as one additional example, there is the bias of overconfidence. Humorist Garrison Keillor labeled this the Lake Wobegon Effect. The Lake Wobegon Effect is when the majority of people rank themselves above average. A specific example is "90 percent of all school districts rank themselves in the top 10 percent." This may seem like a humorous statement – which of course it is intended to be – but real surveys show that the effect is real and perhaps not so funny. For instance, when investors are asked how they think the stock market will perform, and how their own particular portfolio will perform in the next year, a significant majority will state that their portfolio will perform much better than the average portfolio. The bias of overconfidence is when we see that, in general, people believe that they are smarter, more capable, or more in control than the average. By the laws of probability this is obviously false.

A case can be made, however, that there is more to irrational decision making than can be explained by the findings of behavioral finance. Behavioral finance as a field attempts to explain how people act irrationally when making decisions when they are by themselves. However, many if not most of our irrational decisions are made in the context or the presence of others. This leads to a different type of challenge to the concept of the rational economic man that can be called an effect of sociological finance (as opposed to behavioral finance).

As an example of how the social context affects our decision making, consider the simple social experiments performed by experimental psychologist Solomon Asch. The experiment, now known as the Asch Conformity Experiment, involved several test subjects.[3] In this experiment, all but one member of the test group were actors and were acting in coordination with the experimenter. The subjects were shown a card on which a set of three lines were labeled. The supposed role of the test subjects was to tell the experimenter which line on the card was the longest. On the card, one line was obviously much longer than the others. However, all the actors were coached to pick one of the shorter lines as the longest line. Under these conditions, the real test subject would almost always conform to the selection of the actors posing as test subjects. In other words, the real test subject would also tell the experimenter that one of the obviously shorter lines was the longest line. The purpose of the experiment was to show just how strongly we are affected by the thoughts and decisions of others, even though, independently, we might disagree with them.

These experimental results, as well as practical results that we all experience every day, in others and in ourselves, highlight the fact that, individually and collectively, people are anything but completely and consistently rational, as the rational economic man model assumes. We have built-in biases and are affected in our decision making by context and by the presence of others. People do not act according to some identifiable and replicable law of behavior. It clearly appears that there is more to our make-up than can be explained by the simple and fatalistic determinism of philosophers such as Pierre-Simon Laplace and others through the ages. At least when it comes to economic matters, it does appear that we have free will, no matter how irrational or inconsistent it may lead us to be, and our fates are not completely determined by rational considerations.

From the laboratory and from personal experience, we learn that the axiom that people are complicated is inherently false. While in the aggregate we may behave according to certain statistical tendencies most of the time, it is clear that as individuals we are clearly complex rather than complicated when it comes to economic decision making.

Knowledge Is Valuable

It is assumed in business that knowledge is valuable. In certain contexts this is certainly true. If you are valuing the price of a financial security, such as a mortgage-backed bond, it is certainly helpful to know how the security works and some basic financial pricing methodology.[4] If you are running a manufacturing facility, it is certainly necessary to have a workforce that is knowledgeable about how to run and maintain the machinery and operate the production process. It is also necessary to have someone knowledgeable about distribution channels and the relevant regulations in the various jurisdictions to which the company ships its products. However, all these examples describe a complicated task, and the role of such tasks in creating competitive advantage in business is diminishing.

In today's highly connected business environment, knowledge is more and more becoming a commodity. A quick search on the Internet will produce financial pricing models and calculators, as well as examples of how to implement them. Manufacturing can be quickly outsourced to a variety of different specialty manufacturers who are likely using either low-skilled labor or highly automated, machine-run factories. Likewise, distribution and sales channels for many products can and are functions that may be efficiently outsourced.

What matters in today's economy is the knowledge worker. But this is really a misnomer. As most knowledge can be quickly replicated, bought from a specialist, or even downloaded from the Internet, it is not the knowledge worker who is valued but the "thinking" worker. It is thinking, creativity, and risk taking that lead to sustainable competitive advantage. These are qualities that cannot be downloaded from the Web or outsourced to a specialty firm. These are qualities that can only exist in an organization's employees. It is thinking that is valuable. Knowledge is a commodity.

Knowledge is a trait of the "complicated" world. In a complicated world, knowledge is valuable. You want your surgeon to have knowledge, and you want the pilot of the plane you are on to have knowledge. But applying knowledge is very different from thinking, creating, and appropriate risk taking. Thinking, creativity, and risk taking are complex skills. They are the skills that have value and that lead to sustainable competitive advantage. It is what is *done* with knowledge that should be prized.

The rise of computers and robots is exploding the myth that knowledge is valuable. As discussed in chapter 1 and confirmed by many observers, computers and robots are not just taking over what traditionally were thought of as low-value blue-collar manufacturing jobs.[5] Computers and robots are increasingly displacing white-collar workers such as lawyers, financial analysts, and even medical professionals. Furthermore, service jobs are also affected, as robots are now serving customers in some Japanese restaurants.

The philosopher Eric Hoffer once stated that, "in times of change learners inherit the earth; while the learned find themselves beautifully equipped to deal with a world that no longer exists."[6] The axiom that knowledge automatically provides a competitive advantage is a myth. Managers who rely on knowledge alone are likely to see themselves replaced in the near future or, at a minimum, find themselves placed in a series of short-term consulting assignments.

Problems Are Tractable

We assume that the great problems of business have solutions – that they are tractable. If only enough intellectual talent and resources are applied to a problem, then, with tenacity and brain power, it will be solved. The reality is that the most important and valuable problems of business have proven to be intractable.

In addition to being intractable, the most valuable problems of business are constantly changing and evolving. Business is not static; the context of business keeps changing as turnover in an organization changes its staffing, as technological developments change processes and what they can do, as consumers change their appetites, and, of course, as competitors change their own responses. The most valuable questions of business are in a constantly evolving dance that never quite repeats the same steps twice.

Chapter 5, "Managing Complexity," will discuss at length how the task of the manager is not necessarily to solve problems but to manage problems. In part, this is a complexity-management technique, but also in large part it is due to the nature of the problems that managers face. Solving a problem is like hitting a target with a bow and arrow. It is one task to hit a stationary target. However, in business the target is constantly moving in unpredictable ways (see the next section on the futility of planning and forecasting); moreover, most of the target is unseen by the shooter, because a business manager almost never has perfect information or perfect foresight.

Tractable problems are almost always simple or complicated problems. Complex problems are intractable. Although intractable problems are generally the more important and valuable to solve, the best that a manager can do is to try to manage them. As uncomfortable as it may be, the concept of tractable problems in business for the most part is a myth, at least for the problems faced by senior management and a company's board of directors. The reality is intractable problems. This leads of course to the myth that planning is essential.

If business problems were tractable, there would be no need for managers. If all business problems were tractable, computers would almost certainly be capable of making decisions both more optimally and much more quickly than human managers. With an increasing awareness of the difference between complicated and complex tasks, it is likely that many managerial functions will indeed be taken over by computers or robots. The reality, however, is that few important business problems are truly tractable, and thus there will always be a need for decision-making managers.

Planning Is Essential

Chapter 6 will discuss strategy and strategic planning at length. At this point it is important to look at the role that planning plays in creating and reinforcing the "business is complicated" paradigm. Every business school student has taken at least one business school course, and likely more than one, on various aspects of business planning. Business planning is the centerpiece of the command-and-control mindset that is implicit in complicated thinking. Most companies prepare at least an annual business plan, supplemented with a five-year plan and perhaps quarterly plans. Entrepreneurs are coached on creating a business plan before approaching a bank or a venture-capital fund for financing. Of course, employees are encouraged and rewarded for working to the plan. However, the importance and effectiveness of planning are vastly overrated.

Planning works very well for complicated situations. These are situations in which the parameters are known and in which results are predictable. Thus, planning allows a company to see the outcomes of various alternatives and plan to utilize the choice that fits best with their strategy. For instance, delivery van drivers can plan their route based on the drop-offs they need to make and highly predictable traffic patterns. Certain routes will minimize the time and the cost of making the deliveries. Through the use of GPS data and updated traffic patterns, such routes can also be recalculated and the driver rerouted in real time throughout the day if conditions change. The planning involved and the optimization algorithms developed by the large international delivery companies allow for a valuable increase in efficiency. For instance, delivery company UPS estimates that it has saved more than 38 million liters of gasoline in North America in the last decade alone by banning left-hand turns in its drivers' routes.[7] However, unexpected events such as a flat tire or a traffic accident can occasionally render even the best of plans useless.

If business can be compared to war, and there are many similarities between the two to suggest that they are alike, then an old military adage about planning might be appropriate: "No plan ever survived contact with the enemy." A related adage is, "If you want to make God laugh, tell her your plans." Planning is great for a static, complicated world, and later, in chapter 6, it will be argued that planning is a valuable exercise to do even in the face of complexity. However, it is the exercise that is valuable and useful, not the plan itself. Planning in the context of complexity is more of an exercise in creativity than it is the creation of a blueprint for action.

Closely related to planning is forecasting. Admittedly many companies are less confident in their forecasting abilities than in their planning abilities. This is somewhat ironic, as the main input to the planning model is most frequently the output from the forecasting exercise. In any case, it is widely accepted that the future is inherently unknowable, particularly in this age of disruptive technology.

Virtually all forecasting techniques rely in part on projections from the past. When innovation was low and mainly based on extensions of previous technology, the use of past trends was a reasonable basis for forecasting. However, with disruptive technologies, and with the presence of complexity, the past is not a good starting basis for a forecast. Disruptive technologies – such as block-chain record keeping in financial technology, Uber and Lyft in the taxi industry, self-driving cars and trucks, advances in big data, and 3D printing – are creating seismic shifts that make it impossible to guess at– let alone forecast – the future.

Despite the ubiquity of companies that religiously execute planning exercises, a study by Henry Mintzberg found that such planning exercises explained only 20 percent of a company's actions, while almost 80 percent of a company's actions were based on spontaneous decision making.[8] This shows in concrete terms the folly of considering the strategic plan as a blueprint for action.

"Data Is Good"

There is an old joke about a drunkard looking for his keys under a lamppost. A policeman comes along and asks the drunk what he is doing. In a slurred voice the drunk says that he has lost his keys and is looking for them. The policeman offers to help and the two of them search everywhere under the lamppost for the lost keys. After a while the policeman asks the drunk if he is sure that the lost keys are at that location. The drunk responds, "Well, no, officer, I lost my keys over in that dark alley across the street." "Well why are you looking for your keys here!?" asks the policeman in a frustrated tone. To this the drunk replies, "Well it's dark over there and the light is so much better for searching over here!"

Consulting data can make sense, but too often it seems that managers are acting like the foolish drunkard. They are busy analyzing problems for which they have data (i.e., "light," as in the joke), rather than working on the real issues they need to be thinking about but for which they have insufficient data.

For complicated problems, data are generally available. Due to the nature of complex problems, however, data that could be used to solve them are generally not available, even conceptually. This is because the factors that underlie a complicated problem are known, while many of the factors relevant to a complex problem are unknown. You cannot collect data on factors that are unknown. Furthermore, due to the nonlinearity of complex problems and the corresponding Butterfly Effect, even if the factors are known, the precision needed for the data to be useful for a complex problem would not be achievable.

Management guru Peter Drucker once rightly claimed that "what gets measured gets managed." The necessity is for managers to ask if this is always appropriate. Just because there are data available on an issue does not mean that the issue deserves management's time and effort. Often, particularly in cases of complexity, it is situations for which there are no or limited data that most need management's attention.

It is tempting to do research and management where there are data. It gives the manager a feeling of doing something useful. However, managers need to be careful of falling into a trap of managing the measurable rather than managing the important.

Managing to data is relatively easy and rewarding. There is a pleasing clarity to knowing that one is producing answers and on the right track as verified by cold hard data and mathematics, and if not on track, to having a quantified direction of how one needs to adjust to get closer to the answer. Managing without the benefit of data is hard, ambiguous, and, thus, frustrating. One can never be objectively sure of how one is doing. It is not possible to keep score. However, just as it makes no sense for the drunk to look for his keys under the lamppost if he lost his keys across the street in a dark alley, it likewise makes no sense for a manager to manage to data that have no relevance to the success of the business.

"Data is good" is an axiom applicable to the complicated aspects of a business, but a foolish myth that is potentially misleading for the complex questions a manager must deal with.

Frequentist Statistics Will Improve Business Forecasting

Related to the myth of the importance of data is the myth of frequentist statistics. The fallacy of this myth was described in a very insightful and thoughtful book on risk management, *Plight of the Fortune Tellers*, by Ricardo Debonato.[9]

Frequentist statistics involve relying on the statistical trends apparent in large historical data sets. The use of frequentist statistics is implicitly based on the assumption that past trends will continue into the future. For complicated systems this is largely true, but for complexity it is patently false and misleading.

An example of the use of frequentist statistics is actuarial science, which is the basis for setting insurance rates. Take the specific example of life insurance. Based on historical mortality rates, an actuary can calculate with a high degree of precision the mortality of individuals based on certain characteristics such as age, socioeconomic factors, and lifestyle factors such as smoking and whether or not a person takes part in risky activities such as sky-diving. This analysis is valid for an insurance company, since it is dealing with large numbers of individuals and payout rates are dependent on the averages and not on the specific time of death of any given individual. There are a large number of events (deaths versus non-deaths) to consider, and in the aggregate it is quite likely that, barring unforeseen events such as a pandemic of historic proportions, the calculated number of deaths in a large group will indeed be quite close to the actual number of deaths. However, most business decisions are not of the large-sample-size type faced by an insurance company but instead are one-off decisions. This renders moot the accuracy of frequentist statistics. As a simple example, frequentist statistics tell us that the birth rate in the United States for women between the ages of fifteen and forty-four is 0.063 births per year. Obviously no woman gives birth to 0.063 children per year, but in any group of 100,000 women in this age group we would expect to have 6,300 children born.

To further illustrate the fallacy of frequentist statistics, let us consider a variant of the example of betting on the outcome of a coin toss. Imagine that you are offered a bet in which, if the coin comes up heads, you win $1.2 million, but if it comes up tails, you lose $1 million. Most people would not take that bet, as losing $1 million would bankrupt them, even though the expected value of a bet would be on average $100,000. This is a sum of money that would be significant to most people. Now let's assume that the terms of the bet are changed slightly. In the new gamble, the coin will be tossed one thousand times. Each time the coin comes up heads you will win $1.2 million, and each time the coin comes up tails you will lose $1 million. Most people will take that bet, as the overall probability of their losing money on the bet is exceedingly small. Notice that the only difference in the two gambles is that the second gamble is repeated many times, and thus frequentist statistics apply.

In business, few managers get to make the same decision over and over again. Each new hire is unique; every new product launch is unique; every major capital investment decision is unique. The situation for the manager is akin to the position of our gambler in the coin-toss example. Although frequentist statistics tell us that the expected outcome may be positive, we are reluctant to take the risk because we cannot afford to suffer the loss if we are wrong. For this reason, analysis of historical data is often of limited use.

In the case of credit card companies, frequentist statistics can be useful. A credit card company can extend credit to a new card holder based on a variety of numerical characteristics such as income earned, current debt owing, amount of time lived in the card holder's current residence, and a variety of other factors. Here, the downside loss of having individuals default on their credit card debt can be calculated with frequentist statistics, as the credit card company has thousands, or even millions, of card holders. In this case, the averages do hold, and it is analogous to the altered coin-flipping gamble, where the coin would be flipped a thousand times.

Big Data Will Improve Business Forecasting

Also closely related to the myth about the importance of data is the belief that big data will improve forecasting. There is no doubting that the use of big data has been transformative and is likely to continue to be transformative for some time yet. However, whether or not it improves forecasting is debatable.

First, there is a real danger that the rise of big data will only magnify the fallacy of frequentist statistics. Some aspects of business are complicated, or they are repeated again and again. In such cases frequentist statistics have a very valuable role to play, and managers would be wise to utilize all available data sets and the appropriate statistical tools. However, big data and frequentist statistics can be very misleading in cases of one-off decisions, when the environment has changed, or in the presence of complexity. In such cases, prudent managers will use big data with great caution and skepticism.

A second and perhaps more important issue is that big data can only tell you what has happened in the past. While knowledge of the past is helpful, it is of limited use and potentially very misleading when trying to forecast the future. For instance, it is possible with big data to track the movement of a murmuration of starlings through the sky. However, knowledge of such data only allows us to model the starlings' historical movement and is useless in predicting in which direction the murmuration will move next.

In addition, an analysis of the past does not allow one either to see a paradigm shift or to create a paradigm shift. For instance, an analysis of sales of vinyl records would not predict sales of CDs and most certainly did not predict how popular digital music would become. Relying on big data may actually hinder the ability of managers to dream up and develop valuable new products and services.

Brains Win

A pervasive business myth is that "brains win." The essence of this myth is that, with enough talent, brain power, and resources, business problems will be solved. This was also a prevailing myth in science for centuries, where the belief that science could solve the world's problems as well as its mysteries was well accepted. Managers, of course, have a vested interest in perpetuating this myth. After all, it is their brains that are supposedly the major factor behind their company's success.

The counter-argument to the "brains win" axiom is Orgel's Second Rule. Leslie Orgel was a biologist who stated that "evolution is smarter than you are," to explain that any scientist's design for evolution would come up short compared to the actual realized path that one sees in evolution.

There is a natural analogy between Orgel's Second Rule and business development and planning. Events in the business world turn out to be more creative and clever than the best minds can imagine. It is a version of the well-known adage that "truth is stranger than fiction."

With complicated systems, brains and knowledge are certainly helpful. Again, though, we see that the myth has limited application if the system is complex. As will be discussed later, humility and flexibility in thinking may be more important than simply being clever.

Organizations Optimize

Previously in this chapter, the rational economic man myth was discussed and it was concluded that it was very difficult, if not impossible, for people to optimize their personal decisions. However, is it possible for a company as whole to optimize its operations?

For the complicated processes that a company undertakes it is quite possible to optimize operations. For instance an oil refinery can optimize its profits by producing a unique combination of fuel products depending on the type of raw oil it has to refine. A delivery company can optimize the route its drivers take by managing the sequence in which they pick up and drop the various parcels. An airline company can optimize the time its planes are producing revenue by being in the air through appropriate scheduling, although weather and other events cause havoc with the optimization schedules. There are numerous other examples where companies utilize optimization techniques to maximize efficiency.

These optimization techniques are well known and are taught in every business school and engineering program. However, the question remains whether a company can optimize itself. The answer to this question is "No!" The evidence for this answer is clear. At virtually every company in the world where two employees believe they can freely talk to each other at lunch, something like the following sentence will be spoken: "Can you believe how messed up and poorly managed this company is!"

While the comment might be laughable, it is certainly a reality. Businesses are notoriously inefficient in their operations. Optimization and maximum efficiency are the goal but not the reality. Despite this fact, there is an entire industry of efficiency consultants and efficiency planners and project managers. The quest is to apply quantitative optimization techniques to the entire operations of the firm. The problem is that optimization techniques only work for complicated problems, such as increasing the yield of refined products from raw oil. Optimization does not work when a process or a situation is complex.

The belief that organizations are optimizing is not credible. The reality is that companies are satisficing; that is, instead of trying to make the best decision, they are trying not to make the worst decision. Virtually all business decisions are based on a combination of data analysis, intuition, and politicking. The satisficing comes about as each of the different stakeholders in any given decision have a different interpretation of the data, a different set of principles guiding their intuition, and a different set of political motivations. Given such a context, it is remarkable that companies are even as efficient as they are.

The factors that drive decisions in an organization are complex. The unfortunate fact is that complexity and optimization are not compatible. Complexity is the reality, and the statement that companies optimize their operations is a myth.

Experts Know Something

Starting in the mid-1980s, researcher Philip Tetlock examined the forecasts of a wide variety of experts. The forecasts were from a variety of areas, including economics, technology, and politics. The experts were mainly those who had been consulted by various government agencies. As such, they were the foremost experts in their respective fields. Tetlock followed the forecasts of these experts for decades to see how accurate their predictions were. The results he came to were disappointing. His conclusion was that "the average expert was roughly as accurate as a dart throwing chimpanzee."[10]

Companies hire experts in the belief that they know something of value that will be useful to the company in the future. The reality is quite different. This of course does not prevent the business media from constantly bringing forth such experts as part of their journalistic endeavors. As stated in the preface, my experience of acting as an expert for a media outlet was, in part, the impetus for writing this book. The more the media rely on experts, the more the experts' reputation grows, and the more they are relied on by businesses. The ability of the expert becomes a self-perpetuating myth.

The irony is that Tetlock discovered that the more confident and certain experts are, the more unreliable and inaccurate their information is likely to be. Nevertheless, the polished and media-savvy expert who confidently states forecasts as facts will be more highly regarded than the nuanced forecaster who is less confident and states several different possible forecasts or scenarios.

The reality, as we can see, is that complex situations require humility and flexibility. Managers who are considered to be experts are likely to be inflexible or overcommitted in their views and thus unlikely to have the ability to deal with complex situations. The qualities that make them experts also may make them less successful.

There is a very interesting counter-example to the forecasts of experts, and that is the wisdom of crowds. In his book *The Wisdom of Crowds*, author James Surowiecki supplies a wide variety of examples in which the average prediction of a group of non-experts dramatically outperformed the opinions of experts, even though the non-experts had little or no knowledge of the subject.[11] Surowiecki gives examples ranging from the prediction of election outcomes to the future pricing of computer chips. The point seems to be that the value of experts' opinions is highly overrated.

To sum up: a number of axioms are assumed to be important in business and form the unacknowledged base that underlies a lot of business decision making. However, many of these axioms seem to be appropriate only for applications that are complicated. They do not apply in complex situations and may in fact be counterproductive. It is clearly critical to understand whether a given situation in business is complicated or complex.

Of course the most important and the most significant myth is that business is complicated – the subject of the next chapter.

THREE

IT'S NOT COMPLICATED

In 1839 Antoni Patek and Franciszek Czapek joined together to create a company to make watches. Nearly two hundred years later, the name Patek Philippe is synonymous with some of the most complicated, expensive, and sought-after watches in the world. Patek Philippes are known for their "complications" – the functions beyond simply telling the time that can be engineered into a mechanical watch. Complications in a fine timepiece such as a Patek Philippe may include features such as a perpetual calendar that adjusts for the different number of days in each month, a chronograph for measuring two or more time intervals with the same watch, a power reserve dial, a moon phase dial, a tourbillion to adjust for the effects of gravity, and many other possible extras. Often, the more features or complications the watch has, the more desirable and collectible it becomes. Of course, all these complications are created using traditional handcrafted watchmaking techniques such as springs and gears and without modern developments such as quartz crystals or computers.

Fine handmade watches are not only expensive pieces of jewelry, with various precious gems and cases of precious metals; they are also fine pieces of advanced and detailed engineering. That, in part, is how watches with complications get their name. The fine handcrafted detail and design work required to manufacture a watch with complications are truly amazing and worthy of appreciation, and thus provide the rationale for prices of tens of thousands of dollars – and even hundreds of thousands for the most exquisite pieces.

A clockwork world view is analogous to a complicated-thinking paradigm. A fine watch is designed and built by a skilled and talented watchmaker and works with a known level of precision and accuracy. Applying such a world view to business leads to the assumption that the business manager can design and build a business to work like a watch, with a given level of precision and accuracy – if only the manager is clever enough and has the skills to calculate and manage the complications.

In the developed consumer-based world, there is a fascination with complicated things. They tend to cost more, and the engineering skill involved tends to enhance their manufacturers' prestige. The engineers behind the products win awards and get feted within their profession. As consumers we love to demonstrate our complicated products and show off our own personal knowledge and expertise by expounding on the wonderful mechanisms that we have had the means, the sophistication, and the refined taste to acquire.

However, we need to ask whether "complicated" is always better – or even necessary. I first seriously asked myself this question during a very important meeting I attended several years ago. I had flown into the city just that morning, and in my rush to get to the airport on time I had forgotten my watch. As my day was tightly packed with several different meetings I went to a department store before my first meeting to buy a rather generic watch. The watch was nothing fancy, and in fact it was a very simple watch without even a date function. However, it looked respectable even though it was inexpensive. Furthermore, I did not have time to be a picky shopper. As it happened, the key person at my first meeting that day also had a new watch, but his was a very expensive timepiece with several features such as date and day functions, numerous time zones, moon phases, and several other complications. After the meeting started, the person noticed that his watch had stopped. I doubt that it was broken, and we both assumed it had been wound and set incorrectly. (My watch, being a cheap quartz watch, did not need to be wound manually.) The rest of the meeting was taken up with the watch owner's attempts to figure out how to reset and correctly wind his watch. I enjoyed the irony that my $47 watch was functioning just fine, while his $17,000 watch, while certainly more glamorous, was not necessarily more functional.

As with watches and other consumer goods, we also sometimes have a misplaced fascination with complicated systems and processes in business. As demonstrated by such things as the ubiquitous use of elaborate PowerPoint templates and the extensive reliance on consultants and experts, industry loves to believe in the power of complicated thinking and analysis. However, as my unsophisticated watch shows, "complicated" may not always be better – or even appropriate.

This chapter outlines the characteristics of complicated processes in business. Often managers default to a "complicated mindset," and this chapter demonstrates this to be not only inefficient but downright counterproductive. Complicated thinking most definitely has a place and a role, but the truly effective manager will be able to cope with both complicated and complex situations and understand when each mindset is going to be most effective.

Pierre-Simon Laplace

The French mathematician and physicist Pierre-Simon Laplace might rightly be given the title "Father of Complicated Thinking." Laplace, who lived from 1749 to 1827, made numerous important advances in mathematics, astronomy, mechanics, and statistics. He is arguably one of the most talented and important scientists ever to live. He is also the founder of what is called scientific determinism. Laplace believed that if a person knew the position and the momentum of every particle in the world at a given point in time, then, given enough computing power, that person would be able to compute the complete history of the world as well as predict the future.

This was a bold statement with profound implications. Implicit in the statement is that there is no such thing as free will. Everything is completely determined. The past can be completely explained, and the future is calculable with complete certainty. In the context of the eighteenth and early nineteenth centuries, this was a very disturbing and controversial statement with political, religious, social, and philosophical implications that have been debated and dissected by philosophers up to the present time.

It is important to realize that Laplace did not necessarily believe that it would ever be possible to measure the position and momentum of every particle in the world. Nor did he necessarily believe that humans would ever have the computing ability to do the calculations required. The point is that, conceptually at least, Laplace believed that the world was completely determined. One could, in theory, look forward with the same degree of accuracy as one can look backward.

Laplace's scientific determinism was a key concept in the sciences for almost two hundred years, until it was supplanted by a concept known as the Heisenberg Uncertainty Principle.[1] The philosophical and religious overtones of his statement obviously caused significant debate. From the scientific viewpoint, however, it was a very compelling idea. Even today it remains an attractive idea, but its core message seems to have been taken up more by the non-scientist than the scientist.

In particular, the idea of scientific determinism has taken hold in the mind of the general public as a belief in the ability of leaders and managers to control issues as diverse as the economy, the environment, the weather, and, of course, political events. It is implicit in the hopes that we have when we consult doctors and assume that with enough diagnostic tests they will be able to prescribe a pill or a procedure that will cure us of our ills. It is implicit in the self-help industry, where a plethora of books that promote "X steps to a better life" cater to the misplaced hope that there is a formula for success. It is also implicit in our belief that the right formula will enable our managers to develop products or services that will magically increase sales by 10 percent.

What Is "Complicated"?

From the discussion in chapter 1, we understand that a truly complicated system is based on laws or undisputed axioms. It is a world of infinitely repeatable "if … then" relationships. The implication is that if we have knowledge of the complications then it will be possible to command and control for any outcome desired. Physics, for example, for the most part consists of complicated systems. For instance, there is the law of gravity. As with Newton's apple, we know that if we let go of an object it will fall to the ground. Furthermore, as anyone who has taken an elementary high school physics course knows, it is possible to calculate the speed of the object as it falls and the time it will take the object to hit the ground from a given height. While air density and resistance are additional factors, it is possible to calculate the characteristics of a falling object with a high degree of precision. The law of gravity is reproducible in that each and every time an object falls there is certainty that it will fall in the exact same way. Newton's law of gravity is an example of a complicated law of physics that dictates the movement of a falling object; it fits and conforms to a clockwork view of the world.

Processes that are strictly complicated can be distinguished from simple processes based on their level of robustness. In other words, managing a complicated system is exact, while a simple system, which also follows rules, or more accurately rules of thumb, does not require the same degree of exactness to achieve the desired result. In chapter 1 we discussed one such simple system – the making of a pot of coffee. The coffee-making process has a set of rules or processes to follow, but it does not require exactness at each step. The coffee machine would still make reasonably good coffee if a bit too much coffee were added, or if not quite enough water were put into the coffee machine. By contrast, with a complicated system, unless each step is completed with precision, or within tight boundaries, the outcome could be very different from what is desired. For instance, when apples fall out of a tree, they do not "sort of" fall; they fall straight down to the ground. Nor do apples fall with a different rate of acceleration on one day than on another. The same apple, dropped from the same tree and from the same height, falls the exact same way each and every time unless something else comes along to change its path.

In sum, a complicated system is like a well-designed mechanical watch. There are springs and gears that work in a very precise and robust way, based of course on the laws of physics and engineering that apply to springs and gears. By contrast, examples of a modern business, industry, or economy that works like a finely engineered watch are relatively rare. That fact, however, has not prevented complicated thinking from being the most prominent paradigm used in business.

Before proceeding further, we should note that, in the scientific definition of "complicated," the terms "difficult" or "hard" do not appear. While in its everyday sense the word "complicated" does generally mean difficult or hard to accomplish, in the systems sense of the word a complicated process could in fact be quite easy to master. For instance, the daily Sudoku puzzle in the paper is a clear example of a complicated problem. There is a set of rules that a Sudoku puzzle problem solver must follow, and there is only one correct result or outcome. Sudoku puzzles can be extremely difficult or quite easy to solve. Logging into your e-mail program is another example of a complicated task that is quite easy. There are specific steps you need to follow, and some of them, such as entering your password, must be done with precision.

A similar situation exists for our terms "simple" and "complex." A simple system or task is not necessarily easy to do (although it often is). For instance, teeing off in golf is simple. There is a set of guidelines and best practices for doing so. Furthermore, there is a wide variation in how it can be accomplished, so in some sense it is robust. However, many weekend duffers can attest to the fact that it is a very difficult task to do as well as a professional golfer like Rory McIlroy does it.

The Origins of Complicated Thinking in Business

Probably since the beginning of time, humans have been trying to gain understanding of and control over their environment. One can easily imagine the first merchants using knowledge and understanding of how and why people buy and sell things to gain a competitive advantage over their fellow traders. Being able to rely on oneself rather than the whim of the gods has many benefits, including a sense of self-worth, pride in one's skill, and, of course, material wealth and prestige gained through competitive advantage. Thus it is easy to imagine that the rise of complicated thinking in business is as old as business itself.

The rise of complicated thinking in industry began in earnest with the onset of the industrial age. As steam power came to be harnessed and used for industrial purposes, manufacturing and the manufacturing plant began to take off. Advances in science and engineering dramatically changed both the agrarian and industrial sectors of the economy. Complicated thinking was at the forefront of these developments, and rightly so.

Frederick Winslow Taylor, who started out as a machine-shop operator, created the field of scientific management, now commonly known as Taylorism. Taylor's insights dramatically accelerated the rise of complicated thinking in the early 1890s. As an apprentice at a machine shop, Taylor studied the movement patterns of laborers and correctly assumed that with better-designed processes workmen could be much more efficient, and as a result make their companies more efficient and profitable, too. Taylor, who had once planned to be a lawyer, eventually received a degree in engineering and began exhaustive studies of industrial processes, with a focus on the tools and processes that workers used.

Taylor applied a uniquely scientific approach to manufacturing processes. He began by breaking manufacturing tasks into their most fundamental individual steps or parts. Then Taylor used the techniques of time-and-motion studies to measure exactly how long it took the average worker to complete each step of a task. Through the results of his time-and-motion studies in combination with systematic experimentation, Taylor was able to optimize many tasks and achieve large increases in operational efficiency. His thinking created a revolution in manufacturing and established manufacturing and business practices that remain in vogue to this very day.

An example of Taylor's detailed studies is his observation of the use of the lowly but essential shovel. By examining workers' use of shovels, Taylor concluded that the most efficient shovel load was approximately twenty-two pounds. With standardized shovels, workers could increase their output by using shovels designed for each different type of load and for the loaded shovel weight of twenty-two pounds. Thus, different tasks had different-sized shovels.

Taylor's ideas caught on, his personal fame grew quickly, and he became a sought-after efficiency consultant. In a consulting capacity, Taylor would analyze a worker's workspace in detail and design a workspace that optimized the time a worker took to move between segments of an operation. Taylor's ideas were often controversial, as they frequently increased profits for plant owners while resulting in greater workloads and less downtime for the laborers. However, Taylor's ideas became dominant; the principles he expounded are still in wide use today, being taught in virtually every business school and practiced in every plant that relies on high-volume manufacturing. (It must be recognized, at this point, that mass manufacturing is a strictly complicated process.)

Another principle of Taylor's was to adjust the workflow between workers so that each worker spent the same amount of time on a task. This decreased waiting times, prevented bottlenecks, increased a plant's throughput, and led directly to the widespread adoption of the assembly line, which of course was popularized by Henry Ford. The breakdown of an assembly process into its constituent parts, with each step optimized, and with workers for each task completing a specific task within a specified time, led to specialization and much greater efficiency. The role of scientific management and manufacturing, combined with engineering principles in both product design and manufacturing, led to the idea that a company could gain competitive advantage through optimization. Henry Ford's desire for efficiency was so great that he is said to have offered a reward of $25,000 to anyone who could show him how he could save a single bolt in the manufacture of his cars. Thus, scientific management and complicated thinking became deeply entrenched in business.

Another result of Taylorism was the rise of specialization and the concept of comparative advantage. If workers specialized on just one aspect of a manufacturing process, they could more easily and quickly become proficient at that task. Workers could thus be used based on the areas in which they had comparatively better skills. It was an idea that was basically the same as having players specialize in a position in a team sport. For example, although Wayne Gretzky, arguably one of the greatest hockey players of all time, likely would have been a decent defenseman, or an even better winger, his comparative advantage was in playing center, where he could best use his goal-scoring ability.

Scientific management is very well suited to complicated tasks such as manufacturing. In fact, it can be argued that scientific management greatly changed the methods of manufacturing and helped create the modern high-output manufacturing plant. As the importance of manufacturing in the economy rose at the beginning of the twentieth century, scientific management principles became even more popular and widely followed. Scientific management also rose in prominence because of the increasing role of science in the economy. Scientists such as Albert Einstein, Marie Curie, Robert Oppenheimer, Niels Bohr, and others were becoming famous as science made rapid progress not only in the laboratory but also in the minds of society. Scientists were "rock stars" at the dawn of the twentieth century. Scientific management and Taylorism rode the wave of popularity of the scientific age.

Science, scientific management, and complicated thinking continued to gain even more public acceptance throughout the Second World War. The most obvious use of scientific principles was in the development of ever more powerful bombs, culminating in the atomic bombs that were in large part credited with ending the war sooner rather than later. Other science-based wartime developments included radar, sonar, and advances in aircraft design and large-scale armaments manufacturing. Another outcome of complicated thinking was the rise of new communications technologies and the need for secret codes. The German Enigma machine was one such device that was used to great effect by the Germans. Alan Turing, who developed the Turing Test discussed in chapter 1, was a key player in reverse-engineering the Enigma machine and helping the Allies win the war by enabling them to intercept and decode German military messages. These advances highlighted and popularized the use of scientific management and further entrenched complicated thinking.

Robert McNamara, whose ideas will be discussed at length in chapter 6, was a key player in the popularization of scientific management who used the principles of scientific management and process optimization to great effect during the Second World War and then later in the Vietnam War. McNamara and a small group of like-minded analysts used the principles of scientific management for a variety of tasks during the war, including the scheduling of bombing raids and the movement of troops and supplies. The success of the "policy analysis" that McNamara helped to popularize further entrenched complicated thinking as the dominant business paradigm. After the Second World War, McNamara and his team grew in notoriety and become known as the Whiz Kids, which only enhanced their stature and put Robert McNamara's photo on the cover of *Time* magazine.[2]

At the end of the Second World War, it seemed that the possibilities for business to adapt wartime management principles and engineering developments for civilian purposes were virtually unlimited. The rise of the "military-industrial complex" seemed to be the way forward for the growth of Western economies. The command-and-control mindset of the military seemed well-suited to the new technological advances in engineering and manufacturing. These gave rise to the consumer economy, as more products were being made both better and more affordable. Advances were also being made in finance, with the development of new types of securities and advanced ways of analyzing them. The ability of managers to control their organizations, and even the economy, seemed limitless.

Scientific management and the complicated thinking it employed were dominant. The idea that business tasks can be reduced to their parts, with each part analyzed and optimized on Taylorian principles, was very attractive and had obvious commercial appeal. Scientific management promised to provide answers in a logical and reasonable fashion and promoted the belief in the manager as "expert." This "complicated" mindset was one of command and control based on the rules of business. The rise of business as a field of university study certainly helped to accelerate the trend. Master of Business Administration (MBA) programs were developed at several universities to take advantage of the demand for "expert" managers. It is interesting to note that originally MBA programs were designed specifically for engineers so they could continue their engineering studies, the only difference being that the engineering was to be applied to business. MBA graduates began to be highly sought after by corporations looking to implement best practices in managing, manufacturing, and marketing.

Why Managers Like "Complicated"

In 1987, novelist and essayist Tom Wolfe published *Bonfire of the Vanities*,[3] a novel that perfectly encapsulated the "business is complicated" mindset that had become firmly entrenched in the eighties. Wolfe coined the phrase "Master of the Universe" to describe the attitude.

The novel portrays the life of a financial trader during the height of the go-go eighties. The main character, Sherman McCoy, proclaims himself a "Master of the Universe." He is young, he is successful, and he is rich because of his presumed skill in controlling his destiny. For him life is an adrenaline rush composed of feelings of power and control.

Unfortunately, through a series of events in his personal life, his position as a "Master of the Universe" soon turns to dust. McCoy gets into a car accident while having to take a detour to avoid an impromptu roadblock that may have been assembled by some youths to facilitate a robbery. McCoy gets out of the car and is approached by the youths who may or may not have set up the roadblock. His mistress takes the wheel of the car and, in a moment of panic, hits and kills a young black man who she believes was out to ambush them. The incident, which normally would be potentially one of many such accidents in New York City on any given day, gets swept up in a media frenzy that is fueled by racial politics and further inflamed by a community activist, a district attorney who is worried about re-election, and a journalist who cynically and doggedly follows the case, baiting the stakeholders in the hope of resuscitating his journalism career. The story becomes a media and political sensation, and New Yorkers respond accordingly. McCoy, who once thought himself invincible, a "Master of the Universe" in complete control of his destiny through his own conscious and deliberate actions, realizes that he is at the mercy of events that are spiraling more out of control than he ever could have imagined. His Master of the Universe persona is shown to be a mirage.

The "Master of the Universe" syndrome is one of the key reasons why managers implicitly like complicated systems and will almost always default to complicated thinking when faced with a new problem or situation.

Beyond the Master of the Universe syndrome there are a large variety of reasons why managers default to complicated thinking. The reasons range from ignorance of complexity to issues of self-esteem. In essence, it is seductive to want to believe in a complicated world. Things that are complicated are well defined. They allow us to feel intelligent when we master them; they allow us to feel necessary; and perhaps most importantly, they allow us to feel that we are in control.

Intuitively, at some level, most experienced managers understand that the business world is complex. However, the typical business person's formal understanding of the science of complexity is either nonexistent or very shallow. Most managers have a very limited grounding in the physical sciences or the social sciences and even less grounding in the relatively new field of complexity. Given that the terms "complicated" and "complex" are commonly used as synonyms for each other, and that all through school, from kindergarten to university graduation, we are taught to use complicated thinking (though never explicitly), most of us naturally believe that complicated systems are the only paradigm that exists.

Then there is the simple fact that, all things being equal, we prefer more order to less order. To maintain a semblance of order we tend to perceive patterns even when no patterns exist. Stock market analysts claim to be able to predict the stock markets based on charts showing trends in stock prices, despite the fact that investing based on trends has been definitively shown to have little to no added value. Even such a prominent scientist as Einstein craved order when he famously said in his hopeful statement that "God does not play dice."

The trendy Internet shoe retailer Zappos tried an interesting corporate organizational experience in reducing fixed "lines of command" in its management structure. Zappos introduced a management structure known as a holacracy that does away with management hierarchy and bosses. Instead, employees are expected to form their own flexible work groups and find and solve problems worth solving. While the structure is still in the early stages of implementation, it already appears that a record number of employees are leaving the company, as they believe they cannot comfortably adapt to a workplace without structure. Further research seems to indicate that employees really do prefer working in a hierarchy.[4] Employees like certainty and predictability. In other words, we like, and perhaps even crave, a complicated system.

Related to our desire for order is the fact that complex problems tend to be messy. They do not have nice, neat solutions, as complicated problems do. In complicated thinking, the more elegant the solution, the better it is considered to be. Think back to the introduction of this chapter and the discussion of complicated watches. We do indeed like things that are elegant. We like things that can be tied up with a pretty bow. Unfortunately, open-ended complex problems can rarely be tied up with any type of bow at all. Remember that Einstein once said, "If you are out to describe the truth, leave elegance to the tailor."

There is a seductiveness to complicated systems. They make us feel intelligent and they make us feel needed and valuable. Complicated systems allow us the illusion that luck or serendipity played at best a limited role in our success and, thus, that whatever success we have is almost exclusively the result of our own skill and effort. This relates to the findings of a study by psychologists Pauline Clance and Suzanne Imes of what they called the imposter syndrome.[5] The imposter syndrome is experienced by high achievers when they consider their success to be a consequence of luck or fate rather than skill. It produces feelings of unworthiness and creates issues of self-esteem. One way around the imposter syndrome is to hold a firm belief in the fallacy that the business world is complicated and thus that any success must have been achieved through one's own hard work and brilliance. To avoid the imposter syndrome, we need to have a sense that we control our own fate. This is difficult to do while facing the ambiguity and uncertainty that are an inherent part of complexity.

One reason why we like complicated problems is that we like the rush we get when we can solve a problem. Consider, for instance, the popularity of the crossword puzzles and Sudoku puzzles in the daily paper. Essentially these are addictive activities that we use to fill the time on the train during our commute, or while having an extra cup of coffee in the morning as we delay taking on the tasks at hand. Part of the reason we like these puzzles is that they are both doable and finite – they have a definite end where you can unambiguously state that you have solved the puzzle. It is a bit like climbing an intellectual mountain. You can plant your flag at the completion of the puzzle and get a boost of self-esteem because you cracked the puzzle.

Complicated problems in business are like newspaper puzzles. We finish the task and there is a satisfying boost of self-esteem and accomplishment when the "Send" button is hit on the e-mail transferring the project to its destination, or the PowerPoint presentation on the completed assignment is screened for a satisfied group of managers. There is closure. There is a sense of accomplishment that does not exist with open-ended complex problems.

As with puzzles, we also like models. As a kid it was likely that you had a model of some sort, such as a toy car or a doll. We knew they were not real cars, or real babies, but they seemed like a good enough representation of the real world and allowed us to use our imaginations to create our own fantasy worlds. In working with complicated thinking it can be argued that we are doing something very similar. We know that the assumptions for the complicated business model we are using are not an accurate representation of the real world, but making the abstractions concrete through a model allows us to solve a problem, even if it is an imaginary problem that has only a faint resemblance to reality. Models also provide the simplification that allows us to get our heads around a problem in a manageable way. Models make things simpler by getting rid of some of the components of a situation. Often it is the complex components that are assumed away, in turn transforming a complex problem into a complicated one.

Probably the most significant incentive for engaging in complicated thinking is the fear of non-control and its effect on our egos and our sense of self-worth. As will be discussed, there is a limited amount of control that any one person can have in managing a complex issue. The properties of complexity, such as emergence, develop in a leaderless fashion. Our egos find this difficult to take, and we risk succumbing to the imposter syndrome. Consciously or unconsciously assuming that the business world is complicated lets us avoid problematic issues of self-awareness and self-confidence.

Finally, we need to consider whether our bias toward complicated thinking is hard-wired into us or if it is a product of our schooling. In the preface to this book I outlined the case of the top-performing student who fainted out of frustration when there was no "answer" to the case study that was assigned for that week. She was typical of the many students who view education as an exercise in which you learn answers. It can be argued that university business school classes are unfortunately now seen less and less as a place for debate or exploring ideas and more and more as a center for disseminating clear-cut answers. Debate is managed with the use of the Socratic case study method, whereby an objective truth or "the answer" is drawn out by guided questioning and discussion. Increasingly, students perceive that there is not a debate in which there are two or more sides of equal standing. One side always prevails, just as it would in a complicated world based on rules and natural laws.

In his wildly popular TED talk "Do Schools Kill Creativity?," which has been viewed more than 40 million times, education consultant Sir Kenneth Robinson claims that the school system as we know it was constructed for "industrialism."[6] In essence, he argues that curricula with an emphasis on rote learning as well as a focus on literacy and mathematics were necessary to provide workers to staff the factories that sprang up in large numbers at the beginning of the industrial age. At that time children had to be educated to be more productive in their industrial jobs. He plainly states that "education was geared for jobs." He continues to argue that in today's world we have no idea what the future will hold and thus our lack of focus on creativity in education is grossly misguided. The lack of emphasis on the arts is creating an education system where "we get educated out of creativity."

Robinson is not framing his argument in the context of complexity, but his points are very consistent with the arguments of this chapter that the business world is developing complicated thinkers in a context where the issues are becoming more complex. This creates a fundamental mismatch between issues and the ability to address them that will become apparent in the chapter 4 discussion of some of the characteristics and traits necessary for managing in a complex world. Looking ahead to chapter 4, one of the most central and necessary of these characteristics is a mindset that thinks in terms of managing and not solving. This implies managing spontaneously and in the moment, rather than relying on a pre-ordained plan. Constant and ongoing adjustments need to be made using a "try, learn, and adapt" methodology that requires experimentation, creativity, and a tolerance for failure and miscues rather than knowledge, obedience, and conformity.

In direct contrast to such an emphasis on spontaneity and flexibility, the education system rewards those who can objectively respond to test questions, which, guided by testing methodology, are necessarily complicated in their nature. In particular, the multiple-choice test has become the testing method of choice. The multiple-choice test focuses on the ability to think with a complicated mindset. Such tests penalize rather than reward thinking with a complexity mindset. Students at a very early stage of their schooling learn this and thus develop complicated thinking skills. The creative thinkers and the complexity thinkers receive lower marks, are stigmatized, and get poorer placements. It is probably not an accident that so many of the entrepreneurs of leading companies founded in the last twenty years never completed their college educations. The list includes Steve Jobs, Bill Gates, and Mark Zuckerberg, to name just three prominent examples.

The trend of educating for a complicated world is arguably increasing. Education is being prized more than experience, although for most jobs in business there is at best a loose connection between the skills that are needed on the job and the skills that are developed through schooling. To help close the gap between the needs of business and the output of education, a wide variety of professional certification programs and training institutes have emerged. However, these too are mostly based on complicated thinking, with mandatory exams again frequently featuring the multiple-choice test. This emphasis on credentials only reinforces the complicated mindset.

Does It Matter?

Do the shortcomings of complicated thinking really matter? Is this just an academic problem? The answer for the business manager is that it does matter and that it is most certainly of practical importance! The key to competitive advantage for an organization is the ability to manage complex situations. Likewise, the key for progressive managers to making the most of their abilities and their career is also the ability to successfully manage complexity. Technical skills and the ability to do complicated tasks are, admittedly, the traits most likely to get students their first job out of school. However, it is the manager who can grow beyond complicated skills and develop complexity skills who will get ahead and succeed.

Complicated thinking does have a place and role to play. There are definitely necessary tasks within business that need to be completed by someone with the appropriate training. In chapter 1, for instance, I cited the task of completing a company's financial statements as an example of a complicated task that generally needs to be completed by a certified and competent accountant. Similarly, many manufacturing machines and tasks are complicated in nature and must be managed by someone who is a competent complicated thinker. Engineers who design products must know how the laws of physics and electronics will affect the performance of the products they are designing. Ensuring regulatory compliance is another necessary job that requires thorough and sophisticated complicated thinking.

It is instructive to consider a few careers outside of business. For instance, consider the role of medical doctors and lawyers. These are careers that are generally considered to be complicated in nature. Both of these careers require the professional to be certified by a medical board or to pass the bar exam for the jurisdiction in which they are going to practice. Few people in the developed world would seek out a practitioner in one of these professions who did not meet the minimum required standards. However, even these professions require a high degree of ability to deal with complexity.

For doctors, the reality is that the human body itself is complex. We all age, and as we age our bodies evolve. The connections between various organs create feedback loops that make the diagnosis of many illnesses complex in nature. Furthermore, medical tests are rarely unambiguous in their results, and the outcomes require interpretation and judgment on the part of the doctor. For all but the simplest diseases, the task of the doctor is to try a course of action based on knowledge, experience, and judgment, and then make adjustments according to how the patient's body responds. As will be explained in chapter 4, this is a classic complexity-management tactic.

A similar task faces the lawyer. While many legal tasks may be quite straightforward and routine, these tasks are increasingly being handled by paralegals and automated computer searches, and the role of the lawyer in dealing with them is almost solely one of being a quality-control check. The tougher cases require lawyers to be creative in their use of the law. Litigation requires lawyers to read the mood of the judge or the jury and to tailor an argument based on the context in which they find themselves in court. Top lawyers are prized at least as much for their creativity in interpreting and their skill in arguing the law as for their knowledge of the law. In fact, most senior lawyers have a pool of legal interns who do the bulk of the work of researching legal precedents and statutes. The true star lawyer is one who develops the novel solution to solve the issue at hand.[7]

Thus it can be said that the roles of doctors and lawyers, while commonly thought to be complicated, actually involve the addition of value through complexity thinking. Having an ability to deal with both complicated and complex tasks is the ideal for the business professional as well.

Most importantly, a complicated-thinking paradigm and complicated-thinking techniques simply do not work in complex situations. Throughout this book, examples will be presented of cases where complicated thinking failed miserably when mistakenly applied to complex situations. It is often the case that the harder one works on complicated thinking, and the more effort one puts into solving a problem, the worse the ultimate outcome will be if the situation is complex. As chapter 4 – on winning with complexity – illustrates, the tools and tactics for dealing with complexity are quite different from and perhaps even the opposite of normal complicated tactics.

Complicated thinking can be very limiting. Paradigm shifts that accelerate a career cannot happen solely with complicated thinking. If you do everything by formula or by a pre-ordained plan you will not gain in learning, insight, or creativity, and you most certainly will not create a paradigm shift.

To summarize – complicated thinking only works for complicated situations. The problem is that many of the most value-adding tasks the manager or an organization has to deal with are complex. It's not complicated!

FOUR

THE WONDERS OF COMPLEXITY

In 1985, the management of Coca-Cola did what was considered to be the unthinkable: they changed the formula, and thus the taste, of the iconic Coke. A new product introduction is nothing new for a large international consumer product company such as Coca-Cola, but the changing of its iconic recipe from "Coke Classic" (or "Coke" as it was known at the time) to "New Coke" was monumental. Although the introduction of New Coke is one of the most analyzed and studied new product introductions, it is interesting to re-examine it from a "complicated-versus-complex" perspective.

The fundamental reason for the change was that Coke was slowly but persistently losing market share to Pepsi, which was considered by consumers to have a smoother and sweeter taste. In its heavily promoted "Pepsi Challenge" campaign that started in 1975, Pepsi had cola drinkers take a blind taste test of Pepsi versus Coke, with the results showing that the majority of test subjects preferred the taste of Pepsi. The campaign was a marketing coup for Pepsi, which had trailed behind the more dominant Coke brand since its introduction in 1893. Although Coke held the lead for overall cola sales, the lead was largely due to Coke's dominant position in fountain sales and in vending-machine sales. In particular, Coke's sales lead was notably due to the fact that Coke had the contract to provide cola to McDonald's franchises. In terms of store-bought colas, Pepsi had the lead and that, combined with the Pepsi Challenge taste test results, rightly worried Coca-Cola executives. Something had to be done based on the slowly but steadily increasing market share of Pepsi at the expense of Coke.

After a period of development, Coca-Cola thought it might have a solution. Based on extensive analysis, and their own consumer testing, Coke management believed that they had a new formula for Coke that would win back consumers in the cola wars. It was a risky move, and one that was heavily debated within the company's executive ranks. Even the thought that they might change the recipe that had been in place virtually unchanged since 1892 was a closely guarded secret. After all, this was the recipe that was famously locked away in a bank vault that supposedly only three Coca-Cola executives had access to at any time. Everyone involved with the decision had to keep completely silent on the very idea of changing the formula, as even a rumor that they were thinking of changing could lead to a marketing coup for Pepsi.

Imagine that you were a manager who was part of the executive team responsible for the development of New Coke for Coca-Cola in the 1980s. If you were part of the management team you would likely have had plenty of experience with other brand introductions and product-line extensions. Coca-Cola, after all, had introduced many successful new products such as Tab, Sprite, and Fresca, and had extended the Coke line through products such as Diet Coke and Cherry Coke. Protocols and best practices for a new product introduction would be well known and refined. Techniques such as consumer studies, test marketing in selected markets, and market analysis would be standard procedures. While far from perfect, new product introduction is a relatively well-honed science for a global manufacturer such as Coca-Cola.

Despite Coca-Cola's corporate experience, and despite a large and well-orchestrated marketing campaign, New Coke quickly became a marketing disaster. Although consumers preferred New Coke over the old in numerous taste tests, and many stock market analysts were bullish about the prospects for Coca-Cola after the introduction, a public outcry arose and Coca-Cola was eventually forced to reintroduce the old Coke formulation as "Classic Coke." Even then, Coke eventually decided to drop the New Coke formula, as well as the name, altogether. The depth of the analysis and the results of consumer testing did not make up for the emotional attachment that consumers had developed for the iconic Coke brand.

Whenever a company starts on a new endeavor or encounters a novel situation or issue such as the introduction of New Coke, it is imperative to understand the fundamentals of the situation. While marketing is a well-developed field of study and practice, it is important to remember that it is not an exact science like chemistry or physics. Furthermore, when a product's users have an emotional attachment to it, traditional marketing analyses may be unreliable. In such cases, it is critical to appreciate that complicated thinking is not likely to lead to success, and instead that complexity may be the more appropriate operating paradigm. While the failure of New Coke has been extensively studied in marketing case studies, it can be argued that the reason for the failure of New Coke was not complicated; it was complex. How the various elements of complexity led to the failure of New Coke will be discussed in the course of this chapter.

The differences between simple, complicated, and complex were outlined in chapter 1. The basic differences between complicated thinking and complexity thinking have been presented, as well as a basic argument for why complex problems are fundamentally different from complicated ones and thus need to be managed and analyzed quite differently. In this chapter, the focus is on the characteristics of complexity as well as the elements that create complexity.

Complexity arises from having a set of agents (such as consumers or employees) who are subject to a large number of factors both known and unknown (trends, fads, opinions of others, environmental factors) and who have the ability to interact and to change or adapt their behavior and decisions. From these basic elements, an important and intriguing property of complexity known as emergence develops. These characteristics of complexity as well as the properties of emergence are covered in this chapter. With an understanding of complexity, it can be argued that emergence arising out of complexity is ultimately what led to the failure of New Coke for the Coca-Cola company. We start however with an attempt to define complexity.

Defining Complexity

Defining complexity is like defining great art. We know that great art exists, but we cannot quite produce a definition that works for all situations. That doesn't mean that we can or should dismiss great works of art. Likewise, the lack of a precise definition for complexity does not mean that it does not exist, or that it should be dismissed as unimportant.

Within the academic community there are many different ways of defining complexity but no clear consensus on a definition. As such, the differing definitions become more of a taxonomy or classification system of the many different ways that complexity arises and manifests itself.

Perhaps the easiest way to define complexity is by what it is not: namely, something that is most certainly not "complicated" as defined in earlier chapters. This way of defining complexity may be considered to be an intellectually lazy cop-out. However if you consider the current complicated mindset of most business managers, this lazy cop-out definition is in reality a very useful and practical definition. When a paradigm such as complicated thinking dominates, it can be helpful to highlight whatever does not fit the paradigm.

Let us refer back to the classification diagram from chapter 1, reproduced below in figure 4.1. Using this diagram, it is relatively straightforward to classify a situation or problem as simple or complicated. What is complex is defined more by what it is not than by any fixed set of characteristics. The diagram illustrates that it is quite tricky to describe precisely what components make a system complex.

Figure 4.1: Decision Framework for Classifying System Type

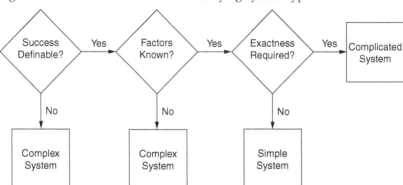

It is paradoxical but useful to realize that the lack of a clear definition of complexity should not pose a practical problem for the manager. A belief in the value of defining and categorizing a problem or a situation is a complicated way of thinking. Complicated thinking is a rational way of having a place for everything and making sure that everything is in its place. Complexity, by its very nature, defies categorization, and thus it is not surprising that it also defies having a clear and objective definition.

One practical problem that arises from the lack of a clear definition is that there is no comprehensive or standard method to measure levels of complexity. Many different methods have been proposed to measure complexity, but they tend to be context-specific. Not all formulations suit all cases. Also, methods differ depending on the type of data that describe the system. For instance, whether the system is composed of quantitative data (such as price movements in the stock market) or qualitative data (such as the emotions of a group of consumers) affects the type of method one might use to measure complexity.

Furthermore, complexity as a practical matter in business does not lend itself to being defined or measured. The lack of a standard complexity measure is problematic in a business context, since in a complicated paradigm the adage "What gets measured gets managed," attributed to management guru Peter Drucker, is frequently true. The fact that changes in complexity cannot be unambiguously measured is likely one of the reasons that the concept of complexity is relatively overlooked in business. It is also a major reason why complexity has been ignored by business academics as well as consultants.

In the case of the introduction of New Coke, we can use the framework to determine whether the situation was simple, complicated, or complex. The first step is to define success. Different observers, however, would have different definitions of the success of New Coke. For some it might be that New Coke stopped Coke's decline in market share. However, for others success might be measured in terms of an arbitrary amount of market share within a given period. When New Coke was introduced, Coke's sales increased significantly, as did its stock price. However, the introduction is still viewed as a classic marketing debacle. Clearly, "success" for New Coke is open to interpretation and not objectively definable. From the beginning we get an idea that the introduction of New Coke may be a complex situation.

The second step in measuring complexity is to determine whether the factors contributing to success are known. Again, the answer is not clear-cut – an indication that the situation is complex. At first glance, one would think that the *taste* of New Coke would be a major factor in its success. Indeed Coca-Cola market researchers did extensive testing, which showed that cola drinkers clearly preferred the taste of New Coke to the Classic Coke formula and also preferred it to Pepsi. However, despite these results New Coke was a flop, raising the question "What was needed to achieve success?" Obviously taste was not a key factor for sales success. One might also reasonably believe that the size of the marketing effort would be important. Again, Coca-Cola put significant resources into one of its largest marketing campaigns ever – to no avail. The traditional factors on which success supposedly depends thus proved to be of little or no consequence. We can therefore say that the introduction of New Coke is complex by our second node of decision.

The third step is to decide whether exactness is required for marketing success. While manufacturing a bottle of Coke obviously requires exactness (and is a complicated process), it is hard to say what exactness would look like in the context of new product marketing. Unlike in product manufacturing, which requires a precise mixture of ingredients combined according to a standard recipe, there is no foolproof recipe or formula for introducing a product. While there were undoubtedly budget estimates, carefully worded publicity releases, and marketing materials based upon extensive testing, there was no formula or set of objective rules available to guarantee success.

Thus, by examining the selection diagram, we can see that the introduction of New Coke is a complex problem. It was not a simple process that senior management could have delegated to a group of interns – as they might have done for a simple project. Nor was it a complicated problem in which experts could have ensured the same result each time by simply following the exact same protocol. The introduction of New Coke was complex, and that made all the difference for Coca-Cola.

The Components of Complexity

Although there is no definitive way to classify a system as complex, the essential components of complexity are straightforward. At the most fundamental level, the following three ingredients are necessary for complexity to occur: (1) several factors or agents, for example consumers of a product, investors in the stock market, employees of a company or the collection of companies in an industry; (2) the ability of the agents or factors to be connected in some way, such as through social media, acting on stock prices, water cooler chit-chat, or market share data; and (3) the ability of the agents to adapt or to make choices, such as consumers choosing to switch to a different brand or supplier, investors selling one stock and buying another, employees choosing to stay with their current employer or looking for a new job, or companies changing their advertising and marketing strategies. As illustrated in figure 4.2, when all three elements are present, then there is likely to be complexity.

Each of the underlying components of complexity exists in almost every meaningful business situation. Furthermore, these components are very common. There is nothing special that has to come about for a complex system to form. The potential for complexity exists in most situations in which people or companies are able to interact and make choices. The issue is how much that complexity behavior will matter relative to the importance of the simple or complicated elements.

Figure 4.2: The Components of Complexity

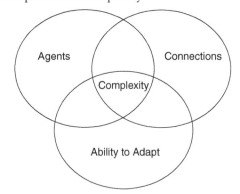

Contrast the elements necessary for complexity to occur with what is needed for a complicated system. For a complicated system there has to be a set of absolute laws or rules. While there are man-made governmental laws and regulations that companies and consumers must obey, they are very different in structure and form from the laws and rules of nature that govern a complicated system. Furthermore, the laws of nature cannot be broken, while man-made laws and regulations are almost asking to be broken or at least stretched on an ongoing basis. Moreover, man-made laws and regulations are somewhat arbitrary and may change from time to time and from one jurisdiction to another. They are not constants.

Similarly, in a complicated system we can say that there are equations that objectively, consistently, and accurately quantify the outcomes, given a set of inputs. In their analysis for changing the Coke formula, it is fair to say that Coca-Cola executives conducted a very thorough and extensive analysis, based on the best marketing practices, of how the New Coke recipe would be received. This analysis, however, when tested against the subjective responses of consumers, proved to be horribly misleading.

In a complicated system, the ability to adapt or change is missing. The laws of physics are unchanging. The regulations that govern such things as financial statements are static and change only infrequently. In a complex system, however, the ability to adapt or change is a central feature. Of course, people have a tremendous ability to adapt and change.

When thinking about complexity in the context of business, it is essential to consider the role of people. Managing a business is, first and foremost, about managing people. It is about managing employees, managing suppliers, managing in the face of competition from other companies, managing the changing preferences of consumers, managing investors, and managing public perceptions. Managing a business is also about managers managing themselves within the context of simultaneously managing all these other management challenges.

People, whether individually or collectively, as employees or consumers, are notoriously unamenable to having their decisions framed according to a set of immutable equations. Recall from the previous chapter that the experiments of Kahneman and Tversky and of Asch (supported as well by the studies of many other experimental psychologists and sociologists) show this convincingly. The factors that drive people and their decisions are not neatly quantifiable and, perhaps more importantly, are constantly changing and shaped by circumstance. Rarely do business managers have available to them a full list of the factors required for success. Second, people, whether they are employees, managers, or consumers, have the ability to connect and interact with one another. This is especially so in our social media world. People have the ability to adapt, to change their minds, to make new decisions and new connections, and to respond to a variety of influences. People adapt and evolve in complex ways. Thus, all the elements of complexity are present in how people behave in a business situation.

When the management of people is in question, whether in a business context or not, the elements necessary for complexity are almost always present. Furthermore, the elements of complexity govern the ways in which people interact. While we may think that people's behavior is either rational or random, in reality people are complex in their actions and decisions.

Since the elements required for complexity are so natural and omnipresent, and since the elements necessary for a complicated system to occur are so unnatural and rare (at least within the context of managing people and businesses), complexity should be the default mode of thinking that managers adopt. However, as I noted in the preceding chapter, the actual default mode is currently that of a complicated thinker. This is one of the paradoxes of modern business practice. Complexity is not something that is weird and unusual. Complexity is the norm; it is complicated issues that are rare and exceptional. This is a fact that the managers of Coca-Cola failed to recognize in their introduction of New Coke.

To better understand how complexity arises, it is instructive to examine individually each of its elements in more detail.

A Collection of Agents

Complexity begins with a collection of agents or factors. These agents could be employees, customers, stakeholders, other companies in the same or even different industries, political factors, geographical factors, the weather, economic cycles, demographics, religious organizations, or a whole host of other factors. Furthermore, the agents or factors have to possess some degree of independence and some degree of choice or adaptability. The degree of independence or adaptability may be small, or even weak, but if there is no independence or adaptability then the system would be a complicated rather than a complex one.

In virtually all business situations, the necessary degree of independence will be present. Only in the most severe situations of working under slave-like duress would an agent in a business situation have such a low degree of independence that complexity could not exist.

The fact that agents have independence means that they can make decisions, whether they choose to or not. These individual decisions may be highly rational, or they may appear to be highly irrational. They may appear to be well thought out or they may appear to be random. They may be subtle or overt, conscious or unconscious. In all cases, agents generally think that they are making rational decisions, although the rationality may only be in their own minds and not apparent to anyone else. The fact that everyone has a different concept of rationality for a given situation is perhaps the most fundamental factor that gives rise to complexity effects such as emergence.

Heterogeneous concepts of rationality and diversity of opinion and thought are what make business management so challenging. They are what make it impossible for a business to be run by a computer. Their presence means that the most talented business managers will always pass a conceptual Turing Test, as discussed in chapter 1, and that business cannot be accurately or meaningfully boiled down to a set of laws or equations. Because of them, business is not complicated but complex.

Let's revisit once again the case of the introduction of New Coke. In this case, there were a variety of agents, all with different motivations and levels of commitment to the success or failure of the change in the Coke formula. To start, there was the management team of Coca-Cola. They had a business problem, namely the declining market share of Coke versus Pepsi. The managers of Coca-Cola were working within the context of the illustrious history of Coke as one of the first truly global consumer products. During the Second World War, Coke was supplied to American GIs around the world, and was a highly treasured product "from home." As a result of this, Coke set up international factories and was as responsible as anything else for the "Americanization" of lifestyles around the world. Without the global success of the Coke brand, it likely would have been much more difficult for other American consumer brands such as McDonald's to spread as rapidly or as widely as they subsequently did. The iconic Coke-bottle shape was one of the most recognizable symbols of America and conveyed a host of emotions that Coca-Cola leveraged as a key part of its global marketing. Coke's smashingly successful 1970s advertising campaign jingle, "I'd Like to Buy the World a Coke," built on and reinforced Coke's global stature and encouraged an unprecedented emotional attachment of consumers to the product.

Coke then, as now, was more than a product. It was, and remains, truly one of the world's greatest brands. This was despite the fact that, in blind taste tests, and even among loyal Coke drinkers and Coke management, Pepsi was preferred to Coke by most taste testers. There was a mismatch between the objective reality of preference as measured by blind taste tests and the perceived status of Coke as an iconic product.

Pepsi, of course, was another very interested and involved agent in this case. The introduction of the New Coke formula was an extremely well-kept secret, and it caught everyone by surprise, including the management of Pepsi. However, it did not take Pepsi long to realize the significance of the change and to seize the opportunity to capitalize on it. From the point of view of Pepsi's management, Coke had essentially declared defeat. To celebrate, Pepsi's chief executive officer at the time, Roger Enrico, took out a full-page ad in several major newspapers and declared a one-day holiday for all Pepsi workers.

Consumers and distributors of Coke were also caught off guard. Despite not yet knowing what the New Coke formulation was going to taste like, Coca-Cola drinkers started to hoard cases of Coke. Soon retail stores were running out of supplies of the old Coke formula. A feedback loop began, as rumors started that retail stores were running out of the old Coke. As these stories spread, consumers became even more anxious about hoarding a stash before supplies totally ran out. Soon there was a run on supplies of old Coke. The media stories became a key catalyst in allowing a movement against New Coke to emerge. They were a way for the disparate agents in the story to virtually connect with each other.

One particular agent plays a special part in this story. His name is Gay Mullins, and he was an avid Coke drinker. There was nothing really all that special about Mr. Mullins. He was not a celebrity or a prominent politician. In fact Mr. Mullins was, from all accounts, a rather ordinary retiree but one who was upset about the change in the Coke formula. This was despite the rumor that when he took a blind taste test between the New Coke and the Old Coke, he too, like the majority of other cola drinkers, preferred the taste of New Coke. Mr. Mullins and a few other dedicated Coke drinkers formed the lobby group Old Coke Drinkers of America. The creation of this network met the second requirement for complexity to emerge.

Connections

For complexity to evolve there needs to be some way for the various agents to connect with each other. For ants this is through the pheromone trails that they deposit in their travels to find food. For many consumers, it is through media and advertisements, which have the potential to spread a message far and wide. Today, of course, a major way to connect is through social media, where a simple message can be spread virally. Twitter, YouTube, LinkedIn, Facebook, and other social media sites are perfect incubators for connecting a widely dispersed set of agents.

Social media sites allow agents to create and form their own networks. These sets of networks are constantly forming and reforming. Most networks and their associated messages die quickly and do not spread very far. Others may lie dormant for a long period before exploding into a world-wide phenomenon. Some of these viral networks have significant staying power. Other factors, of course, can also help a message to spread widely and quickly.

Connections for complexity can be of many different types and are likely to change in nature as they evolve. Connections or links between agents can be strong or weak. An example of a strong link might be one of your best friends. A weak link might be the author of a blog post that someone forwarded to you. Another way that connections can be classified is by the number of connections each link has. For instance, some people have a much larger number of followers on Twitter, or many more Facebook friends, or even a larger number of professional connections on LinkedIn. In many but not all cases, the larger the number of connections a person has, the greater their ability to influence the complex situation. However, this is not always true.

What is important about connections in terms of complexity is the nature and the context of the connection. For instance, a weak connection is paradoxically often the most powerful type of connection for spreading a message. This was the finding of sociologist Mark Granovetter when he studied the actions of job seekers, social mobility, and a variety of other social effects.[1] At first blush this statement is counterintuitive. We generally think that having a strong connection with someone is important in order for them to help us spread our message. Companies spend a lot of time trying to build as strong a connection with their clients as possible, through advertising, social media, and consumer reward programs. Author and marketing guru Seth Godin calls it building a tribe of followers. The issue is that the more connected you are to someone, the more likely it is that they already know the information you know, or already think the way you do, or make similar types of decisions as you, or hold the same opinion on a subject. In a group with strong internal connections, members tend to behave in group-think fashion, and this rarely leads to changes in behavior or emergence. Building a network with people you have a strong connection with is often the equivalent of "preaching to the choir." You are unlikely to change their opinions or actions in a meaningful way that will influence the overall situation.

Often, the best connections are those that are outside your normal set of strong connections. Often, the weak connections you have or are able to form are the types of connections that allow your idea or thought to spread more widely and more rapidly. Weak links, and especially new connections, introduce an idea to a new group, one that may not already have heard of a particular idea or issue. It is the equivalent of having a disease develop into a global pandemic through incidental contact with a stranger on an airplane flight. Unexpected and weak connections often produce key turning points and create emergence.

In the case of the introduction of New Coke, Gay Mullins was not well known; he was not a celebrity or a titan of business. He was simply someone who took action, put out a notice, and watched as his lobbying to get Coca-Cola to bring back Classic Coke grew and seemed to take on a life of its own – probably beyond even his wildest imaginings. Although, in 1985, he did not have the benefit of modern social media tools such as Facebook or Twitter, or even e-mail, he did have an idea that had emotional appeal for a wide variety of people. He also had the weak links being created through media stories that grew in prominence. Rationally or irrationally, people around the world discovered they had an emotional attachment to Coke, and Mr. Mullins tapped into that attachment and made a connection with a wide and widely dispersed variety of individuals with whom he otherwise had no link or prior connection. The weak link was each individual's connection to the classic Coke taste. The catalyst was the media's alacrity in picking up on the story and making it news.

Adaptation, Choice, and Feedback Loops

Another key element of complexity that provides a catalyst for emergence to form is the ability of the agents in a complex system to adapt and make choices. In the case of New Coke, consumers had a variety of choices and adaptations they could make; the management of Coca-Cola had a variety of choices – and did make several adaptations as the introduction evolved; and of course the company's competitors also had the ability to make choices and to adapt to the new formulation. The series of choices and the ways in which each of the agents adapted to the situation led to emergence developing organically.

When the ability to adapt or choose is coupled with connections and the evolution of networks, feedback loops develop and emergence occurs. Gay Mullins made a choice that he wanted to do something about the introduction of New Coke. He started by writing a letter. The letter got picked up by the press, and soon others started to write letters. In addition, Coke consumers started to hoard cans of the old Coke.

These simple acts initiated the stories being played out in the media. Pepsi, of course, decided to celebrate the introduction of New Coke with a full-page ad in a series of newspapers as well as granting its employees an unexpected holiday. This too became a news story.

When people can make choices and adapt, and when they are connected in some way, feedback loops can and often will form. Feedback loops act like a fuel or a catalyst for adaptive change and emergence. With each news story about how consumers were reacting to the announcement of New Coke, other consumers began to think in a different way about their relationship with Coke. Again, it is important to remember that consumer taste tests clearly demonstrated that consumers would prefer the taste of New Coke. That fact, however, did not stop the momentum created by the actions of Gay Mullins and those few select consumers who initially started to hoard a supply of old Coke.

The Butterfly Effect described earlier is an example of how a small change can produce a profound effect through feedback loops. These dramatic changes in the intended or expected outcome occur because of the feedback loops that exist when people are connected and have the ability to adapt and change. It is also interesting to note that the choices that people make do not always have to be conscious choices or even rational choices. In the case of New Coke, it had been clearly demonstrated that people preferred the new taste. However because of the Butterfly Effect and feedback loops, the actions of a relatively few number of people became a major movement.

Even if the actions of a few agents are random, irrational, or even suboptimal, the possibility of feedback loops means that large changes in outcomes can occur. In such cases it sometimes seems as if randomness has taken over. It all depends on the nature of the feedback loops. Some feedback loops are stabilizing in that they tend to return things to normal. Other feedback loops are destabilizing in that a small change can lead to complete randomness.

To illustrate an example of a stable feedback loop, consider a marble at the bottom of a glass bowl. If you move the marble up the sides of the bowl and let it go, the marble will oscillate around the bowl but will eventually come to rest at the bottom of the bowl again.

However, if you turn the bowl over and place the marble on top of the upturned bowl, it may sit there on the flat base of the bowl, but any significant change in the position of the marble means that it will roll off of the flat base of the bowl, down the sloped sides of the bowl, and onto the floor.

When Gay Mullins and a few others started to object to the New Coke formula, they started a feedback loop that was enhanced by media attention. What was an issue for one person became a cause for an unexpectedly dedicated crowd. Peer pressure eventually converted many others. Recall again the experiments of Asch and how they showed the importance of peer pressure on people's decision making.

In the end Coca-Cola capitulated and reintroduced the original Coke formulation under the name Classic Coke. Classic Coke was sold alongside New Coke for a period, but eventually sales were such that New Coke was quietly dropped and Classic Coke became simply Coke again.

Emergence

The primary consequence of or outcome from complexity is a phenomenon called emergence. The dictionary defines emergence as "the rise of a system that cannot be predicted or explained from antecedent conditions."[2] It is an evolving situation where the whole is more than the sum of the parts. It is something for which there is an obvious pattern but for which there is no way to predict how the pattern will continue to evolve. Emergence is both the mystery and the substance of complex systems, and is ultimately the reason why a business manager needs to care about complexity.

Emergence is a state that is somewhere between order and anarchy. Complexity researcher and author Scott Page calls complexity the "interesting in-between."[3] It most certainly does not have the complete predictability of a complicated system, yet it is not without any form whatsoever, like chaos. There is a recognizable structure to emergence, and there is generally a pattern, but there is no predictability. As previously stated, an excellent example of emergence is a murmuration of starlings in the sky; the birds move as a group and with some form of obvious pattern or coordination, but the coordinated movement of the group appears to change continuously in a random way.

One of the many mysteries of emergence is that it often appears to be leaderless. Unlike in the Coke example where there were a few leaders such as Gay Mullins and the Old Coke Drinkers of America to lead and organize the movement against New Coke, there generally is not an obvious leader in a complex situation. In truth, one cannot tell definitively if the actions of Gay Mullins had any effect. It is quite likely that most of the consumers clamoring for Classic Coke had never heard of him. It is also plausible that the New Coke saga would have turned out the same way even if he had not played a role. With complexity and emergence it is not possible to tell.

The stock market has already been put forward as an example of a complex system. The stock market is an almost perfect example of a generally leaderless complex system. On most days stocks will move in discernible up and down patterns, but there is no individual or group of individuals that dictate the movements of the market. Influential commentators and analysts of the markets may occasionally have some effect, but on most days the market moves based on the leaderless collective will of investors. Even in the case of Coca-Cola, the movement to retain the original formula was largely leaderless. While Gay Mullins and the Old Coke Drinkers of America may have started a small movement, they most certainly were not directing the evolution of the story in any meaningful way. In fact, one could argue that the Old Coke Drinkers of America and Gay Mullins were led by the leaderless groundswell of support among others trying to bring back Classic Coke rather than being the leaders of the movement themselves.

To the management team of Coca-Cola, the emergence of events after the announcement of New Coke must have been quite baffling. They obviously suspected that some consumers would want to keep the original Coke. They were also keenly aware of the iconic status of Coke. However in their decision making they likely never imagined that things would spiral out of control as much as they did.

Serendipity

In the scientific literature, serendipity is generally not considered to be a natural or a necessary trait of complexity. For business, however, it seems quite reasonable to include serendipity when considering the role of complexity. Virtually everyone can think of a chance meeting or event that proved to be significant in changing the trajectory of their personal life as well as their professional life. It could be a chance reading of a quotation, a brief encounter with a stranger, or perhaps an epiphany that seemingly came out of nowhere. Of course, one might consider serendipity to be a special form of weak tie. However, when considering serendipity in the context of business, it is potentially useful to include it as a separate element on its own.

Consider for a moment the components and traits of complexity that have been discussed so far. The list includes connections, adaptation, nonlinearity, feedback loops, and emergence. Put together, these characteristics explain that the serendipitous events of our lives are both a by-product of complexity and a potential source of complexity.

Emergence coupled with serendipity brings about another very important property of complexity that has significant implications for management. That additional property is the holistic nature of complexity. A complicated system can be dealt with in a reductionist way; that is, the pieces of a complicated system can be dealt with individually and separately. With complexity, because of connections, emergence, and serendipity, the system can only be understood and managed as a whole. It is not possible to reduce a complex system to its individual component parts. This reality will be explored further in chapter 5.

Is Complexity Just a Metaphor?

It is reasonable to ask if complexity is simply a convenient metaphor. Perhaps it is just a convenient way, with the benefit of hindsight, to explain the unexplainable. Perhaps it is just a convenient excuse. After all there is no clear definition of complexity, and the definition provided earlier focuses more on what complexity is not than on what it is. It is equally rational to ask if complexity is simply a function of not knowing enough about a given problem. In other words, if we just had more knowledge, or more data points, or a greater understanding then perhaps we would be better able to model a given decision as a complicated problem and then use complicated optimization techniques to make business decisions.

It can be argued, however, that this is a shallow, naive, and wishful-thinking way to view complexity. Indeed, complexity science is currently relatively undeveloped. There are many aspects of complexity that are unknown, uncertain, and not yet fully understood. A mature understanding of complexity is particularly lacking within the realm of business, where complexity is rarely discussed or studied. However, there is ample evidence that there are times in business when something fundamental keeps a project from being handled as a complicated or simple set of decisions.

One beginning argument for complexity is the very limited success of complicated thinking in handling business problems. Coca-Cola no doubt had the best engineers, market testers, food scientists, and marketing analysts, to say nothing of an extremely large marketing budget. The decision to change the Coke formula was not taken lightly; the utmost due diligence was observed in analyzing the advantages and disadvantages of the change. It was also done with the utmost care to continually monitor and manage the unveiling of the new formula. Coca-Cola executives, as well as the army of investment analysts who follow the company, kept a close eye on Coke's sales as well as the public's perception of New Coke. Yet despite all of this hard work and attention to detail, the introduction of New Coke failed, and failed badly as well as embarrassingly. Coca-Cola applied the very best complicated business practices as well as the accumulated experience of years of very successful marketing. Despite this, instead of succeeding, the company wound up with an embarrassing flop that handed a huge moral and market-share victory to its rival Pepsi.

Another compelling example of how complicated thinking is unproductive is its inability to predict the behavior of financial markets. In chapter 8 the financial markets and complexity will be discussed at length, but at this point it is useful to use the financial markets as an example of how complicated thinking comes up short. Perhaps there is no area of business or the economy in general in which more effort and resources are put into complicated analysis than the financial markets. Each and every day, thousands of highly trained and highly compensated financial analysts with advanced degrees in business, mathematics, and finance and the use of the most advanced computers try to come up with a model that will predict where financial prices are going. The rewards for doing so are tremendous. Yet the result is that almost 75 percent of all financial managers actually underperform the simple task of buying and holding a diversified basket of stocks. In other words, you actually have a better chance of outperforming the money managers by choosing your financial investments by throwing darts at a listing of potential investment assets.

Clearly there is something at work in the financial markets that prevents the most sophisticated complicated thinking from being successful. Likewise, there is something at work that limits the ability of companies like Coca-Cola to know how to conduct a successful new product introduction. That element appears to be complexity.

Complexity has been studied to a greater extent in the sciences and has been successfully applied to an understanding of how a wide variety of different types of scientific systems work. An early advocate of complexity in science was the British biologist Robert May. Dr. May was one of the very first researchers to warn against an over-reliance on mathematical models that ignored the effects of complexity. May's early work on complexity in the 1970s introduced complexity to the natural sciences and has proven to be very influential and effective in a variety of fields ranging from anatomy to climate change to zoology.[4]

The main reason for believing that the concept of complexity has validity is the success of the principles of managing with complexity that will be discussed in the remaining chapters of this book. During the Industrial Revolution, complicated thinking proved to be very useful and valuable. However, in the current highly connected and global context of business, complicated thinking has increasingly proved to be of limited value, while the techniques of managing with complexity thinking have been shown to be increasingly useful. While complexity does not lend itself to an absolute measure of success, outcomes can be better managed if complexity is accounted for.

People

The ultimate argument for managing with a complexity mindset is that business is about people. All business transactions involve people – employees to make things, managers to manage them, marketing experts to determine what is to be made, and of course customers to buy things. People at their fundamental core are complex in their decisions and actions. Since all business is done through people, it thus stands to reason that business is complex.

Complexity can be frustrating to deal with. It goes against our natural mindset, and furthermore may be conceptually troubling. The fact that events might emerge and evolve in ways that are beyond our direct control is troublesome to many. This does not however diminish the reality of complexity.

Conclusion

After Coca-Cola withdrew New Coke and returned to the Classic Coke formula, many observers speculated that the introduction was an extremely clever and sneaky marketing ploy to bring a new form of attention to Coke and its iconic position in American society. To this, Coca-Cola executive Donald Keough had this to say: "Some critics will say that Coke made a marketing mistake. Some cynics will say that we planned the whole thing. The truth is that we are not that dumb, and we are not that smart."

He continued with a statement that sums up the complexity of the situation perfectly:

> The simple fact is that all of the time and money and skill poured into consumer research on the new Coke could not measure or reveal the deep and abiding emotional attachment to original Coca-Cola felt by so many people. The passion for original Coca-Cola – and that is the word for it: passion. Something that caught us by surprise. It is a wonderful American mystery and you cannot measure it any more than you can measure love. This is the twist to this story that will please every

humanist and will probably have the Harvard professors puzzling for years.[5]

In summation, it's not complicated; it's complex.

Dealing with complexity is not an art, nor is it a science. The next chapter explores some of the specific and sometimes counterintuitive strategies and tactics for dealing with complexity.

FIVE

MANAGING COMPLEXITY

The characteristics of complexity may make it appear to be hopeless to manage. The nonlinearity of results to inputs, emergence and its randomness, non-centralized control, the holistic nature of complexity and the impossibility of reducing it to its separate parts – these are all factors that do not bode well for a manager who wishes to harness and perhaps even leverage complex situations. It may seem an exercise in futility even to hope to manage much less exploit a situation with these characteristics. However, it is not as hopeless as it first appears, and in fact there are major advantages to dealing with a complex situation for the astute manager who is willing to venture away from the paradigm of complicated thinking.

To explore the feasibility of managing complexity, consider the following two questions: Can you recognize your friends by their fingerprint? Can you recognize them by their irises? Unless you are an identification expert, the answer is likely no. However, let's alter the questions a bit. Can you recognize your friends by their faces? Of course you can – even if they happen to be wearing a wig, sporting a new hairstyle or a silly hat, or even wearing new glasses. Can you tell by their facial expressions whether they are happy, sad, or angry? The answer again is that you probably can. Finally, based on their facial expressions, would you know how to react to them and greet them appropriately based on their mood? I suspect that you most certainly could. When walking down the street, if you saw an old friend who seemed to be in a particularly good mood you would wave and greet them with a big smile and an expression like "Great to see you!" However, if they were sitting on a park bench sobbing uncontrollably, your greeting to them would be very different in both tone and substance, along the lines of, "Oh, my gosh! What's wrong?!" You would have a different response and express a different form of empathy in each case.

Now ask the same questions of a computer. Computers are very proficient at recognizing fingerprints. You may have a laptop that has a fingerprint scan instead of a password as a login control. Eye scans, as well, have progressed from a gimmick seen in spy movies to practical, real-life applications. However, a computer is not yet very good at recognizing faces, particularly those that might be in some sort of disguise. Furthermore, computers are lousy at determining emotional states and even worse at responding to them. Although it would be a best seller, no one has yet developed a computer that can respond to your moods, nor are they are likely to do so in the near future. Computers are poor at recognizing emotions and inadequate at conveying empathy, as emotions and empathy cannot be digitized.

This simple example illustrates that managing and dealing with complexity are skills natural to humans but not to computers. Fingerprints and iris patterns are all complicated human features. Facial expressions, emotions, and empathy are complex. As humans we can recognize faces and emotions but are less adept at recognizing fingerprints and iris patterns. Computers may have an advantage in dealing with complicated problems, but it takes a human to make sense of complex situations.

Just as you can perform the complex task of recognizing a friend, you can also perform the task of managing complexity. Likewise, just as a computer is better at recognizing the complicated features of a human, a computer may also be better at managing the complicated tasks required in an organization.

In our social interactions, we all "manage" within a complex system on a day-to-day basis – we just do it instinctively. The issue, as discussed in chapter 3, is that with business situations and problems we seem to automatically switch into complicated thinking mode. Thus, the manager needs to consciously think about managing complexity. Consciously managing complexity in a business context is broadly a function of four different strategies or tactics. They are: (1) recognize which type of system you are dealing with; (2) think "manage, not solve"; (3) employ a "try, learn, and adapt" operating strategy; and finally, and perhaps most importantly, (4) develop a complexity mindset.

Identify System Type

Before anything can be managed, it must be recognized for what it is. This is especially important for complex versus complicated systems. The manager needs to consciously take a mental step back and classify the issues. Using the framework discussed in chapter 1, it is relatively straightforward to ascertain which elements of the situation are simple, which are complicated, and which are complex. Simply getting the context correct automatically sets the manager on a better course for success.

Obviously, each type of issue needs to be managed in a way that is consistent with its characteristics. Simple systems need to be managed as simple systems. Well-known recipes, procedures, or rules of thumb need to be followed and adhered to. In his bestselling book *The Checklist Manifesto,* author Atul Gawande makes a compelling case for using simple checklists as a way to manage simple systems.[1] Dr. Gawande would likely argue that even your grandmother should follow a recipe for baking her favorite cake. Simple systems are generally easy to manage, but that also can produce hubris that leads to mistakes.

One example of a frequently encountered simple system is the task of packing for a business trip. I travel, on average, three times a month on business. After twenty years of this you would think that I would be an expert on packing for a trip. However, I hate to admit the number of times I have wound up discovering I forgot something as basic as a dress shirt. To prevent this, I have developed a packing checklist that takes less than a minute to go through but avoids those costly and sometimes embarrassing situations where, for instance, you show up at a meeting in a day-old dress shirt that you obviously slept in on the plane.

Complicated systems require more expertise in their management, but, as long as the proper expertise is available and used, the attractiveness of complicated systems is that they generally can be successfully managed. Complicated systems, by definition, adhere to a comprehensive and robust set of axioms and rules, and thus it is a matter of making sure that the proper models are being used for the situation at hand. The handling of complicated systems can be managed by the appropriate teams of experts. The more complicated the issue, the greater the need for experts or specialists but, ironically, the higher the probability of success. Business situations with a high level of complication are well defined, and the solutions to them are also well defined.

The default response for a lot of organizations is to hire a team of experts or consultants when faced with what appears to be a complicated issue. For a truly complicated problem, this is a reasonable thing to do. Often, however, the results of the experts' or the consultants' actions are less than satisfactory. Almost by definition, experts and consultants are good at complicated thinking – they know a lot about a subject that is concrete and based on rules, regulations, laws, and axioms. However, that makes them less suitable for dealing with complex situations – unless of course their field of expertise is dealing with complexity.

Complex systems are nuanced and require a nuanced approach. The one thing that will not work is a rigid, rules-based, complicated approach. Taking the time to make an accurate judgment about the type of management problem at hand helps to avoid the arrogance of complicated thinking. Complicated thinking leads managers to think that they are doing something purposeful when in reality they are not, and in fact they are likely doing more harm than good.

Almost everyone is familiar with the beginning of the serenity prayer by Reinhold Niebuhr. It goes, "God, grant me the serenity to accept the things I cannot change; courage to change the things I can; and wisdom to know the difference." When dealing with the differences between complicated and complex systems, the prayer could be modified to read, "God, grant me the serenity to accept the things that cannot be calculated; courage to calculate the things that can be calculated; and wisdom to know the difference."

Having the wisdom to know which system is appropriate and the courage to apply the proper techniques for that system are the first and perhaps the most effective steps to gaining competitive advantage with complexity.

Think "Manage, Not Solve"

The children's game of tic-tac-toe and the adult game of chess are both examples of complicated systems. Tic-tac-toe is a game that can be solved. That is, you can predetermine a precise set of rules that lead to the optimal results each time you play.[2] Theoretically, you can also do the same for chess, although the computer large enough to do so has not been invented yet (and perhaps will never be developed). The number of possible combinations of moves in chess is simply too large for even the most powerful computers to calculate. Thus, the most experienced chess masters only try to anticipate a few moves ahead and play more for position than solving of an optimal problem. It is a "manage, not solve" mentality.

Tic-tac-toe and chess illustrate that complicated systems can be either very easy to understand or so complicated that they are virtually unsolvable. Now consider the game of business. Is business more like tic-tac-toe, in that there are a limited number of moves and combinations, or is business more like chess? The quick answer is that business is more like chess, in that there are an infinite number of combinations that can be played out in any business situation. Furthermore, in business there is the presence of emergence, so the task of "solving" becomes even more impossible. So if it is not possible to "solve" a game of chess, does it not also make sense that it is not possible to "solve" business problems?

Complex situations do not lend themselves to a solution, and it is folly to spend the time, energy, or effort even to attempt to create solutions. Yet this is exactly how the complicated way of thinking works. It is in evidence when companies try to optimize complex activities such as marketing strategy, production schedules based on demand, or long-range planning. This form of thinking is especially evident in economics, as politicians all promise solutions to economic ills.

When playing chess you have to play in the moment, based on the actions of your opponent, keeping in mind as well your relative position at any given point in time. It is not possible to plan out all situations, and of course the unexpected can always happen. For instance, your opponent may make a particularly ill-advised move. Perfectly rational planning would imply that such an event could not occur, as that would imply that your opponent is stupid and irrational. Any businesses that are run stupidly and irrationally are soon replaced by more astute rivals. Likewise, your opponent can make a particularly spectacular move that you will unexpectedly need to defend against. In chess you have to try to manage the situation. A similar strategy also works for business. The key is to think "manage, not solve."

"Manage, not solve" may be a humbling strategy to use but, as already discussed in chapter 3, a lack of humility might be one of the reasons why managers default to complicated thinking. "Manage, not solve" can also be an unsettling strategy to use, as it implies that you have to rely on your in-the-moment thinking. "Manage, not solve" is based on a strategy of thinking and making relatively spontaneous decisions under uncertainty. The assumption in the complicated world is that knowledge facilitates control, while "manage, not solve" implies uncertainty. It also implies that true answers can only be experienced with hindsight. Unlike in a situation of total randomness or chaos, where any action of management is as good as any other, complexity implies that there is a level of control available; but it is not complete control, and the situation is not completely manageable. This mode of management can be quite stressful if the manager has a complicated mindset that abhors ambiguity and uncertainty.

"Manage, not solve" does not imply that managers should not plan in the face of complexity. In fact, they should do extra planning and develop creative scenarios to understand as many of the possible outcomes as possible. In the end, however, they have to remember Eisenhower's saying, that in preparing for battle, "plans are useless, but planning is indispensable." The planning helps one to envisage how things *might* unfold but cannot explain exactly how things *will* unfold. The value of planning is in the exercise of planning and the creation of alternative scenarios and alternative responses, not necessarily in the result of the planning.

Try, Learn, Adapt

You may recall the example from chapter 1 of the Post-it Notes that are one of the most successful products of 3M. When they were first test marketed under the name Press 'n Peel, the product was a dud. 3M engineers and marketers kept trying to remarket the product in various ways, each time changing and adapting their approach. Eventually, Post-it Notes became the very successful product we have all come to depend on. A rational, complicated-style approach which relies on yes or no answers would have killed product development after the unsuccessful premiere launch. 3M was acting in a somewhat random manner, allowing the product line to tweak itself and find a profitable use. It was a bold management move that has paid, and continues to pay, big dividends for the company.

The Post-it Notes saga illustrates our second useful tactic for dealing with complexity, which is to try, learn, and adapt. In the top-down command-and-control paradigm of complicated thinking, a "grand strategy" or comprehensive plan is developed. The plan is then followed through as writ, and at the conclusion success or failure is determined. If 3M had followed this paradigm with Post-it Notes, the product would have been considered a flop. Recall that the purpose behind the original project was to develop a heavy-duty adhesive. What was created was the exact opposite – a very weak adhesive. 3M, however, did not stubbornly stick to the original plan. It tried something that did not work, but it learned from the experience, adapted the strategy, and tried again.

In a complex environment it is truly rare that a grand plan or strategy will work as intended. Successful managers, however, are not discouraged by this. They learn from their missteps and use their learning to move forward with a new angle on the problem. They essentially learn as they go. Furthermore, they expect to learn as they go. Complicated thinkers tend to get too intellectually invested in an idea and refuse to let go, despite sometimes overwhelming evidence that the plan is not working. Complexity thinkers have the humility and flexibility not to get trapped into this low-probability strategy.

With a try, learn, and adapt approach, organizations have to allow for mistakes to be made and for risks to be taken. They do not take large bets on grand projects or get too invested in comprehensive plans. A key characteristic of complexity is adaptation. To succeed with complexity, an organization must also be continually adapting. It is important to note that this does not necessarily mean getting better or continually improving. It is quite possible to keep continually improving on all of the wrong things. Kodak continued to improve its film products, but when digital photos replaced film, all of the continual improvement was for naught. Adapting means developing a keen sense of how elements of the system are changing and trying new ideas to see how they work in the context of the shifting environment. Ultimately, adapting means changing along with the environment rather than trying to get the environment to change.

A specific version of the try, learn, and adapt technique is being popularized in entrepreneurship. Perhaps there is no scenario in business as complex and with as low a probability of success as that of starting a new company to manufacture a new type of product or deliver a new type of service. This, of course, is the situation of the start-up entrepreneur. One of the latest business models for entrepreneurs that is becoming widely touted is the "Lean Start-up." The Lean Start-up is a model that has been created and popularized by serial entrepreneur Eric Ries.[3] The Lean Start-up model encourages entrepreneurs to create and market a "minimally viable product" as quickly as possible. This is so entrepreneurs can learn from market feedback and adjust their product offerings appropriately. The Lean Start-up cycle has three parts: (1) Build, (2) Measure, and (3) Learn. It is a methodology that is being taught in many business schools and entrepreneur workshops. It is also a great model for dealing with the complexity faced by the entrepreneur. Starting lean is a practical application of the try, learn, and adapt approach to complexity management.

For a complicated thinker, adapting to changing and evolving situations can be difficult. It is not easy on the ego to admit that a well-thought-out plan is not going to succeed. However, having the humility and the risk-taking ability to adopt a try, learn, and adapt approach is necessary for success in the presence of complexity. Ecologist and complexity researcher C.S. Holling sums it up best when he states, "in complex systems, wealth should not be measured in money or power, but in the ability to adapt."[4]

Develop a Complexity Mindset

Perhaps the most useful complexity management strategy is to develop a complexity mindset. Managing complexity is more of a mindset than it is a set of steps that can be learned. By now it should be clear that, almost by definition, one cannot manage complexity in a mechanistic way. Such a course of action would of course be reverting to complicated thinking. Complexity requires an open mind and the ability to be humble and flexible. It also requires a willingness to try things, to experiment, even at the risk of being wrong. It goes well beyond developing a knowledge set.

A complexity mindset is simply a mindset that accepts that complexity exists, accepts that complexity needs to be dealt with differently, and accepts that there are certain limitations on what the manager can control in complex situations. Furthermore, and perhaps most importantly, a complexity mindset embraces complexity and the challenges and opportunities that come with dealing with complexity.

While it is not necessary to be a genius to manage complexity, it is helpful to consider for a minute the difference between a genius and someone who is really smart. Throughout your schooling you probably knew someone whom you considered to be a genius. Perhaps you were that person. The "genius" was the student who got top grades in everything, and for them school seemed to be easy. They were the first to hand in assignments, the ones who finished exams early, and the curve-breakers who aced the exams while everyone else got an average mark. At the time, you probably thought these people were geniuses, and indeed they were probably taunted as such in the school yard. However the odds that they were a genius are quite small. The kids who got the best marks in school were just very smart – and being smart is quite different from being a genius. A smart person is someone who thinks more efficiently, thinks more quickly, and remembers more facts than the average person does. However, they don't necessarily think differently from the average person; it is just that all of their thinking is done more efficiently, quickly, and effectively. A genius, however, is someone who thinks very differently. Geniuses seem to have their brains hard-wired in a unique fashion. They do not think in conventional ways, and because of that they frequently do not excel academically in the traditional sense.

The name "Einstein" often springs to mind when the word "genius" is uttered. While the story that Einstein did not do well in school is a myth, the reality is that Einstein thought differently. The truth is that he was certainly an above-average mathematician but not a mathematical genius. A little-known fact is that most of his mathematical problems were solved by others, including an assistant, Walther Mayer, who solved many of the mathematical equations and did most of the calculations that Einstein's theoretical musings required. Einstein called Mayer "the calculator." Mayer was obviously a very knowledgeable and talented mathematician. He was not, however, a genius like Einstein. Einstein's genius was mainly confined to abstract physics and thinking about physical systems in unique ways that were novel, innovative, and creative. The originality and power of his "Gedanken-experiment," or thought experiments, are what made Einstein such a remarkable scientist. As a mathematician Einstein was good, but not great, and most certainly not a genius. As a physicist, however, he has few peers, and for that he is considered a genius, while the talented Mayer barely registers as a footnote in history. Einstein was a complexity thinker while Mayer was a very good and very intelligent complicated thinker.[5]

The difference between being super smart and being a genius is relevant for understanding the difference between having a complicated mindset and a complex mindset. Smart people – those who are very efficient in their knowledge of facts and very fast in applying that knowledge – do very well with complicated thinking. Complexity thinkers, however, think differently. Einstein could be classified as a complicated thinker when it came to mathematics, at which he was good, but not great, and as a complexity thinker when it came to physics, at which he is one of the greatest physicists of all time. While you do not need to be a genius to be successful at complexity, you do need to think differently. Thinking harder, smarter, and deeper is the complicated mindset, but it is not sufficient, and furthermore is likely a hindrance for dealing with complexity.

Steve Jobs and Steve Wozniak provide an interesting case study to illustrate the difference between someone who is very smart, and someone who is considered to be a genius. The co-founders of Apple had very different personalities, strengths, and weaknesses. It was the synergy of their differences more than the pairing of their strengths that led to the eventual success of Apple. By all accounts, Steve Wozniak, or "Woz" as he is often affectionately called, was an excellent electronics engineer and almost single-handedly responsible for the functioning of the early Apple products. Conversely, Steve Jobs was the marketing genius. Wozniak understood how to put the electronic components together much better than Jobs, but it was Jobs who saw the vast potential for such products. Wozniak was a complicated thinker. He had mastered computer development. Jobs was the marketing genius. It was Jobs who mastered the evolution of the computer for the masses. The two had very different thinking approaches. One, Wozniak, was very good at understanding and developing the existing knowledge about electronics and computers. Jobs, however, was very good at seeing a potential for the world of personal computers that very few others did. Wozniak knew things, while Jobs dreamed about things. Wozniak was extremely smart and talented; Jobs was a genius.

A complexity mindset is a creative mindset. It focuses on what can be, rather than what is. A complexity mindset is an imaginative mindset, as different from a complicated mindset as the difference between thinking and knowing. Thinking is a creative process, while knowing is an information-retrieval process. Recall the TED talk by Ken Robinson, "Do Schools Kill Creativity?," discussed in chapter 3. Robinson's major claim is that schools kill creativity by focusing on a rote-learning approach that is better suited to the past industrial age than to the current career climate for which today's students need to be prepared. He argues that the arts are just as important as the more traditional science, writing, and mathematics-based curriculum. He emphasizes the need for creativity and self-expression so that school children can develop their talents in the way best suited to them and their passions.

Looked at another way, though, Robinson's views can be seen as an argument to allow complexity mindsets to develop as well as complicated mindsets. School curricula with their focus on mathematics, science, and literature focus on the transmission of existing knowledge rather than the development of creative abilities. Schooling, including post-secondary education, is set up for developing complicated thinking skills. Robinson claims that this is in part because it is a system that has changed little since the start of the Industrial Revolution. At the beginning of the Industrial Revolution there was a need for standardization in knowledge, as workers migrated from an agricultural background to the factories. To be successful in a factory required the ability to understand and work with machines. Creativity and imagination were not desired in the factory worker. Furthermore, there was more than enough development work in exploiting existing technology, so that engineering skills, such as the type exhibited by Wozniak, were what were needed and in short supply in industry. Imagine for a moment how Steve Jobs would have fared in the mid-1800s with his futuristic ideas of how personal computers would develop and how consumers would welcome an integrated product such as an iPhone. It is likely that someone with Wozniak's technical skills would have been a valued engineer, while Jobs might have been stuck in a grimy factory role.

In an ideal world, managers would develop both their technical knowledge and their creativity. In a sense, the manager would become a new kind of Renaissance Man. However, instead of possessing knowledge across many different fields, the modern-day "Renaissance Manager" would develop both complicated thinking skills and a complexity mindset. There is an approximate parallel between complicated thinking / complexity thinking and being a left-brain thinker versus a right-brain thinker. Being left-brain dominant is associated with being logical and analytical, while being right-brain dominant is associated with being more intuitive or creative. To excel in complexity requires flexibility in what side of the brain to use. In other words it requires one to be able to flip between being right-brain dominant and being left-brain dominant. You need to be creative as well as analytical.

This duality has sparked the beginnings of an educational movement to focus not only on science, technology, engineering, and mathematics – the STEM subjects – but also to enthusiastically include the arts, or create a STEAM curriculum.[6] Appreciation and understanding of the arts can be valuable in dealing with complexity. The arts allows us to be more creative in envisioning how emergence might play out, just as Steve Jobs envisioned how the iPod and iTunes might emerge to forever change how we select and listen to music.

The final aspect of developing a complexity mindset is to learn to embrace complexity. Complexity is a fact of business. As long as there are economies, organizations, workers, and managers, there will be complexity in business. The sooner one recognizes and makes peace with this fact, the better. Complexity is not going to go away. Trying to make complexity disappear or to make it a nonfactor is unproductive and even harmful.

While it may at times appear to be strange and unknowable, complexity is not something that is to be feared. Yes, complexity involves uncertainty and risk, but with this uncertainty and risk comes not only danger but opportunity. If there was no complexity in business there would be no need for managers or workers. As previously discussed, all the operations of a business could be run by computers or by robots if this were the case. Business decisions would be based on a master optimization program. The input of managers would be redundant at best and, more likely, suboptimal. A computer can calculate optimization problems much better than any manager or group of managers, but only a manager can emerge along with complexity.

A complexity mindset recognizes that complexity creates both challenges and opportunities. It also creates an avenue for competitive advantage. If for no other reason, this should be more than enough motivation to develop a complexity mindset.

Additional Tactics to Manage Complexity

Use Complexity to Manage Complexity

Using complexity to manage complexity sounds like a tautology or a circular argument. However, that is how the natural world aligns itself, and there are some useful analogies and lessons in this for the business manager and the business organization. The very traits that lead to complexity, such as randomness, diversity, connections, and emergence, are also the tactics that we can introduce to leverage complex systems.

As a first example, consider an ant colony. Perhaps no animal has been studied as much in the context of complexity as ants. Ant colonies are a perfect example of a complex system in that they exhibit emergence, adaptability, randomness, and self-organization. Ants are also one of the most successful species on earth. An ant colony is an example not only of a complex system but of a working organization that successfully exploits complexity.

Contrary to popular belief, ant colonies do not appear to have a clear leader. The queen ant's role, despite the regal title, appears to be limited to reproduction. Instead, ant colonies, both internally and in their dealings with other ant colonies, appear to rule themselves by self-organization. There is no central command, and there is no central commander. Yet ant colonies are extremely successful and adaptable.

One of the key tactics employed by ants is to leverage randomness to create complexity and serendipity within the colony. Ant colonies exhibit several forms of randomness that would appear to be counterproductive but instead are key to their success. For example, consider how ants find their food sources. You probably learned in high school biology that as ants search for food they leave behind a trail of scents or pheromones. When an ant discovers a food source it will go back to the ant colony and, along the way, develop a pheromone scent trail. The pheromone trail in turn marks a path to the food that attracts other ants, and soon a column of ants is seen making the trek between the colony and the food source. The stronger the pheromone trail, the more ants will be attracted to it, and thus it becomes a self-reinforcing feedback loop.

However, this is not the full story. If the feedback loop was all there was to ants finding food, then all of the ants would quickly be attracted to the same food source, which in turn would be quickly used up, and the ant colony would eventually starve. What prevents this from happening is a less well-known fact. An ant colony will have some ants that do nothing but randomly search for food. This random searching might seem like a waste of effort, particularly when an acceptable food source is already known and being used. However, it appears these "random" ants are part of a complexity strategy that embraces ambiguity and randomness by "assigning" them the role of continuing to search in case a better food source is to be found or in case the existing food source dries up or ceases to exist. This random searching appears to be one of the keys to success for ants, and it is one of the ways that they embrace complexity.

It is interesting to note that, with complicated thinking, the "random ants" would be acting suboptimally. They are not working on what is known as a successful strategy, namely exploiting a known food source. Instead they are engaged in a low-probability exercise of randomly searching for food. Furthermore, there does not appear to be a coordinated effort in this random searching. It appears as if each ant is doing its own thing, which in turn involves ants in randomly searching the same areas in a redundant and inefficient fashion. However, ant colonies are extremely effective at surviving and thriving in many different types of environments.

A corporate example of embracing multiple models and randomness is the famous skunk works projects that were made famous by 3M and that have been imitated by many other companies since. A skunk works project is an employee-driven project that is done with the support but without the interference of corporate managers. Skunk works projects are separate from the normal workflow and business processes of the operation. They operate on a principle of "business not as usual," and management is strictly hands-off. There is no central command, by design. The "ants" in a skunk works project get to forage randomly, even if this creates redundancies and inefficiencies.

The random behavior of the ants helps them to avoid local maxima. Any given food source for the ants will be a local maxima. It will eventually be used up, and the ants will need to find another food source, or in mathematical terms, another maxima. Managers and companies that focus on one idea and one idea only are like ants that rely on a single food source. As management guru Peter Drucker observed, the last buggy-whip manufacturer was likely a model of efficiency in its use of best business practices. However, the last buggy-whip manufacturer was also stuck on local maxima. It needed to branch out. It needed to copy the ants' tactic of randomly searching for food – only, in the case of an organization, the search would be for ideas and markets. Counter-intuitively, organizations need to purposely introduce randomness into their operations for complexity success.

Encourage and Seek Diversity

One of the ways to avoid being stuck on local maxima is to intentionally introduce diversity into an organization or into one's thought patterns. Developing diversity in a workforce is a well-established "best practice," but like many good ideas it is easier said than done. The biggest imped-iment to organizational diversity is the "hire like me" syndrome. It is well known that managers like to hire those whom they believe they will like. In turn, similarity in traits, education, and background are the key components of increasing the likeability factor. As a result, "hire like me" can create a self-reinforcing spiral of diminishing diversity until almost complete conformity is achieved.

Complexity only exists in the presence of diversity. Complexity arises in a competitive environment of diverse agents. It is thus a good idea to intentionally introduce diversity into the management structure. Too little diversity leads to groupthink and an inflexible organization. However, too much diversity can lead to chaos. There is an optimal amount of diversity to have in an organization, just as there is an opti-mal amount of complexity. Determining this ideal amount is more an art than a science. Furthermore, the amount likely changes over time and as business conditions change.

Organizations are social structures, and the hiring process does as much to form the corporate culture as any of the other deliberate or unintended actions of management. Smart organizations (and smart potential employees) know that a candidate's "fit" with the organi-zation is as important as the candidate's skills and knowledge. Great potential employees will look for organizations and positions that are slightly outside their comfort zone, places where they will be stretched and have the opportunity to learn, take on new challenges, and develop new skills and attributes. Organizations rarely think this way, particularly when it comes to hiring from outside the organization.

It takes discipline and conscious effort for an organization to introduce the right amount of diversity into its workforce. One way is to consciously experiment with hiring from different sources (schools and geographic areas) but also from different educational and experiential backgrounds. While technical skills may not be transferable (a surgeon may not make the best computer-chip designer, and vice versa), managerial skills such as a complexity mindset for the most part are transferable. Again we are brought back to the dichotomy between complicated and complexity skill sets. Skills in complexity are adaptable and transferable, and this transferability should be exploited more. There is no reason to suspect that sales skills in the pharmaceutical industry cannot be transferred to the marketing of packaged consumer goods, yet that is not the common mindset of either employers or people who are looking for work. It is part of the assumption that business is complicated.

A lack of organizational diversity leads to groupthink – the quick forming of consensus within a group around a specific idea without considering a wide range of potential ideas. Groupthink kills good ideas and stifles creativity, leaving a company vulnerable to rapidly changing competitive environments and unable to spot new opportunities. The demise of Kodak, the once-dominant producer of film, is a tragic example of how a lack of diversity can negatively affect a company. While the rise and popularity of digital pictures quickly and dramatically changed the picture-taking universe and, more directly, the use of film, the turn to digital photos by itself was not the cause of Kodak's demise. In fact, Kodak had been an early innovator in producing digital cameras. Where groupthink let Kodak down was in keeping the company's focus on single-purpose cameras. Kodak's management totally failed to see, or did not sufficiently appreciate, the rise of smartphones as a viable substitute for cameras. Smartphones, with automatic connectivity to social media sites such as Facebook and LinkedIn, completely changed the picture-taking habits of consumers, moving them away from single-use cameras. It turned out that it isn't the photos that are important, it is the sharing of the photos. Kodak was left with only niche markets in which they had dominance or expertise. Although

Kodak was a leader and an innovator in digital photography, it totally missed the broader implications of that market development because of a lack of diversity in its thinking and blindness to the ways in which its market might change.

Build Connections

To respond nimbly to complexity, the members of a diverse workforce need to have some way to connect or network. Building connections and networks is thus another key strategy for managing complexity. The ease and effectiveness with which employees can build connections, both within an organization and externally, are key to building a complexity-savvy organization.

Bank of Montreal's (BMO) corporate training facility is called the Institute for Learning, or more commonly the IFL. The IFL has many innovative features, and one is built around the Managing by Walking Around (MBWA) philosophy and the value of making connections. Unlike most corporate training facilities, which are composed of unused office space in corporate headquarters, the IFL is a purpose-built learning facility. Furthermore, it was intentionally built in the suburbs, away from the corporate head office. However, it was not seen as a retreat. Instead, its distance from head office was so that guests (as they are called) of the IFL could focus all of their attention on learning and on making connections.

To begin with, the architecture of the IFL is specifically designed to foster connectivity, emergence, and MBWA-type interactions. There are two very distinct halves to the IFL, connected by an architecturally stunning central corridor. The formal training spaces and classrooms are all on one side of the building, while the dining and living facilities are on the other side. The central corridor is fashioned in the shape of a sail so that it funnels traffic in such a way that guests of the IFL have a maximum opportunity of spontaneously meeting people. The open-plan design encourages guests to stop and meet with others. The fact that everyone has to navigate this space between their rooms and the training facilities acts as a catalyst for serendipitous meetings. This space is designed to develop connections, both planned and accidental. The outcome is that guests from diverse parts of the operations of BMO can more easily meet and learn from one another. These chance meetings are reinforced by having communal tables in the dining areas, facilitating – even compelling – the development of conversations and new connections. The IFL was intentionally designed to allow complexity to flourish.

The design of the office spaces of many social media companies is based on similar principles. Instead of having the traditional cubicle, or even the more limiting separate offices with closed doors, modern workplaces feature flexible working spaces that encourage people to wander, to play, and to interact with each other in a variety of different contexts. Play rooms complete with ping-pong and foosball tables are interspersed with private spaces furnished with couches and/or more open conference centers. These open and fun workplace designs encourage and facilitate MBWA as well as LBWA (learning by walking around). They foster connections, corporate learning, and emergence and help to develop the complexity-management capabilities of the organization. They are the contemporary version of the traditional water cooler and coffee-break room. It is probably not by accident that these workspaces are favored by social media companies, as they are the companies that are best at exploiting complexity in their business models. To manage complexity you need to create complexity, and one of the best ways to do that is LBWA.

It is also wise for individual workers to build their own personal networks of connections. In today's social media atmosphere, all savvy business professionals are aware of the need to build a strong personal social media presence. The previous chapter discussed two kinds of links – strong links and weak links. The concept of links is aligned with diversity. Strong links are those connections that you are regularly in touch with. For instance, they may be members of the group you eat lunch with on a daily basis, or the set of people who most often post on your social media sites. Your strong links are the group that you associate with and that is associated with you. Weak links are those connections you have that you only see or know of sporadically. Your weak links are those friends of friends whom you may have met only once or twice in passing.

As I discussed in chapter 4, sociologist Mark Granovetter's research demonstrated that weak link connections are often the most effective source of leverage. While it is obviously easiest to spread ideas among your friends and close acquaintances, the reality is that ideas shared in this way are not likely to go far, nor will they be developed much further. Your close friends likely have a similar background to yours, and they likely think much the way you do. The ideas that you learn from them are likely to be similar to ones that you have already had or thought about. It is the same with the ideas you present to them. This is the "preaching to the choir" syndrome. However by counterintuitively striving to develop weak links, your world and your world of ideas have the potential to expand exponentially. While it is important to have a connection to strong central nodes, it is also extremely helpful and valuable to attempt to establish connections with people who are very different from you. As an additional feature, weak links also tend to be more correlated with diversity, and thus are useful in that way as well.

Besides the value of incorporating diversity, the tenets of complexity teach us that connections are key. The networked and social media world in which we now exist is one of the key drivers behind the need to understand complexity. As management guru Henry Mintzberg has stated, "Management is not to control people. Rather it is to let them collaborate."[7]

Become a Learner

Individual managers need to take responsibility for building and developing their own diversity coefficient. It is imperative to avoid mental ruts if we want to progress professionally. While it takes work to develop an attitude of openness to new and different influences, the good news is that it can be a very fun and fulfilling endeavor. Charlie "Tremendous" Jones, a popular motivational speaker in the 1960s, counseled that your future progress is a direct function of "the books that you read and the people you meet." His point was that, to develop and progress, we need to expand our portfolio of ideas and our knowledge set by reading a variety of books. In addition, we also need to expand our networks by making it a point to meet new people from a variety of walks of life. It is a great tactic for increasing one's managerial complexity value.

The Renaissance was a period of great development in science, the arts, and government in fourteenth- to seventeenth-century Europe. The term "Renaissance man" referred to a person who excelled not only in the arts but also in the sciences and humanities – a person with an understanding of a broad range of ideas and disciplines and with a variety of interests. Of course, the vast store of knowledge that has accumulated since the Renaissance means that a meaningful level of expertise in multiple areas of study is no longer possible. We are living in the era of specialization, where experts know increasingly more about an increasingly narrow field of knowledge. Specialization, however, moves us farther away from the concept of "Renaissance man."

We need to revive the concept of the Renaissance person to cope with an increasingly connected world that is becoming more complex and less complicated. "Complexity" is expansionist, while "complicated" is reductionist. "Complexity" is eclectic, while "complicated" is didactic. The need for individuals whose knowledge and interests range across a variety of fields and disciplines is greater than ever. It is regrettable that the current prevailing educational paradigms seem to run counter to this. Liberal arts programs have declining enrolments, while specialist programs and concentrated certificate programs are on the rise. Unfortunately, society celebrates the specialist but considers the generalist a commodity.

Successful organizations will be those that develop a Renaissance mindset. Organizations must actively promote diversity, not only of culture but also of mindsets, if they are to compete successfully in a complex environment. They must proactively train people in different knowledge and skill sets. They must recruit from a diversity of backgrounds and from different fields of knowledge. They must work to cross-train managers to a greater extent than they are currently doing. The challenge of management lies in allowing diversity to function – tolerating and even welcoming differences; it is the only way that an organization can grow and learn. Perhaps this is why many leading companies actively recruit employees who have held a variety of different positions at different organizations.

Managers must also take personal responsibility for opening themselves to new influences and ideas. Managers who make a point of developing in as many ways as possible will be the ones to gain the fresh insights and spot the emergent trends that complexity presents them with. Managers need to learn to become diverse learners. They must get out of the comfort zone that made them successful and develop new skills and new ways of critically looking at the world. Random learning is a counterintuitive but key strategy to deploy. Examples of random learning include reading magazines far from one's normal areas of interest, taking part in unique cultural or artistic events, and talking to professionals from vastly different areas of business.

As Eric Hoffer once said, "In times of change learners inherit the earth … while the learned find themselves beautifully equipped to deal with a world that no longer exists."[8] In this era of complexity, this statement has never been truer. Complexity mocks the learned and rewards the learner. Learners can make and understand the connections necessary to manage complexity, while the learned are stuck with a rigid and inflexible knowledge base.

Playbooks, Not Rulebooks

So far it may seem that there are no rules for dealing with complexity. Actually, complex behavior can be mathematically developed out of a small set of very simple rules. Ants, for example, have a propensity to follow a pheromone trail, and the stronger the trail, the more likely it is that other ants will follow it. Note that the rule is simple – with a given positive probability of following a pheromone trail, the stronger the trail, the higher the probability that it will be followed. However, this rule leads to a very complex ant society. Note also that the rule is not absolute. The rule has randomness built into it. We have already discussed the importance of introducing randomness and diversity into a system. Here the focus is on keeping the rules simple. Complicated systems are based on a large set of very rigid rules. Complexity is based on having a very few simple heuristics. The complexity manager keeps this in mind and keeps the heuristics to a minimum. Complexity is not an absence of rules but a minimization of rules.

Jeff Swystun, the chief communications officer at advertising giant DDB (Doyle Dane Bernbach), interprets this approach as "playbooks, not rulebooks." In other words, you want to have a few general principles in place (the playbooks) but not encumber employees with a plethora of rules. This simple philosophy allows for the flexibility (as opposed to total chaos) that is needed to manage complexity effectively.

Minimizing rules while introducing randomness means that at any given point in time there will be apparent inefficiencies in the system. In other words, a complicated approach would appear to have savings in terms of costs and utilization. These inefficiencies have to be expected and planned for – again, a trait that goes against the intuition of the modern manager. Optimization, which is often the goal of modern business practices such as "just in time inventory management," tries to minimize slack whenever possible, and, for certain complicated tasks such as keeping a factory functioning, this makes sense. However, for complex systems this approach prevents the system from learning and developing more efficient processes that are more suitable for emerging contexts.

Embrace Emergence

A key trait of complexity that can be exploited by a manager is emergence. Emergence arises out of connections and social interactions. These social interactions could be internal to the organization, or external, between the organization and its industry or even between the organization and the larger economy. Emergence itself cannot be directly managed or predicted, but it can be imagined, and the catalysts to allow emergence can be put in place by an enlightened manager.

To appreciate the potential of emergence one needs to think like a sociologist. The empathy can be on a personal level from a manager to an employee, or an organizational empathy, where the manager consciously tries to develop a feel for where the organization is headed socially. In addition, senior managers need to develop an economic empathy – a feeling for where the general mood of the economy might be headed and, if possible, for why the mood of the economy might be changing.

C.W. Mills, who is considered to be the godfather of sociology, calls this a sociological imagination. Having a sociological imagination requires one to attempt to understand not only individuals but also the sociological context within which individuals exist. This is perfectly consistent with trying to understand or model emergence. Emergence occurs when individuals participating in a joint relationship, both independently and as a leaderless collective, take cues from their social context, make individual decisions based on that context, and then act. This "check context, make decision, act on context" loop is what produces the leaderless patterns we call emergence. It is the interplay between individuals and their social context, and it is the sociological imagination framework that Mills originated.

Emergence can be either intimidating or inspiring to the manager. It behaves in weird and unpredictable – as well as uncontrollable – ways. It can also be an overpowering force, as the management team of Coca-Cola found out. Emergence cannot be controlled, but perhaps it can be nudged. If nothing else, alert managers can be aware of it and perhaps adjust and adapt their strategies accordingly. Being aware of emergence and being willing to work with emergence rather than fight it are key. However, doing so requires managers to be sensitive to the broader context of business operations and willing to abandon rigid frameworks and strategies that do not allow for the company to quickly change course.

Emergence can give a competitive advantage to the nimble organization but is the enemy of the rigid behemoth. For example, consider the privately owned grocery store chain Trader Joe's. Trader Joe's has created almost a cult around its stores and the products they offer. In its quirky stores, the employees wear Hawaiian shirts and specialize in extremely high customer service. What makes Trader Joe's unique is that the stores stock less than 10 percent of the number of products that a traditional grocery store does but are estimated to make more than twice the profit per square foot. Known for such things as its Two Buck Chuck, which is a bottle of wine that retails for $1.99, or its quirky Speculoos Cookie Butter, a spread made out of crushed cookies,

Trader Joe's is a company that is embracing emergence and gaining a competitive advantage because of it.

What makes Trader Joe's unique is that it is much more nimble than other grocery store chains. Many of the low-turnover basics that other stores carry – for instance, mundane products such as toothpicks – do not make the shelves at Trader Joe's. Also, its selection of goods is very eclectic. The chain thrives on surprising customers with goods they cannot get elsewhere, and it does this by selling over 80 percent of its products under its own brand name. The company is very close to the customer and does not hesitate to drop any product that is not selling quickly enough. Thus the customer comes into a Trader Joe's expecting to be surprised by the products on offer.

Trader Joe's has developed a connection with its customers through creating a "neighborhood store" feel through its smaller spaces and superior customer service, and by letting its customers spread the message to their friends about the newest quirky food product they have "discovered" at Trader Joe's.

Through its willingness to experiment with new products and quickly pull those that are not meeting expectations, Trader Joe's is exhibiting the complexity management tactics of encouraging diversity, absurd thinking, and "try, learn, and adapt" management. It essentially tries things and lets its connections with its customers (and its customers' connections) allow the winning products to emerge. It is one example of a company that has embraced complexity thinking and emergence in its operating strategy, and the strategy has worked extremely well.

Empathy

It has already been discussed that business complexity most frequently arises through the interactions of people. People are empathic, and the manager with a complexity mindset needs not only a sociological imagination but also a well-developed capacity for empathy. Columbia Business School professor Rita McGrath has explored the importance of empathy in an article titled "Management's Three Eras: A Brief History."[9] McGrath argues that in the first era of management, during the Industrial Revolution, execution of mass production was key.

The next era of management, during the mid-twentieth century, emphasized expertise and can be represented by the rise of the principles of scientific management. Today, McGrath explains, we are entering into a new era where the emphasis must be on empathy.

McGrath's three eras are consistent with the change of the manager's role from that of a complicated thinker to a complexity thinker. During the Industrial Revolution, the main problems were simply figuring out how to get things done. As businesses became more sophisticated, scientific management and complicated thinking came to the fore. However, the world is now more global and more connected and thus more complex. McGrath argues that work is done more through networks than through lines of command – again, consistent with the change from complicated to complex. When the lines of command shift to networks, the emotions and the personality of the worker become more important, and the complexity mindset manager needs to take account of this.

Have Fun with Complexity

As I have previously noted, complex systems cannot be mastered. They are a continually evolving and emerging portfolio of activities. This implies that the manager's style needs to be continually evolving as well.

Successful managers will learn to have fun with complexity. While it is true that "getting to maybe" may be frustrating, it is a need that must be acknowledged. It can also be discouraging to realize that complete command and control are not achievable through extra effort or exceptional skill. However, it is also true that complexity brings surprises, and for each surprise there is a new area to exploit and profit from.

Complexity is a reality. It is a fact. It is not a fad, and it is not going to go away. It is not going to diminish in importance; it is only going to grow in importance. Managers and organizations can come to accept the new reality or continue to remain ignorant of complexity and its implications. However, only acceptance will lead to "maybe," while the path of ignorance will almost certainly lead to obsolescence.

In the run-up to Super Bowl XVLI between the New York Giants and the New England Patriots, one reporter's story focused on how Tom Coughlin became such a successful coach. One of Coughlin's players noted that Coughlin stressed the teamwork philosophy of "adjust and mystery." If football players can adapt to "adjust and mystery," then so can business managers.

Managers and their organizations should not be intimidated by or afraid of complexity. They need to embrace it and enjoy it for what it is. They need to have fun with it, or, as author Daniel Pink would say, they need to embrace it and "play."[10] It's not complicated.

SIX

THE COMPLEXITY OF STRATEGIC PLANNING

"The essence of strategy formulation is coping with competition," wrote business strategy guru Michael Porter at the very beginning of his classic 1979 *Harvard Business Review* article "How Competitive Forces Shape Strategy."[1] Competition is the defining characteristic of business, as it is of war. Business strategy and war strategy have often been compared to each other – and with good reason. The parallels between war and business, especially in the way they demonstrate complexity, are too obvious to miss.

In both war and business you have two or more sides that are competing against each other for territory, whether it is land, political power, or the wallet of the consumer. There are connections and linkages between the protagonists. There are high stakes combined with high uncertainty. Both are also open systems with no guarantee of a definitive end, as the battles, both military and commercial, can continue and evolve as new players enter the fray while others leave or are defeated.

Strategic planning is considered a cornerstone of every company's activities, just as it is a critical and essential part of any military campaign. The strategic plan guides the activities and tactics of the firm in the long term as well as on a day-to-day basis. It is the foundation of a business and the foundation of military operations. We celebrate the winning business strategist as we do the winning military strategist.

Despite the perceived importance of strategic planning, Dwight Eisenhower once famously said that "in preparing for battle I have always found that plans are useless, but planning is indispensable."[2] His point makes good sense in a complexity context. There is significant value in planning, as it is through planning that the strategic team is forced to get creative about possible future scenarios. The exercise of planning stimulates learning and creativity. It also aids in contingency planning and in risk management. However, strict adherence to a strategic plan only makes sense if the assumed future that was used to construct the plan is aligned with an actual future. It is this impossibility of accurately predicting the future that renders plans useless in the heat of battle.

Another component that is frequently given short shrift in planning is the actions of the other stakeholders. In war it is the enemy. In business it is both the competitors and the customers of the firm – as well as competing forces within the firm, as its employees and managers often have their own competitive agendas. All of a firm's stakeholders are, explicitly or implicitly, making and continuously revising their own plans. Furthermore, those plans may be subject to swift and radical change. Stakeholders are continually adapting and responding to the actions of others in an ongoing dance of adaptive complexity that defies complicated thinking in even seemingly straightforward cases.

The fundamental weakness of strategic planning is that it is static and linear. Strategic planning is based on a vision for the future. However, the best one can do to predict the future is to imagine what it will be like from a present-day perspective, assuming that future events will unfold in much the same way as they have in the past. As such, most scenario planning is at best a linear extrapolation of existing trends. This works well for complicated systems. The underlying rules and laws of complicated systems are based on the premise that the future will be a reasonable linear extension of the present, barring any new technological developments.

However, as we observe with starlings flying in concert, twisting and turning in beautiful but random patterns in the sky, the patterns that exist for complex systems are continuously changing in mysterious and unpredictable ways. There are definitely patterns, but the patterns are continually evolving and are not reproducible or predictable. In a similar manner, the buying habits of consumers are complex. The actions of competitors are complex. The internal culture of a firm is complex. The interactions between a company, its target market, and its competitors are complex. Linear extrapolations of existing trends usually provide wildly inaccurate predictions for business-planning purposes, quickly rendering the most well-laid plans obsolete.

War is not complicated; it's complex. Strategic planning is not complicated; it's complex. Strategic planning is a key area in which managers need to make the transition from a complicated to a complex mindset.

Strategy and Complexity

One of the key requirements in managing complexity is the need to continuously observe and react to patterns and trends rather than focus on a fixed target – to maintain a "manage, not solve" complexity mindset, as discussed in chapter 5. Developing a strategy, simply stated, is the management function that looks at patterns and trends and sets the general direction for a company's operations over an extended period. Strategy involves taking the long view rather than focusing on the more mundane tactical decisions that determine the day-to-day operations and outcomes of the firm. Strategic thinking sets in motion a myriad of decisions and actions that a firm will implement going forward.

Selecting a strategy that is both appropriate and flexible enough to respond to the unexpected can therefore be a major component of a company's ability to manage complexity successfully. However, as with most things involved with systems thinking, we see that the task is not quite that simple. As this chapter will attempt to make clear, strategy itself is a field that demonstrates all the previously identified hallmarks of complex systems, including connectedness, ambiguity, feedback loops, randomness, emergence, adaptiveness, and nonlinear relationships.

The strategic direction of a company is at the locus of a complex set of complex systems. It is, if you will, a "complexity-squared" juncture. A company is part of an industry, which in turn is part of a national economy, which in turn is part of the global economy. Looking inward, the strategy of a company in part determines the corporate culture, the prevailing corporate values, and the management practices that the company employs. These strategic decisions in turn affect the employees of the company and their interactions in the broader society.

Of course, how the employees of the company react to the strategy and the tactics employed to enact the strategy also loop back into how well the strategy is executed, and how well a change in strategy is accepted and managed. In this way strategy setting becomes the hub of a universe of complex systems, which individually are complex, and taken together as a whole are also complex. It is layers of complexity within complexity.

It is therefore imperative that the management team of a company explicitly acknowledge the presence of complexity, both when making strategic decisions and, perhaps more importantly, when implementing and managing the consequences of those decisions. As with all aspects of managing in a complex system, it is essential that managers adopt an attitude of humility with regard to their decisions and actions. Becoming overcommitted to a particular set of strategic decisions can be one of the most detrimental traits of a business manager. While persistence and belief in an idea are necessary for success (as even the best of strategies face hurdles in their implementation and need time to mature and find acceptance), the manager who understands complexity will constantly be looking to see whether the original assumptions and decisions are still valid, as the overall business systems, both external and internal, are adapting and evolving. Even the most successful strategy will not succeed forever. Companies need to adapt their strategies as the business landscape evolves.

Robert Strange McNamara: The Whiz Kid Extraordinaire

Perhaps there is no one who epitomizes the parallel between war planning and strategic business planning as much as Robert Strange McNamara. The most prominent of the so-called Whiz Kids, Robert McNamara rode the "manager as technocrat" wave of the 1940s to become a leader in both industrial and military circles as the first non-Ford chief executive officer of the Ford Motor Company and the Secretary of Defense under Presidents Kennedy and Johnson. He later concluded his illustrious career as head of the World Bank.

Robert McNamara received an undergraduate degree in economics (with minors in mathematics and philosophy) at the University of California at Berkeley and then a Masters of Business Administration at Harvard in 1939. After a brief period working as an accountant, he returned to Harvard Business School as a professor. His academic training was to influence his thinking greatly. He was the model for the rational economic man; a person who put his faith in extensive analysis and a supposedly unbiased focus on making decisions based on a strictly rational analysis of data. He was the poster child for scientific management and complicated thinking, just as faith in complicated thinking was on the ascendant in America.

During the Second World War, McNamara was in the Statistical Control Unit of the U.S. Air Force. He and his peers analyzed all aspects of the war using a disciplined, data-driven approach. From procurement operations to the efficacy of bombers, there seemed to be little that escaped the calculations of the Statistical Control team. Compared to the sometimes inconsistent and chaotic decision-making style that had existed in the military before then, the decision-making style supported by analysis from the Statistical Control team was unemotional, objective, and rational and produced more effective and efficient operations. After the war, McNamara and nine of his peers from the Statistical Control unit joined the Ford Motor Company and continued applying scientific management and rational, data-driven analysis to increase efficiency and decision making. It was while at Ford that the group of ten got labeled the Whiz Kids, with McNamara as the acknowledged leader. McNamara quickly rose through the ranks within Ford, and in 1960 he became the first non-Ford family member to become president of the Ford Motor Company.

Less than three months after achieving the top job at Ford, McNamara was called to be Secretary of Defense by President John F. Kennedy. McNamara served as Secretary of Defense for seven years under first President Kennedy and then President Johnson. Presumably, his mandate was to continue his focus on complicated, data-driven thinking and embed it into the strategic planning and operations of the Armed Forces, and he carried out this mandate with enthusiasm.

If McNamara's storied career had stopped here, it would provide a strong case for complicated thinking. The assumption underlying McNamara's approach was that an effective management technique was to deconstruct problems into their constituent components, analyze the trends that were apparent within each of those components, implicitly make the assumption that those trends or patterns would continue, and use statistical forecasting tools to project the future, comparing the outcomes from alternative strategies and choosing the optimal strategy. This technique was a classic use of the command-and-control paradigm of complicated thinking, supported by the principles of scientific management and driven by spreadsheet analysis. It was straight from the business-school classroom and demonstrated a textbook approach to complicated thinking and decision making.

By any measure McNamara's career had been a success up to the point at which he became Secretary of Defense: the youngest professor at Harvard, on the cover of *Time* magazine in 1963, president of one of the mightiest corporations in the world (albeit for a very short time), and then Secretary of Defense. Unfortunately for McNamara, over time, slowly and painfully, he came to appreciate the severe limitations of his strict adherence to complicated thinking.

The event that McNamara is most associated with is the Vietnam War. His views and approaches to managing the Vietnam War were his first major failure and demonstrated the weakness of his complicated thinking approach to strategic planning. However, it is also likely that a slow but persistent sea-change in society was the catalyst for change that led to a re-evaluation of the efficacy of complicated strategic planning.

After the Second World War, Western economies and the U.S. economy in particular were booming. There was pent-up demand for goods and services, and corporate America was only too happy to satisfy that demand. The 1950s gave rise to the conglomerate corporate structure in the quest for manufacturing and marketing efficiency. In the 1960s, investment in stocks of the "Nifty Fifty," as America's leading corporations were called, was seen as a formula for guaranteed financial success. Based on improved technological and managerial performance, and also on the application of scientific management principles to marketing and sales, growth in the American economy seemed assured.

Prosperity led consumers to make decisions based upon wants rather than needs. This trend was facilitated by the rising role of the creative advertising agency, which promoted products based on detailed scientific testing of consumer behavior, in essence creating a demand where little had existed during the Depression. The rise of the suburbs, shopping malls, and the car culture accelerated the consumer trend. Convenience and lifestyle became the issues that concerned consumers and, by extension, corporate America. These were consumer demands based on the heart and emotions rather than need.

The mood in America also began to shift, influenced by the growth of "flower power" demographic change. As the boomers began to exercise their power in both business and politics, subtle but profound changes started to occur.

Within this context of relative prosperity and change, the Vietnam War and the Cold War were defining factors. The Vietnam War is probably one of the most critically analyzed events in American history, second probably only to the U.S. Civil War. McNamara and his scientific analysis played a key role. Many of those opposed to the war for a variety of reasons derisively labeled it "McNamara's War."

With or without McNamara and his scientific decision making, the role of the United States in the Vietnam War would have been controversial. However, McNamara's insistence on running a "spreadsheet war" struck some as callous and others as strategically short-sighted. There were major questions concerning the validity of the data that were coming out of the war. Perhaps more importantly, there were many things that the data, flawed or not, could not reveal about important factors that ultimately influenced decisions and the outcome of the war. For instance, one of the most important elements that the numbers did not capture was the determination of the North Vietnamese. In addition, there was the apparent inability of the South Vietnamese to mount a significant effort despite a sometimes material superiority in weapons and resources. The leader of the North Vietnamese Communist forces, Ho Chi Minh, is quoted as saying, "You can kill ten of my men for every one we kill of yours … But even at those odds you will lose and we will win."[3]

Many reasons have been put forward to explain the United States' failure in Vietnam, ranging from a misunderstanding of the on-the-ground conditions and the Vietnamese culture to inaccurate casualty data leading to misguided analysis of how the war was going. All these explanations notwithstanding, there were forces at work in Vietnam that did not involve military power, and that were not covered by the analyses that McNamara relied on. What had seemingly worked so well in the Second World War did not work in Vietnam. Unlike the laws of physics, the strategic planning of war was not reproducible.

After he retired, McNamara himself provided extensive analysis of the war from his point of view. This included his complete involvement in the aptly named 2003 documentary by Errol Morris called *The Fog of War: Eleven Lessons from the Life of Robert S. McNamara*. The documentary was in part based on the 1995 memoir that McNamara wrote with Brian VanDeMark, *In Retrospect: The Tragedy and Lessons of Vietnam*.[4] In both the movie and the memoir, McNamara looks back on his thinking and his actions while Secretary of Defense and offers a list of lessons that should be taken away. Some of McNamara's thoughts are especially relevant for a manager who is trying to understand the link between strategic planning and complexity, coming as they do from one of the most celebrated complicated thinkers of his era.[5] In particular, there are three lessons that McNamara emphasizes in the documentary that are worth examining in the context of complex strategic planning.

The first applicable lesson is "Rationality will not save us." This is a most unusual and unexpected statement to ascribe to Robert McNamara, given his reputation for rational analysis and decision making. However, it is a blunt admission that human beings in the collective do not always act in a rational manner. There is human nature at work, and human nature is not a machine, nor does it act like one. This is particularly true when it comes to aspects of culture or politics. McNamara reinforces this insight with the supplementary insight that "You can't change human nature."

The lesson here for strategic planning is clear. Human nature is what it is, and that is not always what we want to believe it is or what we perceive it to be. Furthermore, it is subject to change. As discussed before, planning based on the ideal "rational economic man" will likely lead to misguided analysis and interpretations. Strategic planning needs to allow for culture in the broadest sense. In today's social media world, culture can be defined along more than just geographic, racial, or religious lines. With increasing globalization, the concept of culture is becoming more and more fluid, such that individuals, during the course of a single day, may relate to several different cultures, including a parent culture, a professional culture, a sporting culture, an age-related culture, or even a specific hobby culture such as car or stamp collecting. What is rational for an individual in one culture may be irrational in relation to another culture. This shifting of rationality creates challenges and opportunities for the strategic planner. The challenges, however, are greatest for the complicated thinker, while more opportunities present themselves to a strategic thinker who thinks in terms of complexity.

McNamara and others misjudged the resolve of the North Vietnamese. They also misjudged the changing political mood at home in the United States. In hindsight, it seems that, more than anything, these two factors explain why the United States, and by association Robert McNamara, lost the war not only abroad but also at home in the minds of the electorate. It wasn't necessarily a misinterpretation of the numbers; it was a lack of awareness and appreciation of factors the numbers could not convey.

A second lesson from McNamara, outlined in his memoir, is "We did not recognize that neither our people nor our leaders are omniscient." This statement follows directly from "Rationality will not save us." A strategic plan may be regarded as foolproof (omniscient) or as a worthless document. Neither of these perceptions is completely accurate. Although people will make mistakes in calculation, in interpretation, in judgment, and in implementation, the fact that they are not omniscient does not negate the value of their thoughts, analyses, and judgments. It simply means that there needs to be an ongoing healthy respect for the fallibility of any type of plan, no matter how thoughtfully it is developed. This is not to dismiss the plan but to recognize the presence of complexity – that there is a limit to how well the human mind can predict the future.

The final lesson for strategic planning that we can draw from McNamara is also the final lesson he provides in his memoir. "We failed to recognize that in international affairs, as in other aspects of life, there may be problems for which there are no immediate solutions." He continues: "at times we may have to live with an imperfect, untidy world."

This can be interpreted as a straightforward admission that it is essential first to determine what type of system you are faced with – complicated or complex – and then to learn to accept "maybe" as a possible result in the presence of complexity.

Complicated thinking belongs in the world of "organized and tidy," while complexity characterizes the imperfect untidy world, but also the world in which managers most often find themselves. McNamara perhaps regretted that he did not acknowledge this fact earlier in his career. He certainly seems to imply as much in his memoirs. Unfortunately, it is often hard to learn "in the moment," and would have been particularly so for McNamara, given his success with complicated thinking up to that time. Frequently, it is only with time and through reflection that such lessons are learned and appreciated.

To summarize, the reflections of Robert S. McNamara are very interesting, insightful, and valuable for strategic planners, since McNamara was considered to be the poster child for rational strategic analysis and complicated thinking.

McNamara, at the conclusion of the documentary, explains the term "fog of war" as follows: "the fog of war means war is so complex it is beyond the ability of the human mind to comprehend all of the variables. Our judgment, our understanding are not adequate …"[6] There are a couple of discussion points arising from this comment. First, McNamara is using the term "complex" interchangeably with the term "complicated" here. Second, his statement is essentially implying that, with better data and more comprehensive analysis, many of the problems experienced could eventually have been solved. The science of complexity would imply otherwise, and it behooves strategic planners to take this into account. It's not complicated; it's complex.

Porter's Five Forces

It is widely acknowledged that strategy setting is a difficult if not an impossible task to optimize – even without acknowledging the presence of complexity. In large part this is why CEOs of companies, who are also de facto the chief strategic officers of their organizations, are so well compensated. To make the strategic decision analysis more manageable, academics, business analysts, and strategic consultants have developed multiple models, schematics, and frameworks for strategic analysis and planning.

Although many popular strategic frameworks exist, one of the most widely used frameworks for conducting a strategy analysis is Porter's Five Forces. Porter's Five Forces was developed by Harvard Business School professor Michael Porter, outlined in his book *Competitive Strategy,* published in 1980.[7] Porter's framework helped both to popularize and to standardize strategic analysis. It provided a rigorous academic basis that legitimized the practice of strategic analysis and remains at the core of strategic planning even today, more than thirty years after its initial publication.

Porter's Five Forces are as follows: (1) the threat of new entrants, (2) the threat of substitute products or services, (3) the bargaining power of suppliers, (4) the bargaining power of customers, and (5) the intensity of internal competition within the industry. Using the Five Forces framework, companies analyze their strategic positioning within an industry and develop tactics and strategies to improve or at least defend their position and profitability. Viewed with a complexity lens, the framework also provides a useful framework to illustrate the challenges of strategic planning and the role complexity plays in understanding business strategy.

Before considering Porter's framework in the context of complexity, let us recall from chapter 4 the essential elements that give rise to complexity. They are: (1) several different agents, (2) the ability of the agents to be connected in some way, and (3) the ability of the agents to learn and thus adapt or make choices. Using Porter's Five Forces framework in light of the components of complexity, one can easily understand and appreciate that strategic planning is a complex exercise. The Porter Five Forces model does a wonderful job of breaking strategy analysis into digestible component pieces. However, it also provides a framework for understanding how complexity enters into strategy. When we examine each of the components of the Porter model, it becomes apparent that the elements of complexity are present in all of them.

The purpose of Porter's model is to examine each of the five components in turn and analyze the relative strengths and weaknesses of a company as well as the threats and opportunities that exist. A thorough and thoughtful Porter analysis allows a strategist to see more clearly the interconnections between the factors affecting the firm, and thus provides a picture of how a company might move forward most successfully.

Consider the first element of Porter's framework: the potential entrants to an industry. In our increasingly globalized world the potential for new entrants is in constant flux. Given the ease with which financing flows around the world, the financing of new entrants has become ever more difficult to forecast. When Porter originally developed his model, the world economy was becoming global but at a much slower pace and to a lesser degree than it is now, more than thirty years later. In addition it has become more apparent now that certain industries are strategically important, with the result that developing countries in particular are becoming more active in developing their own entrants into those industries, if not creating whole new industries themselves. The presence of strategically important industries is an idea that Porter put forth in his companion book, *The Competitive Advantage of Nations*.[8]

Ironically, one of the industries where the dynamics of determining new entrants has evolved most is in the capital markets and finance industry. Developing countries are realizing that strong capital markets are a key determinant for the development of ideas, which in turn drive economic growth. Thus, even though there has been a consolidation of stock markets around the world, the number of financial exchanges continues to increase. The proliferation of financial markets has in turn increased the number of financial products available. It has also dramatically increased the global sophistication of the markets. The volume of trading in financial products and ideas continues to grow around the world, and a large part of that derives from new entrants into the system.

The threat of new entrants, and the potential impact they might have is a function of many things. In large part it is a function of the perceived attractiveness of an industry. The perceived attractiveness of an industry in turn depends on context. Many mature industries in the developed world look relatively unattractive from a strategic point of view, while the perception in the developing world might be very different.

The mere act of developing a view on an industry has changed with the changing of the economy from one based on physically manufactured goods such as cars and refrigerators to one based on concepts and ideas, as in technology-based industries. For instance, the iPhone is as much a concept as it is a physical device. The world of the Internet is another example that is almost purely conceptual. Google has no physical products; it has no manufacturing facilities in the conventional sense of the word; yet few would argue against the statement that Google has in effect created a brand-new industry.

Uber and Lyft, the apps that allow users to summon a driver, are a different sort of disruptive technology that has fundamentally changed the taxi industry and that forces us to think differently about what exactly the threat of a new entrant is. While taxis are obviously real physical objects, Uber and Lyft are companies that do not own cars but simply provide a phone app. Instead of providing a new competitor, they have provided a new way of doing business.

The threat of new entrants and the barriers to entry – from the ability to source financing and build a manufacturing plant to the ability to finance and implement an idea – have changed. With the globalization of the financial economy, the barriers to financing a new company have become considerably lower. Even more significant, there are few if any barriers to the creation of an idea. This has dramatically changed the calculus of determining the threat of new entrants since Porter first developed his model.

Perhaps the most important consequence of a context in which the rise of ideas is the catalyst for new entrants is that ideas emerge much more rapidly than manufacturing plants do. Ideas are also copied much more quickly and can be very difficult to brand as one would brand a physical product. A complement to the role of ideas as new entrants is the role of substitute products. For example, when looking at the iPhone from smartphone rival and prior dominant industry leader RIM's point of view, it is reasonable to ask if the iPhone was a new entrant (Apple) in the mobile phone market, or a substitute product. The answer is probably a bit of both.

Ideas are nonlinear. Ideas are also generally highly connected, and they depend on connections for their growth. They evolve and emerge from other ideas. Of course, whenever we observe nonlinearity and connectivity we are likely to observe complexity. As an example, consider AOL and Netscape. AOL and Netscape were the two dominant leaders in the early days of the Internet when home computers were in the process of becoming ubiquitous. AOL and Netscape were among the first major companies to conceive of a personal Internet service provider and an Internet search engine, respectively. However, the way ideas about the Internet industry developed led to a highly diversified set of Internet providers, while Google quickly took a near-monopoly position among search engines. These examples demonstrate a bifurcation of results that strategic analysis and classical economic theory say should not exist.

Thus, if ideas and disruptive technologies are thought to be a major competitive factor, then one must take complexity into account when analyzing the threat of new entrants.

Complexity also plays a significant role in the second component of Porter's model – the relative power of buyers. For example, the existence of Internet shopping has dramatically changed consumer buying habits and with it the relative power of buyers. Even if one does not purchase goods over the Internet, one is likely to be highly influenced by the medium. For instance, the ability to comparison shop in terms of price is greatly facilitated by online shopping. The ease of comparison shopping online has had a transformative impact on bricks-and-mortar retailers.

Nowhere is this more evident than in the influence Amazon has had on the book-retailing industry. Even before the advent of e-readers such as the Kindle, readers' book-buying habits changed dramatically when Amazon came into the market. Bricks-and-mortar bookstores rapidly went out of business as they could not compete on price, convenience, or even service. This affected not only the regional and independent booksellers, but also former giants of the industry such as Borders. Now the only competitive advantage bookstores have is immediacy, as you can get delivery of a hardcover book right away by driving to your local bookstore. However, even that advantage has eroded with the rise in popularity of e-readers, which provide virtually instant access to the book you want without your even having to get up out of your chair. Furthermore, the role of booksellers as adjudicators of quality has also been overtaken by online reviews, which are also readily available. The wisdom of crowds expressed through online reviews has almost totally replaced the influence of traditional judges of literary taste such as book clubs or the *New York Times* book review section.

One consequence of online customer reviews is that in large part companies have lost control of their message. To complicate their marketing challenge even further, the proliferation of Internet and other alternative media outlets has made it much harder for companies to change their message and rebrand a company through advertising. The traditional channels of advertising, such as broadcast television and influential magazines, have been supplanted by the Internet and multiple media sources delivered through mobile technologies such as smartphones. The reach of social media gives consumers the power to influence others by posting reviews – again, making it harder for a company to control its message and branding.

Online reviews are an example of the power of complexity to alter the dynamics between the company and its consumers. By fostering a strong relationship with its customers, a company can positively impact its online brand and presence. Conversely, improperly managed, a company's brand can be irreparably damaged by the power of online consumers. The speed with which buyers can change the positioning and value of a brand, for better or for worse, increases the complexity of assessing and managing buyers' power for the strategic manager. It is another example of the power of connectivity and complexity and how they impact the development of strategy.

The third leg of Porter's model is the threat of new substitutes. As previously mentioned, the threat of new substitutes is particularly strong in the world of technology, where ideas are the substitutes rather than a physical product. With globalization and the ever-increasing speed with which products can be manufactured and brought to market, the threat of substitutes might be the most fluid and dynamic of the forces to be discussed.

For instance, if three-dimensional printing continues to develop at its current rapid pace, it is possible that in the relatively near future each home will have its own manufacturing facility, in the way that most households have at least one computer today. If three-dimensional printing in the home becomes a practical reality, then products will truly become virtual, and the pace of industrial change will be altered by an order of magnitude. This development could lead to a large cottage industry of product developers and reinvigorate the "garage tinkerer," in much the same way that the iPhone has led to a large cottage industry of app developers.

The fourth leg of Porter's model is the power of suppliers. In the context of the market, when Porter was originally developing his model, suppliers were the manufacturers or suppliers of specialized parts. They were also the commodity suppliers. In the world of physical products these are still important factors. However, more and more products are outsourced for production purposes, as manufacturing continues to move to the lowest-cost and most efficient provider. For manufactured products, all of the manufacturing may be done by suppliers, with the company itself existing solely to provide design and marketing services. Consider Nike, for example. Nike does not really manufacture anything in the traditional sense. Almost all of its products are made by third-party suppliers. Nike as a company exists mainly for design and marketing purposes. This is a fundamentally different model from that of a traditional manufacturing company such as Ford, with its famous River Rouge plant that was fully integrated for the production of cars. As one way of achieving the flexibility needed to manage complexity, numerous companies, like Nike, have in essence become virtual companies.

In the context of commodities, however, a different dynamic is at work in the supply chain. The rise of financial instruments for the trading of commodities as investment or speculative instruments has changed the dynamics of how manufacturers need to deal with commodity suppliers. Even the largest players in the markets cannot control the market dynamics affecting commodity prices, which rise and fall with the expectations of speculators, which in turn are based on judgments about the future. The financial markets for commodities, just like all financial markets, exhibit all of the usual characteristics of complexity, including connectivity, nonlinearity, adaptation, and emergence. The ability of companies to control their commodity costs has evolved to make them vulnerable to a volatile market-driven process.

Finally, we come to the final leg and the centerpiece of Porter's model: the degree of competition within a given industry. The competition within an industry depends on many factors, and again most of these factors exhibit characteristics of complexity. Uber versus taxi companies, Amazon versus brick-and-mortar retailers, or virtual companies such as Nike versus traditional manufacturers are just a few of the countless examples of the increasing complexity inherent in examining industry rivalry. The very nature of industrial competition makes it easy to see how complexity plays a key role in this aspect of a Porter's analysis.

One of the key factors affecting industry is demographics. In many industries, demographics are significantly impacting industry structure and dynamics. Demand for skilled workers of various types goes through ebbs and peaks. There is almost always a delay between the demand for labor of a given type and the supply of that labor. A classic example of this is occurring in the oil sands project in northern Alberta, in Canada. The demand for pipefitters and welders for this huge project in what is a thinly populated part of the country means that the supply of labor needs to come from all across Canada. This changes the supply of both skilled and unskilled labor in other regions. Complicating the picture is the fact that the forces influencing labor supply and demand are global. This in turn affects immigration policies, adding another layer of complexity.

These cycles in labor happen in virtually all professional and technical occupations. There are cycles of supply-and-demand imbalance in law, business school enrolments, nursing, physics, teaching, and so on. Part of this volatility is driven by demographics and the change in the age distribution of the overall population, while some of it is driven by regional factors, such as the Alberta oil sands project. A fact that is often overlooked is that younger workers want and expect something different from their working careers than perhaps previous generations of workers did. The traditional concept of working for a single company for your entire life is now all but a quaint relic of the post-Second World War generation. The gold watch for years of service has been replaced with iPods, which are given as retention bonuses for employees who remain for as little as a full year of service to a single company.

As David K. Foot highlights in his book *Boom, Bust & Echo*, dramatic differences between the demographics of different countries also influence the behavior of the labor market.[9] In general, the developed world is getting much older, while parts of Asia and the Middle East are getting much younger. This creates asymmetries and conflicts in government policies, and puts stresses on international population flows.

The important point, however, is that the dynamics of the demographics of the global (and regional) workforces are very similar to those of an ecological system – such as, for example, the fluctuations in the balance between foxes and hares in nature.

With greater ease of movement of workers, the supply of workers available to companies within an industry can change dramatically in a relatively short time. This in turn changes one key variable that companies can compete on: namely, their workers – including their ideas and the culture they create within a firm. It is important to realize that the ability to attract talent is a major factor in the struggle for competitive advantage within an industry and has a direct impact on strategy development. It is increasingly a company's ability to recruit creative thinkers with a complexity mindset that will separate the strategic winners from the losers.

Competition within an industry is also influenced by the culture of the industry as well as the culture of the individual companies within the industry. In all industries, companies compete with one another, but in some industries the competition is more intense and vigorous. A large variety of factors determine the level of competition in an industry. Some of these factors are clearly defined and well known, such as the relative market share of companies and the amount of industry competition, the profitability of the industry, as well as the degree of globalization of the industry. Arguably, however, one of the main competitive factors is the speed of change within an industry.

The faster an industry changes or emerges, the more internal competition it is likely to foster. Changes in an industry lead to new ways to compete and new opportunities to exploit. Consider the North American car industry in the 1950s and 1960s. During these boom years for the industry, the appearance of car models tended to change significantly every two or three years, whereas today the "look" of car models changes more slowly. The average age of cars on the road has also changed from approximately five years thirty years ago to almost twelve years today. With buyers changing cars much more frequently in the past, there was more opportunity to compete and thus more competition. There was more to be gained by significantly changing models every two to three years, as consumer tastes were also changing more rapidly and consumers were buying new cars more frequently. The opportunity to win a new customer came up every two or three years, rather than every six or seven as it does now. Thus you had more competition.

In terms of complexity, the main thing in determining competition in an industry is how much the actions of one competitor affect the outcomes of the other competitors. This, in turn, is influenced by the degree of interconnectedness among companies and their ability to adapt. In relatively low-tech industries such as mining, the actions of one competitor have a limited effect on the others. The connections between companies are limited, and the ability of companies to change or adapt their mining operations is almost nil. However, in a technology-based consumer market, the effects of one company's actions can be dramatic, as occurred with the introduction of the iPhone in the mobile phone market or Uber in the taxi industry.

Each of the elements of Porter's Five Forces model has embedded within it an element of complexity. Each element of the model has its own inherent feedback loops, nonlinearities, and sources of emergence. However, when Porter's model is taken as a whole, the amount of complexity multiplies. There are two main reasons for this. The first is that the model is based on a forward-looking analysis. In this it is often incorrectly assumed that each of the players in each of the segments of Porter's model will have relatively homogeneous and static views about the future. However, the presence of a diversity of views and the actions taken that are based on these different views increase the complexity of the system. The second and more important reason is the connectivity between the segments of the model. The actions of suppliers affect the actions of the industry participants, which in turn affect the actions of buyers, suppliers, substitutes, and new entrants. Each and every segment affects the actions and relative power of each of the other segments in unpredictable and often counterintuitive ways.

The actions of suppliers – for instance, a chip maker producing an insufficient supply of high-quality chips – impact the competitiveness of a given company within an industry. When Microsoft introduced the Xbox 360, the company was not able to produce the machines quickly enough to meet demand. This in turn led to Xbox's going for premium prices on online auction sites such as eBay. The balance of power was thus shifting to the alternative sellers, who were the early buyers, or perhaps even independent speculators, who were now selling their machines on eBay. The lack of supply potentially had an initial impact of increasing demand for the product, as gamers competed to get a game that was in short supply. However, it also increased the incentive for industry competitors to speed up and enhance their own product offerings, and, in the long run, created more competition for the Xbox. The delay also allowed handheld gaming consoles and smartphones to gain a larger foothold in the gaming market than they would have otherwise. This introduced a new set of entrants into the gaming market, including the iPad, which in turn is helping to spawn a new set of game application developers who are changing the dynamics of the gaming industry yet again.

Since each segment of Porter's model affects the actions of every other segment, the connectedness of the players and the speed with which they now adapt and change their strategies imply that complexity and emergence are inherent elements. Thus, despite the simplicity and common-sense rationality of Porter's model, it is really an accurate tool for analyzing only the current state of an industry, rather than predicting the future state, which is the primary concern of strategic planners. Thus it is not so much a model for strategic planning as it is a framework to explain the key role of complexity in strategic analysis and outcomes.

Another important consideration that is not included in Porter's model is the role of factors or agents that are external to an industry – factors such as politics, changing demographics, changing opinions, natural disasters, technological change, and even serendipity. The role of the strategic planner is indeed complex.

Scenarios and Stories

Porter's Five Forces analysis gives one a very comprehensive picture of the current state of an industry. However, it cannot forecast the future. All the Porter analysis can do is highlight some of the current strengths, weaknesses, threats, and opportunities that exist. Strategic decision makers ultimately have to make decisions based on their view of the future and how that future might evolve going forward. In essence, strategic decision makers need to make decisions that will enable the firm to be optimally positioned based on what Porter's analysis will look like five or ten years hence. This requires long-term foresight and planning.

In a classic treatise on strategic planning, *The Art of the Long View*, Peter Schwartz (at the time – in 1991 – the head of scenario planning for Royal Dutch Shell)[10] essentially takes the approach that the future is fundamentally unknowable to the degree necessary for traditional strategic planning but that it is still an instructive and valuable exercise to practice scenario planning. This view is consistent with U.S. President Eisenhower's claim that "plans are useless, but planning is indispensable." Schwartz takes a very different approach to the role of strategic planning than Porter does – one that is more aligned with complexity.

Schwartz advocates the creation of scenarios solely as a tool for thinking strategically (or for what I would call complexity thinking) rather than as a tool for prediction. It is strategic planning as storytelling. Stories, as we know, have twists and turns. Stories involve surprises as well as conflicts, challenges, problems, and setbacks. A good story, just like a good novel, can also have multiple sequels, and, as *Star Wars* has taught us, perhaps even prequels.

As Schwartz highlights in his book, if you want to be able to plan for the future, you cannot go to conventional sources of information, nor can you simply extrapolate from the past. The future is always evolving, and strategic planning based on current knowledge and trends is likely to be misleading and to miss paradigm shifts in the business environment.

For Schwartz, a good scenario is one that leads us to ask better questions. Note how this contrasts with the strategic analysis of Porter's Five Forces, which has as its goal the ability to provide better answers. Scenarios do not provide answers, but they provide possibilities. Good scenarios involve making connections and visualizing how elements can evolve. It is more dreaming and conceptualizing than analysis. It also is more creative and subjective than it is objective and rational. As implied in Schwartz's title, strategic planning and analysis are more "art" than "science."

Management strategist Henry Mintzberg is another well-known academic and consultant who is also skeptical of the complicated thinking that is implicit in most strategic planning. In a *Harvard Business Review* article, Mintzberg argues that there is a distinct difference between strategic planning and strategic thinking.[11] Strategic planning, in Mintzberg's definition, is the analysis of what is. It is an objective exercise with limited value and utility for an organization that wants to successfully compete in its industry. Strategic thinking, however, is the consideration of what might be and what should be. It is an exercise that cannot be codified; nor is it subject to the successful use of frameworks or schematics. Mintzberg's argument is that "the most successful strategies are visions, not plans."[12]

For Mintzberg, strategic thinking is a complex and messy exercise that is not subject to frameworks that rely on complicated thinking and analysis. As Schwartz also implies, much strategic planning as currently practiced involves extrapolation from existing ideas rather than the creation of new ideas. Mintzberg's arguments are thus also consistent with the assertion that strategy development is a complex activity.

Concluding Thoughts

Admitting that strategy is complex can be humbling for many CEOs and business professionals. The fact that strategy is complex means that all of the superficially undesirable traits of complexity come to the fore in strategic planning: the unpredictability; the lack of reproducibility; the lack of control; the role of serendipity; the randomness; and the inability to use superior skill, knowledge, and complicated training. However, another way to look at it is that a strategy that is designed with complexity in mind has a much greater probability of leading to long-term competitive success. That is, a company that is flexible and creative – that leverages connections, has the ability to react to patterns, and has a strategy that takes advantage of the complexity mindset of its leaders – is a company that is more likely to experience competitive success.

Strong and capable managers should relish the thought that strategic planning and implementation are complex. Gaining competence in a complicated field is relatively easy to do. In essence, if complicated thinking is the key to success, then all one has to do is get the proper training and go through the proper procedures each time. If that was all it took to formulate and implement strategy, then the role of the manager would become a commodity that could be replaced by a computer or a strategy robot. However, since strategy is complex, the role of the competent manager is forever safe from computer competition. Although computers and robots are well suited to dealing with extremely complicated problems and situations, they cannot think about or deal with complexity. Only human managers willing to develop and trust their wisdom and learn to embrace complexity will be able to successfully deal with the complex nature of strategy. It's not complicated; it's complex.

SEVEN

THE COMPLEX ECONOMY

The economy is the framework within which businesses operate and the context within which managers manage. Traditional academic economics paints the world as a complicated system, and complicated thinking has governed the study of economics since Adam Smith published his famous treatise *The Wealth of Nations* in the late 1700s.

The Wealth of Nations is widely considered to be one of the founding texts of the study of economics and, although Smith's work is almost 250 years old, the ideas presented in it still form the basis for much current economic thinking. *The Wealth of Nations* introduced Smith's famous "invisible hand." The "invisible hand" analogy described how the economy works as a system in which self-interested, greedy, rational, economic individuals perform as separate agents to produce the best desired economic outcomes, as if guided by an invisible hand. Historically, this has produced an understanding of economics that is predicated on an equilibrium between supply and demand that in effect sets prices for goods and services. *The Wealth of Nations* laid the foundation for a view of the economy as a complicated system, and that is the predominant paradigm from which economics has developed. However, that way of thinking about economics is now being challenged by other perspectives.

This chapter explores some of the evolving ideas in economics, and in particular the role that complexity thinking is playing in changing how economists view the world. Increasingly, complexity is seen as an alternative – and better – way to explain and understand many areas of economics, such as the occurrence of market crashes and the development of fads. However, complexity economics is still in its infancy as an area of study and thus still very much takes a back seat to classical economics.

To illustrate some ways in which the economic climate within which the modern manager must function has changed, I offer two comparisons of companies that attained dominance in different economic eras. The first comparison is between *Forbes* magazine, the stalwart of business media from the 1920s through to today, and *Fast Company* magazine, a modern business magazine that started with the digital age in 1995. The second comparison is between the corporation ITT, the face of conglomerates in the 1960s, and Facebook, the corporate face of today's generation.

Classical Economics

Almost every business school student has been treated to at least one semester, and more likely two semesters, of economics. "Principles of Macroeconomics" and "Principles of Microeconomics" are staple courses at universities globally. "Macro" and "Micro," as they are commonly called, have laid the foundations upon which generations of managers, politicians, and regulators, as well as the general public, have based their economic ideas, plans, and policies.

Traditional, or classical, economics is based on complicated thinking. Classical economics employs a reductionist way of thinking that assumes that one can simply scale the completely rational actions of a single individual up into the collective whole. It is a system of thinking that assumes that equilibrium is always the final as well as the desired state, based upon negative feedback loops and diminishing rates of return. It is a field of study where trends can be forecasted and wages and prices explained by supply and demand curves. It is a discipline that has produced competing schools of thought that have heavily influenced government policy since formal governments arose. It is also the field of study that has earned the moniker "the dismal science."

As an academic field offering rules for predicting economic outcomes, traditional economics is seductive. The axioms of economics are based on reasonable principles that few could argue with. These axioms include the following: all things being equal, individuals prefer to have more wealth than less wealth; all things being equal, individuals will look after their own interests first rather than being concerned about the common or public good; all things being equal, individuals will gravitate toward activities that make them happier and avoid those that make them less happy; and, all things being equal, individuals will become satiated with any good or service, and thus the rate of increase of demand will decrease and the price of a good will also decrease as more and more of that good becomes available. The problem is that, with complexity, as in the real world, it rarely happens that "all things are equal."

Traditional economics is also seductive because the set of simple axioms used by economists leads to an extensive set of mathematical laws. Classical economics holds the promise of providing order and predictability and control. As was discussed earlier in chapters 1 and 3, these are all characteristics that appeal to individuals, managers, regulators, and politicians – in fact, to anyone who wants to have the illusion that it is possible to predict and manage the future. Economics gives the illusion that one can foresee and control the future, in large part by controlling either supply and demand or prices. This promise of economics is the rationale behind wage and price controls, farm subsidies, production quotas, the setting of interest rates by central banks, and the need to regulate utilities.

Economics has admittedly been quite successful in explaining many phenomena in both the global economy and local business systems. However, its failures have perhaps been more spectacular than its successes. The major successes of economics have been in describing and predicting what happens in "closed systems." These are interactions where outside influences are nonexistent. For instance, where there is just one seller, a group of buyers, and only one commodity or product for sale, then supply and demand analysis can help determine what the price of the good will be. However, business and management, especially in today's world, are dealing with anything but a closed system. Competitive markets for all goods and services are global, and new competitors and new products continually enter into the "system" of the global economy. Consumers are continually changing in their demand for goods, workers are continually evolving in terms of their skills and their demands, and companies are constantly producing new goods to appeal to consumers. And all of this is happening in the context of disruptive ideas and products.

The simplistic view of the explanatory power of supply and demand analysis likely had more validity in an earlier era when the actions of consumers were more focused on meeting basic needs for food, clothing, and shelter. However, as the basic needs of consumers are met, more complex elements influence consumer decisions. The shift from a needs economy to a wants economy necessitates a shift from complicated thinking to complexity thinking.

For instance, the coffee company Starbucks started to sell coffee at higher prices than traditional coffee shops did. Although Starbucks coffee was generally made from premium coffee beans, it is not clear that the quality of the coffee alone justified the significant price difference that Starbucks introduced. Instead Starbucks focused on more intangible qualities such as the "hipness" of the ambience of their coffee shops, the snob effect of offering premium coffee, and the customization of coffee orders, allowing customers to order various combinations of their drinks based on milk choice and sweetener choice. Starbucks took what was considered a commodity product – coffee – and turned it into a highly customizable and unique personal beverage experience. This focus took classical economics beyond the two-dimensional demand-supply graphs and introduced pricing and economic factors such as personalization, "hipness," and "customer experience" that simple two-dimensional graphs (and the associated mathematics) cannot easily deal with. Classical economics would have predicted that charging higher prices for a commodity good would have severely limited demand for the product. Starbucks, however, changed consumers' attitudes about coffee and also changed the purchase of coffee from the simple acquisition of a commodity good into a more subjective "beverage experience." The success of Starbucks is a simple example of the breakdown of classical economic theory as well as an example of how a company created a paradigm shift by exploiting complexity.

Another feature of classical economic thought is the belief that one can understand the economy from a bottom-up perspective – the purview of microeconomics – and manage the economy from a top-down perspective – the realm of macroeconomics. For example, the frequent interventions of central banks and governments to prop up national economies during economic downturns are based on the belief that the economy can be "fixed," somewhat like a broken mechanical watch. It is a paradigm that relies upon reductionist thinking and linearity. One outcome of this belief is the idea that our actions as individual economic agents (either as consumers or producers) can be analyzed in isolation and our collective actions aggregated and summed to create the economic outcomes observed in the market. However, the reality is generally much more complex than that. The observed net economic outcome is almost always substantially different from the sum of the predicted aggregate actions of rational individuals.

Take the case of marketing. In a marketing-driven world, consumer goods are bought as much to satisfy desires as they are to meet "needs." This is in large part the result of advertising, whose goal is to increase the subjective "desire" component rather than focus on the objective "need" component of a product or service. Advertising is designed to encourage buying behavior that is based more on emotion than on reason. However, in a complex world, clever advertising is not the only influence motivating the individual economic agent. The emotional "desire" for a product is stimulated as much, if not more, by considerations of how others will view our ownership of a product as by our idea of how the product will contribute to our own well-being. We purchase many products in the belief that they will make us appear better than others, not necessarily because they will actually make us better or make our lives better. To a considerable extent, it is the influence of our environment and connections that drives our buying behavior. Of course, this is complexity at work in its effects and in its actions – a process that calls into question the validity of reductionism in economics.

A related assumption of classical economics is linearity. In essence, classical economics postulates that if you double a variable, such as an input, you will proportionally affect other variables – for example, producing a doubling of output. In a digital or a knowledge economy this is simply not true, and there are numerous counterexamples. The work required to produce this book you are reading is the same whether one person reads this book or ten thousand people read this book. This is especially true if everyone purchases the book in electronic format. No marginal effort or additional resources are required to produce the second electronic copy of this book, or the tenth, or the thousandth. The input is the same, while the output can vary greatly. This effect is particularly prominent with products or services that "go viral." Think of the popularity of the music video *Gangnam Style* by Korean pop star PSY, which has been viewed more than two billion times on YouTube and has spawned thousands of knock-off imitation videos. As a video or any other product or service goes viral, the demand for the product or service increases exponentially. A positive rather than a negative feedback loop is formed. The more people who view the video (or buy the product), the greater the demand is for others also to see the video (or buy the product). The linearity assumption of classical economics clearly fails in such cases, which are more and more prevalent in the Internet economy.

The restriction imposed by a requirement for equilibrium is an underappreciated core aspect of classical economics. "Equilibrium" is the basis for virtually all of the mathematical modeling that is produced by economists. Equilibrium is the concept that allows for the ability to make economic predictions. The promise that this concept will allow us both to explain and to predict is a very potent drug for both the economist and the manager who use economic principles. Given its power, the concept of equilibrium is somewhat of a sacred cow in economics. The reality of real-world global economics, however, is the ubiquity of disequilibrium. It is obvious that there are peaks and valleys in the economic cycle. There are stock market bubbles and stock market crashes. There are dislocations such as Detroit's evolution from being arguably the manufacturing capital of the world to being a bankrupt city in less than fifty years. Economists allow for paradigm shifts, and for the need for economies to find a new equilibrium after each paradigm shift, but when the global economy seems to be nothing but a continual series of dislocations and paradigm shifts, then perhaps it is better to think of disequilibrium rather than equilibrium as the norm.

In traditional industries, such as heavy manufacturing, there is a point at which economies of scale start to turn negative. For instance, in the steel industry, huge mills such as those of Bethlehem Steel dominated from the rise of the industrial age until the late 1970s. As mills such as Bethlehem Steel's became ever larger they achieved economies of scale that were thought to be safe from competition. However, changes in technology, along with demographic and workforce changes, led to the rise of mini-mills – smaller mills that served specific purposes and that were much more efficient at producing customized and smaller runs of steel products. The large mills were trapped by their size and lost both their economies of scale and their dominance. As a result, Bethlehem Steel filed for bankruptcy in 2001.

In public goods there are also diminishing economies of scale. Consider a highway from the suburbs into the heart of a city. A bigger highway increases the speed and ease with which commuters can get into the city for work or entertainment. However, as more and more families move to the suburbs, the highways eventually become clogged and public transportation becomes more attractive. There are diminishing returns to driving to work, and an equilibrium between individual commuting and public transportation is created.

We know that the demand for hotdogs from a fan at a football game does not increase exponentially. Similarly, as the number of people driving their cars into a city's core cannot expand exponentially, the need for public transportation in most major cities is evident. Even in steel production, if the size of a mill grows unchecked, it becomes too unwieldy to manage successfully. Thus, in traditional economic scenarios, increasing economies of scale lead to chaos and unpredictability and essentially eliminate the prospect of competitive markets. It is no wonder that diminishing returns to scale became the favored paradigm of economists.

In today's digital knowledge economy, however, cases of increasing returns to scale are common. Consider the textbook case of Microsoft. The cost to produce and sell an additional copy of software in the cloud is virtually nil. There is no diminishing return to scale for digital products. Furthermore, the more users who become familiar with the Microsoft suite of Office products such as Word, Excel, and PowerPoint, the more incentive there is for them to continue to use familiar Microsoft products. The more companies that install Microsoft Office, the more comfortable and familiar it becomes to an ever larger pool of business professionals. The incentives to keep using Microsoft Office products keep growing and the disincentives to switch to non-Microsoft products for word-processing or spreadsheets and presentation software also grow. Increasing economies of scale produce significant first- or early-mover advantages. The company that creates an established base in a product category or industry will increase that base at a rate that potentially grows exponentially. The larger the lead, the bigger and faster the lead will grow. Traditional economics is stood on its head. The world as assessed by an economist is the opposite of that predicted by theory.

The same argument concerning increasing returns to scale can be made for virtually any creative activity. There is no limit on ideas. Furthermore, ideas do not get used up or worn out, and can be recycled and reformulated endlessly. Although they may appear to be individually scarce, ideas are not commodity goods that are subject to the availability of resources or effort or time. Understanding this is key to understanding and appreciating the economics of a knowledge-based economy.

With diminishing returns to scale, a mathematical equilibrium model can be established. With equilibrium, coupled with linearity and an illusion of control and prediction, there is a set of optimal outcomes that classical economics produces. As with every other type of activity where complicated thinking is the paradigm, optimal solutions are considered to be both achievable and desirable. The reality, however, is often something quite different.

Economics: The Dismal Science

In the time and place of Adam Smith, the world more or less behaved like the complicated system that economists envisaged it to be. Limitations on communication and travel in the 1700s, as well as an economy that served to provide the necessities of life rather than luxuries, enabled the models of classical economics to work well.

However, consider how much things have changed since the 1700s. Today, in the developed world, the daily needs for survival of most people are easily satisfied. Food is plentiful, and most people have their basic clothing, health care, and accommodation "needs" met. The main concern of most consumers is to purchase things that are designed to satisfy their "wants." Happiness rather than survival is the main issue governing many purchasing decisions, but happiness is a subjective and relative concept. In terms of the actions of economic agents, economic activity whose goal is survival is an objective and complicated process, while economic activity based on desires is more subjective and complex.

Economics, as it is commonly expressed in academic circles, was developed in response to the conditions of a different era from ours. Furthermore, like all fields of study, its adherents naturally want to build on what has been developed before. Unfortunately, a discipline based on complicated thinking cannot adapt or even evolve to align with the very different paradigm of complexity. However, although the two are not compatible, they are natural complements to each other.

The main components of complexity that were described in chapter 4 are the following: (1) several independent factors or agents, such as consumers or producers of good; (2) the ability of the agents to be connected in some way, such as through social media, or being competitors in an industry; (3) the ability of the agents to learn and thus adapt and make choices. These components obviously exist when one is discussing the economy. Furthermore, they are components that are increasing in their significance as the world economy becomes more globalized and connected. The relatively isolated villages of Adam Smith's day are no more. The social structure required for classical economics has fundamentally shifted to exhibit complexity. While classical economics still has much to say and value to add to our understanding of the fundamentals of many aspects of business, it provides an increasingly incomplete picture that needs to dramatically add new components to its thinking to keep pace with the present-day reality of business economics.

Perhaps there is no better laboratory in which to study the effectiveness of classical economics than the stock market. If classical economics is correct and the actions of rational economic agents, such as investors in the stock market, can be aggregated to explain the whole, and to produce equilibrium, then the stock market is the ideal laboratory. The stock market has a large number of investors (so the mistakes of any one agent or investor can be averaged out); there is a pure profit motive (if it is assumed that the number of people who invest in the stock market solely for "fun" is limited); and each day brings a new trial or experiment whose effects can be studied. The stock market is also where some of the most highly trained and highly compensated economists ply their trade. It is an arena in which "survival of the fittest" rules and where the rewards for being right are enormous.

A casual examination of the popular press would lead one to assume that the stock market truly does reward the best and the brightest. Investment magazines and television shows applaud the performance of successful managers, and investment firms are all too ready to showcase the investment prowess of their star money managers. Indeed, it is a profession where many earn significantly larger than average incomes. However, study after study seems to show that success in the stock market is more a matter of luck than of skill, knowledge, or implementation of a specific economic model or paradigm.

For instance, a study by academics Gary Porter and Jack Trifts shows that while successful money managers do outperform their peers, they do not outperform a naive strategy of passively investing in benchmark index funds.[1] Those managers who perform best tend to have more successful and longer careers, but they do not perform better than the average passive investor who builds a diversified portfolio. Winning managers also attract more investment money as a function of their better-than-average returns compared to losing money managers, but again, that only means that they collect larger fees, not larger profits for their clients. Winning at the game of money management seems like the old joke about two people in the woods who come across an angry grizzly bear; the objective becomes not to outrun the bear but to outrun the person you are with. Investors who place their money with winning investment managers are confusing relative performance with absolute skill over a naive strategy. The lack of demonstrated skill by professional money managers calls into question the usefulness of classical economics.

In the current context of a connected, global, knowledge-based economy, the ability of economics to explain and predict economic events has become severely diminished. Perhaps at no time in history have so many governments around the world used economic policy so extensively to prevent economic collapse with such limited success. The financial crash of 2008 and the subsequent European economic crisis are two such examples. Japan has had anemic economic growth for more than a decade, following strong growth in the 1980s and early 1990s. Nor can classical economics explain the rise of high-tech companies that have billion-dollar valuations but no revenue streams. It is for these and other failures that classical economics is often called "the dismal science." It appears to be time for the dismal science to reconsider some of its fundamentals. The surprising vote in the United Kingdom in favor of leaving the European Union, despite the overwhelming advice of economists that to do so would be economically disastrous, is an indication that the general public has little regard for the verities of classical economics. There is obviously another paradigm that is playing a role.

Complexity Economics

Complexity economics is a new field of economic thought that is being developed by a relatively small group of innovative economists. Complexity economics is an attempt to re-examine the underlying axioms of classical economics and develop a field of economics based on the principles of complex adaptive systems. As a field of economic study, it does not necessarily claim that classical economics is wrong. Instead complexity economics is developing as a complementary field of study and analysis. Just as a manager needs to think in terms of simple, complicated, and complex systems, so does an economist. It is not that one way of systems thinking is correct and the other is wrong; it is simply that there is more than one type of system at work in the economy, and the paradigm chosen to analyze a given economic or business issue should depend on the underlying characteristics of the system under study. The spread of globalization, changes in technology, the expansion of social media, and the shift away from manufacturing toward services in developed economies enhance the need for complexity economics as an additional set of concepts and a way of thinking for economists to add to their toolbox in order to understand and explain the economy.

There are several unique cornerstones to complexity economics. One of the distinguishing features of complexity economics is its explicit recognition that humans (economic agents) are not perfectly rational or consistent in their choices. Rationality depends on context, and in particular social context, which is itself complex. Complexity economics also incorporates the fact that in a knowledge- and ideas-based economy there can be increasing returns to scale. Complexity economics allows for the fact that the economic world more often than not is naturally in a state of disequilibrium and that it is equilibrium that is rare. Finally, complexity economics deals with the observed fact that economic outcomes are qualitatively and quantitatively different from the sum of their constituent parts. In effect, complexity economics attempts to deal with observed real-world economic issues and their complex nature.

Behavioral finance is a field that bridges classical economics and complexity economics. In chapter 2, the ground-breaking work of Daniel Kahneman and Amos Tversky in the study of behavioral finance was briefly introduced. Behavioral finance discusses how the assumptions of the concept of the rational economic man are consistently violated. Complexity economics picks up from behavioral finance. Behavioral finance looks at how the individual makes seemingly irrational and inconsistent choices. Complexity economics attempts to model and explain how these irrational and inconsistent choices are connected and, through this connectedness, result in complex outcomes. In a way, behavioral finance is akin to psychology – a study of how an individual acts and behaves. Complexity economics takes this further and looks at a how a group of people behaves and so is more akin to sociology, in that sociology focuses on the collective and the resulting connections between individuals in a social system, which in turn give rise to complexity. This social complexity, combined with the structure of our increasingly knowledge-based economy, can also lead to increasing returns to scale.

Brian Arthur was among the first economists to utilize the concept of increasing returns to scale. His story was first popularized in journalist M. Mitchell Waldrop's excellent book *Complexity: The Emerging Science at the Edge of Order and Chaos*.[2] Arthur, who was academically trained in operations research and started his research in studies of population growth, is most often associated with his work at the Santa Fe Institute, where he was the Citibank Fellow in Economics and is currently an adjunct associate. The idea of increasing returns to scale was initially not well accepted by classical economists and remains controversial despite numerous instances of it in our modern economy.

The concept of increasing returns to scale has several implications for complexity economics. In particular, it suggests that wealth creation and economic activity have shifted from a complete reliance on manufacturing (which is subject to decreasing returns to scale) to an economy where knowledge, creativity, and service industries are becoming more important. There is no natural limit or constraint on creativity or knowledge. In addition, the efficiencies of scale in many service industries are also quantitatively and qualitatively different from those in industries centered on the production of goods.

J. Doyne Farmer is another economist who is a leader in the promotion of complexity economics. Trained as a physicist, Dr. Farmer has been active in both the academic study of complexity economics and its practical applications. Currently a professor of mathematics at the University of Oxford and an external professor at the Santa Fe Institute, Farmer was a co-founder of the Prediction Company, a financial-analysis and money-management firm that was founded in the early 1990s to create mathematical models that would predict financial markets.

A particular focus of Doyne Farmer's work is the use of computer-based models of complexity to model economic activity. Adaptive, agent-based modeling using computer simulations produces results that are more consistent with observed real-world outcomes than other models. The issue, however, is that they often produce multiple equilibria, which of course is an anathema to classical economics.

Classical economics and its reductionist approach explicitly assume that a singular solution or equilibrium exists for each economic situation. One of the main problems with multiple equilibria is that prediction, a cornerstone of classical economics, becomes impossible. Conceptually, and using computer models of complexity, economists like Farmer argue that multiple equilibria should be allowed to exist. This, of course, is consistent with real-world observations and with the complexity notion that accurate prediction is not usually possible.

J. Doyne Farmer is also co-director of CRISIS (Complexity Research Initiative for Systemic Instabilities), "a consortium of universities, private firms and policymakers that aims to build a new model of the economy and financial system that is based on how people and institutions actually behave."[3] CRISIS was formed after the 2008 financial crisis and is financed by the European Commission.

The multidisciplinary team of researchers at CRISIS is attempting to develop better and more realistic models of the economy based upon the principles of complexity economics. A large part of the work that CRISIS is doing uses novel approaches such as agent-based modeling, experimental analyses of how people behave, and econophysics.

Econophysics is closely aligned with complexity economics. Econophysics uses the techniques of statistical mechanics, which is the study of how large numbers of objects interact. For instance, statistical mechanics explains how the billions of gas molecules in a confined space will interact in response to heat and pressure differences – a problem that it is not possible to analyze using classical Newtonian mechanics. Likewise, in an economy there are many different economic agents interacting, and the interactions of these agents are too numerous to study using classical economics. Econophysics provides useful analogies to facilitate study of the large number of economic interactions that take place between consumers and producers in an economy. Econophysics provides economists with new tools and concepts that help further the study of complexity economics.

Using a portfolio of principles from econophysics, agent-based modeling, computer simulations, and principles of complexity science gleaned from other fields such as weather forecasting, the team at CRISIS is building a series of computer models to replicate global economics. While such a model will likely not be very useful for predicting the next financial or economic crisis, it does provide regulators, policy-makers, and economists with a new tool for looking at and analyzing real-world economics that is free from the restrictions and limitations imposed by classical economics.

For instance, one of the phenomena being studied at CRISIS is the development of a systemic lack of confidence in the financial markets. Researcher Jean-Philippe Bouchard, a professor of physics at École Polytechnique in Paris and one of the research heads at CRISIS, compares the development of a lack of confidence in the financial markets to the way an audience stops applauding at the end of a concert or the way in which starlings form their flight patterns. It is an economic model that depends on connections and the adaptive behavior of agents, and is an obvious example of the application of complexity thinking to economics. Professor Bouchard and his team are hoping that their work will provide fresh insights into how economic changes such as crises get started, as well as clues to how these economic shifts might be better recognized and managed.

Criticisms of Complexity Economics

Like any new field of study, complexity economics is not without its critics. There are two main criticisms of the field. The first is that complexity itself is not a theory; nor is it based on a set of axioms like that of the "rational economic man." The second criticism is that, unlike classical economics, complexity economics explicitly does not allow for the making of predictions. The two criticisms are related but also largely irrelevant.

The first criticism can be countered by asking whether or not the evidence is consistent with the axioms – self-evident and obvious truths – that underlie classical economics. Consider the "rational economic man" axiom. One can argue that, extrapolating from the eccentric antics of a rich person in the movies (and some in real life), the wealth created in the developed economies of the world diminishes the value of the concept of rational economic man. As we have seen, much of the economic activity in the developed world is based not on survival needs but on consumption wants. Consumption wants are not prone to objective rational thought. They are more closely related to emotional needs, which the classical economist intentionally ignores.

Another cornerstone axiom of classical economics – that of scarcity of resources leading to diminishing returns – is also not consistent with a knowledge-based economy. Although the axiom is more a philosophical than an economic principle, it is reasonable to assume that there are no limits to the human mind, and thus creativity and ingenuity and decisions based on emotions are not scarce resources.

The second criticism of complexity economics, that of not enabling prediction, can be quickly countered by asking whether it is preferable to have no prediction or an incorrect and potentially misleading prediction. As in management, there are aspects of economics that lend themselves to complicated thinking and the application of classical economic analysis, and to the possibility of prediction. However, if the situation is complex – as is increasingly the norm in economic matters, then it would be sensible to admit that the best answer is "maybe." Although the ability to predict is often considered a critical cornerstone of a true science, it does not necessarily mean that its absence should rule out complexity economics as a field of serious study and research.

Related to the criticism of lack of predictive power is the criticism that the possibility of multiple equilibria is absurd and inconsistent with a true understanding of an issue. This argument is perhaps best left to the philosophers of science. The reality is that there are many times in real life where there are multiple answers to a given situation. Anyone who has bought ice cream as a child knows that there are many excellent choices that are impossible to distinguish between or to rank in order of preference.

Classical economics has at its foundation a set of theories. The need for prediction is part of an implicit strategy to have the field of economics accepted as a true science like chemistry or physics, which have as their hallmark the ability to predict.

Complexity economists tend to have varied academic backgrounds. For instance, Brian Arthur first did work in demographics and was academically trained in operations research. J. Doyne Farmer was initially trained as a physicist. This diversity is probably not a coincidence. Economics, like business management, needs new ideas such as complexity, and only through a willingness to think in new ways and to embrace a holistic approach can we make the necessary paradigm shift toward complexity thinking. Complexity economics represents an evolution in thinking that appears to align with how the economic world of business is evolving. And that, ultimately, is the best test of the worth of a field of study.

Comparison of Economic Eras, Part 1: Business Media – *Forbes* Compared to *Fast Company*

To appreciate the impact of these changes in economic thinking upon business and business professionals, it is useful to compare how companies operated in the period from the 1950s to the 1980s and how companies operate today. Let us first compare the factors influencing the success of *Forbes* magazine and *Fast Company* magazine.

All forms of media have undergone major changes in the last twenty-five years. The Internet has fundamentally changed the business model of virtually every type of media outlet. With this as a given, it is interesting to examine how business media in particular have changed. After all, the media reflect the sector of society that they report on. *Forbes* magazine and *Fast Company* magazine are both stalwarts in the world of business media. Both are considered leaders in their field and both cover the business world, although from very different perspectives and using very different styles. Given that the subject matter of both is business, the differences in their approach are instructive.

Forbes magazine was founded in 1917 and is one of the icons of business publishing. *Forbes* developed its audience as North America was developing its industrial economy. With the tagline "The Capitalist Tool," *Forbes* profiled the dominance of the corporation in society and, with its manager profiles and company stories, helped create the business professional as celebrity. *Forbes*'s ascendancy began in the 1950s and 1960s. By contrast, *Fast Company,* a much younger magazine that was founded in 1995, caters to the generation of business professionals who grew up in the digital economy. Although both magazine franchises are adapting to the new reality of media in the digital era, the differences in how the two magazines produce their content highlight differences in the way their contributors think about business and the economy, in the times in which the magazines were first developed, and in the audiences they attract.

Forbes magazine is perhaps best known for its list of the richest Americans, while *Fast Company* is known for its lists of the "Most Innovative Companies" and the "Most Creative People in Business." The first focuses on something as concrete and (relatively) objective as wealth, while the second focuses on the more subjective categories of innovation and creativity. As "The Capitalist Tool," *Forbes* saw the objective of business as generating wealth. For *Fast Company* the objective is primarily the generating of ideas, with the implicit assumption that success will follow. In an industrial economy, the focus is on scale and return on investment. Wealth is the barometer of success. By contrast, in a digital economy the focus is on ideas. From the "lists" that they are respectively known for, the two magazines reflect the changes in the economic mindset of the two eras in which they emerged.

In *Forbes*, the focus of the magazine was traditionally on the company and the company's leaders, and most often a company's chief executive officer. In *Fast Company*, the focus is on the people with ideas, and not just the strategic thinkers. *Forbes*'s focus on the organization and its leader is a function of top-down, command-and-control thinking. It is a paradigm where leaders reign supreme. *Fast Company*'s focus on individuals and their ideas is characteristic of a disruptive economy where ideas rule and the actions and interactions of the crowd (the employees of the firm) are significant.

Forbes magazine traditionally celebrated the leaders, the industrial giants. *Fast Company* more often features the up-and-comers. In an industrial economy, size and economies and efficiencies of size and scale matter, and *Forbes* has traditionally reported on these aspects. For *Fast Company* readers and the knowledge economy, nimbleness and speed are more important ingredients of competitiveness – a fact that is enshrined in the name of the magazine itself.

In *Forbes* there are a large number of opinion and advice columns written by experts and well-known pundits. This is consistent with the idea of the ability to command, control, and predict outcomes. In *Fast*

Company there are fewer op-ed columns that analyze how future events will unfold and how one might be able to exploit or manage them.

In *Forbes*, the reporting on innovative companies features those that were pushing the envelope of existing techniques by developing new and more efficient ways of doing a traditional business task. In *Fast Company*, the focus is on companies that are producing paradigm shifts – not companies that are doing things differently but companies that are doing different things.

In *Forbes*, the traditional focus has been on cash flow and return on investment. One of the magazine's main functions has been to provide an insight into companies and industries so investors could ascertain their investment potential. Investments and a building of wealth have always been cornerstones of the content of *Forbes*. The capital markets and the performance of a company in the capital markets are central to the stories. By contrast, at *Fast Company*, the focus is on venture capital funding and burn rates of companies.[4] Many of the companies profiled in *Fast Company* are private or controlled by a collection of private investors, venture capital firms, and private equity. Capital plays a different role in the knowledge economy than it does in an industrial economy. The capital markets have also changed as the role of the individual investor has been supplanted in large part by the rise of the institutional investor and passive investing strategies using investment instruments such as exchange traded funds (ETFs).

The focus on investment potential in *Forbes* stands in sharp contrast to the ability to scale for users or connections that is so common in *Fast Company*. It is frequently stated that a knowledge-based company, such as a social media company, needs to be able to scale to build its user base first. Only after a user base has been built will the company start to work on a business model that will generate cash flows. In *Fast Company*, the important variable is connections with users.

The differences between the two magazines are consistent with the differences between a classical economy based on manufacturing and diminishing returns to scale and a knowledge-based economy based on ideas and connections. They illustrate the contrast between classical economics and complexity economics.

While it is tempting to focus on the new and the novel, it is important to remember that, in managing, it is just as important to understand and be able to manage complicated systems as to be able to understand and manage complex systems. Each way of thinking has its place and its own respective advantages and disadvantages. Neither should dominate; instead they should coexist and complement one another. Thus, I still continue to subscribe to and read both *Forbes* and *Fast Company*.

Comparison of Economic Eras, Part 2: Leading Companies – ITT and Facebook

Forbes and *Fast Company* are emblematic of their respective eras and dominant economic paradigms. So too are ITT and Facebook. ITT Corporation was begun in 1920 under its original name of International Telephone and Telegraph. Under the leadership of Harold Geneen, its CEO in the 1960s and 1970s, it became one of the world's most dominant companies and a symbol of the conglomerates that ruled that business era. Facebook, a much younger company, was founded in 2004 by Mark Zuckerberg and some of his college friends. However, in less than ten years, Facebook has become one of the dominant companies of the digital era, and equally a symbol of the social media era of business. As with *Forbes* and *Fast Company*, ITT and Facebook provide an interesting contrast in business economics.

ITT is best known for becoming a conglomerate of companies during the heyday of conglomerates between the 1950s and the 1970s. Under the leadership of CEO Geneen, ITT made more than 300 acquisitions and likely would have made many more if anti-trust legislation had not prevented it from doing so. Branching out from its original business of producing telephone switching equipment, ITT made acquisitions in hotels, bakery products, cosmetics, auto parts, education, insurance, and televisions, and even attempted to get into television programming by trying to purchase the ABC television network – an acquisition that was blocked by anti-trust regulators. ITT was one of the "Nifty Fifty" stocks, a group of companies of such "obvious" investment potential it was thought that all an investor had to do was invest in these fifty leading companies and forget about them, as they would unfailingly produce safe and consistent investment returns. During the 1960s, annual revenues at ITT grew from less than a billion dollars to almost $8 billion. However, with the passage of time, and following a rapid shedding of divisions and company reorganizations, current annual revenues of a radically streamlined ITT are approximately $2.5 billion.

Facebook is a company that has grown rapidly from a university-dorm-room start-up to having current annual revenues of almost $8 billion. Created as a social media website, it quickly surpassed Myspace, a social media site that was founded just over a year before Facebook. The early growth of the company was organic, but Facebook has recently begun to use its hoard of cash, as well as its market share, to make acquisitions and grow its share of the social media market. In particular, Facebook's offer to buy the start-up instant-phone-messaging company WhatsApp for $19 billion in 2014 shows that it is serious about building a dominant market position.

ITT became a conglomerate of companies to create economies and efficiencies of scale in operations, centralizing such activities as finance and administration. In the bigger-is-better thinking of the era, ITT had a voracious appetite for acquiring companies to build scale. Facebook, however, seems to be acquiring companies to build scale of connections, rather than scale of assets. The aim of social media companies like Facebook is to become a conglomerate of ideas and users and connections. With ITT it was to become a conglomerate of assets and cash flows.

In addition to creating synergies in funding and administration, conglomerates like ITT were formed to manage the supply chain both upstream and downstream in order to achieve efficiencies by controlling the process. With Facebook, the strategy is to let the users control the development of the process while retaining access to the data flows and the connections that its users create. It is a backward form of control that is consistent with moving from a complicated command-and-control paradigm to a complexity paradigm, where outcomes are allowed and encouraged to emerge.

To achieve economies of scale in administration, conglomerates like ITT focused on centralizing as many functions as possible. Conversely, at New Age companies like Facebook, the environment is generally one of decentralization where all employees are encouraged to put forth their ideas. Perhaps paradoxically, this tends to create a more intense work environment, as more responsibility for producing is in the hands of the individual employee, by contrast with a top-down command structure, where responsibility for decision making and idea generation is largely out of the hands of middle managers and non-managerial employees.

Because the ITT conglomerate's capital structure included high levels of leverage and a constant need to source funding from the capital markets, its accounting and finance functions were generally dominant. The constant need to produce returns to satisfy shareholders and debt holders required a continuing focus on the cash flows of the company. In contrast, at a social media company, it is programming and design along with idea generation that drive the process. Instead of managing cash flows, the more pressing need is to scale users and user experiences. The main competitive task is to keep the design sharp so users will continue to use Facebook and its associated sites, enabling the company to retain its dominance in the social media sphere.

The funding schemes for major companies have also changed dramatically since the era of ITT-like conglomerates. From the 1950s until the late 1980s, the stock market and the public debt markets were the dominant sources of new funding. Beginning in the late 1990s, however, venture capital and private equity funding have been the vehicles of choice for companies like Facebook. Although Facebook did indeed go public just eight years after its founding, the initial funding was from a series of venture capitalists. Even rival Microsoft made an early and significant investment in the company.

While venture capital has always played a role in the start-up funding of new companies, the role and importance of venture capitalists (VCs) has changed quite significantly in the last twenty years. When a bank grants a loan to a company, the fundamental question for the banker is whether the bank will get its money back or not. The key question a banker asks is, "How much am I likely to lose?" Bankers never grant a loan if they expect to lose money on that loan. VCs, however, know that they are investing in very risky projects. As such they expect to lose money on the majority of the deals they invest in but also expect to more than make up for those losses on the few deals that are successful. A rough rule of thumb is that VCs will lose their investment almost completely on six or seven out of every ten deals they invest in. They also expect to more or less break even on one or two of their investments, and hope to have a huge return on one or two deals out of ten. The problem is that because of the nature of the risk with start-up companies, particularly ones that rely on complexity for success, VCs essentially have to rely on intuition and the odds to generate returns. So, while a bank asks how much it can lose, VCs ask how much they can make. It is a profound and fundamental shift in investing philosophy. The bank is looking for high cash flow and low-risk investments, while VCs are looking for high risk and high potential for scaling in their investment. Traditionally, stock-market investors have also wanted steady returns in the form of consistent dividends and steady capital appreciation. Wild fluctuations in stock prices have not been considered to be desirable. Slow and steady has been the mantra for most conventional equity investors. Now, however, a growing number of investors are much more excited by the prospect of enormous capital gains.

This attitude signals a fundamental shift in the mindset of the providers of capital. It takes the classical economics model of equilibrium and turns it on its head. In turn, this attitude requires a change in how companies present themselves to investors. While ITT needed to show stable and positive cash flows emanating from its investments, Facebook needs to show extreme upside potential, even if it means potentially placing the company's survival at risk. Many "dot.com" companies went bust in the early 2000s, leading to the moniker "dot bombs." Those that survived, however, such as Facebook and Google, have produced spectacular returns for early investors who gambled on their survival and ability to grow.

Another characteristic of this new approach is a different attitude to "failing." Expansion for a company like ITT was based on careful consideration and extensive analysis of the downside risks. A company embracing complexity economics is more likely to accept a scenario of "fail fast and try to adapt fast," taking the complexity management strategy of try, learn, and adapt and incorporating that philosophy on a company-wide scale. Such an approach is the opposite of a focus on planned economies and rationally thought-out strategy.

These contrasting mindsets are also seen in different views about the characteristics of desirable employees. Companies such as ITT (which, by the way, was a "high-tech" company for its day) would hire for technical skill and knowledge. Facebook and its ilk, however, hire more for creative talent and ambition. While employees or managers might spend their entire career at a company like ITT, aiming to receive the gold watch at retirement for thirty or more years of service, the market for talent is now much more fluid. Employees are looking for different types of experience – and experiences. New Age companies are constantly renewing their talent pool, as doing so helps to keep employees fresh, as well as creating connections across companies that, in a time of complexity, also help with competitiveness. The shift is from that of an employee as a bureaucrat to that of an employee as a freelancing entrepreneur.

Companies like ITT tried to create competitive advantage through technical expertise protected by patents and trade secrets. In acquiring WhatsApp, Facebook stated that it wanted to provide "connectivity and utility to the world" and make the "world more open and connected."[5] Perhaps more than anything else, this change in competitive philosophy signals the difference in how companies compete in a complex economy versus a classical economics economy. Knowledge becomes a commodity; it is through ideas and a focus on evolving with complexity that competitive advantage is now achieved.

The different operating philosophies of *Forbes* versus *Fast Company* and ITT versus Facebook can in large part be attributed to the different economic contexts in which they emerged. The economy today is more connected, global, and ideas-based than ever before. In short, it is now more complex than complicated.

Revisiting Adam Smith

This chapter started with a brief discussion of Adam Smith and his publication of *The Wealth of Nations*, the book that essentially started the study of classical economics. Blaming Adam Smith, however, might be a bit unfair. For anyone who has studied economics, it is likely that the only thing they remember of his ideas is the concept of the "invisible hand," the idea that self-interested economic agents will act as if guided by a mysterious invisible hand so as to produce an optimal package of goods and services. It is time to postulate that the mysterious invisible hand is nothing more than complexity at work, as economic agents produce emergent outcomes. Perhaps what Adam Smith was really trying to tell us is that economics is not complicated, it's complex.

EIGHT

RISK MANAGEMENT AND COMPLEXITY

When one mentions risk management and crisis management, many examples come to mind, but few in recent years have had the business impact of the BP Gulf of Mexico oil spill. The *Deepwater Horizon* oil platform explosion created one of the world's largest oil spills and ultimately cost BP's CEO, Tony Hayward, his job.

Facebook represents a different side of risk, namely upside risk. If you think of risk as the chance that something unexpected will happen, then who in early 2004 could have foreseen that a website designed for a select group of students at Harvard University would, less than nine years later, become a member of the *Fortune* 500 list of companies with a value greater than $90 billion.

These two very different events, the BP *Deepwater Horizon* disaster and the unprecedented rise of Facebook, show the complexity of risk and risk management. Both instances are concrete examples of complexity in action and illustrate how complexity and risk management are intertwined. They also illustrate the folly of relying on complicated thinking in the presence of complexity.

"Risk" has many different definitions, depending on who is providing the definition. It has become a very popular subject in fields as diverse as ecology, health sciences, politics – and, of course, business. If asked, the typical lay person would likely respond along the lines that "risk is the possibility that something bad may happen." Conversely, business school students learn several quantitative definitions that all boil down to the fact that risk is the possibility that bad *or* good things may happen. Thus according to the academics, risk is two-sided. Risk can be good or risk can be bad.

The reason for this slightly different definition is literally complicated. It has to do with the fact that the mathematics of risk measurement works much better if risk is considered to be two-sided and symmetrical than if it is considered to be one-way (i.e., bad only). Some analysts differentiate between upside and downside risk by labeling them separately. For instance, many risk analysts speak of "loss" and "opportunity," to differentiate the two-sided nature of risk.

A widely adopted definition of "risk" is "any activity that prevents an organization from meeting its strategic objectives." You will note that this definition is also two-sided, and this is as it should be. Ultimately, risk management is about undertaking actions that increase the probability and magnitude of good risk events while decreasing the probability and severity of bad risk events. A firm wants to have as few negative surprises as possible and also to make their effects as small as possible. Conversely, a business also wants to have pleasant surprises and to have those pleasant surprises occur with the greatest possible frequency and with the greatest possible positive impact.

Perhaps a more practical way of thinking about risk is that risk management is about making decisions under uncertainty. The world is uncertain, even if you believe it to be complicated rather than complex. Risk management is the field of management that explicitly takes this uncertainty into account and attempts to manage it.

All business managers are managers of risk – whether they acknowledge it or not or whether they have a risk-related title or not. The role of any type of risk manager is both complicated and complex. There are definite steps that the risk manager can take to guard against known risks and hazards, as well as other concrete steps that increase the probability of achieving the desired and planned-for outcomes. However, the risk manager also needs to be concerned about the "known unknowns" and the "unknown unknowns" that inevitably alter the plans of even the most prepared and risk-averse organization.

The role of risk management extends into the regulatory sphere of influence as well, with regulators being charged with preventing systemic risks (albeit one-sided negative risks) to everything from fish stocks, to drinking water, to the financial markets. The natural tendency for regulators is to apply more regulation to prevent mishaps; however, as we will see, the regulations themselves can have unintended consequences. In fact, we will argue that the rigidity of regulation frequently makes matters worse, as a heavily regulated system does not have the flexibility to respond appropriately to complexity. As an example, later in this chapter some of the root underlying causes of the 2008 financial crisis will be examined. It was a crisis brought on by naively trying to impose regulations based on complicated thinking upon the complex world of financial markets. Essentially, it was a crisis of unintended consequences – an all-too-frequent outcome of applying complicated thinking to complex systems.

Market-based regulatory systems, much like natural systems, tend to unintentionally create a Darwinian form of evolution that is unique to each system. Rules-based regulation is, unfortunately, almost always based on complicated thinking. As such, the complexity of the markets necessarily means that complicated-type regulation is almost always doomed to failure, in large part due to the production of unintended consequences. It is yet another example of Orgel's Second Rule (previously mentioned in chapter 2) that "Evolution is smarter than you are."

A Very Short History of Risk Management

In his entertaining book *Against the Gods: The Remarkable Story of Risk,*[1] author Peter Bernstein tells the tale of the ageless human quest to tame the unpredictable and to understand, control, and master risk. In his history of risk management, Mr. Bernstein points out that, although risk management is currently a popular topic, it is not a new one.

Early forms of derivative contracts for managing risk are observed from around 2000 B.C. for rice traders in China, olive traders in Greece, and slave traders in other parts of the world. Later, insurance contracts were constructed and became a part of daily business and personal life, and the modern insurance company came into being in the late 1600s.

Up until the late 1970s, risk management was a profession of probability management. By studying historical trends, actuaries could develop elaborate tables and charts that plotted the probability of a wide range of risks. Insurance contracts and prices were based on these actuarial studies, and the role of speculators was relatively minor. The tasks of the risk manager were to ensure that the sample size on which the statistics were developed was sufficient for the accuracy needed and that the portfolio of risks undertaken was aligned closely enough with the actuarial sample so that insurers had reasonable confidence that although they would have to pay out on some contracts, the portfolio overall would be profitable.

It was a game of numbers, with a realization that the numbers were not controllable and would be subject to the will of the gods. The underlying premise was the mathematical principle called the central limit theorem. The central limit theorem, simply stated, is that, with a large enough sample, the normal bell-curve distribution will adequately characterize the realized distribution of all outcomes. Thus, insurance companies were content with the concept that, although they would have no realistic idea of whether or when a given policy holder would trigger a claim, they could be comfortable in the aggregate, knowing that the results would be in line with their probability-based actuarial assumptions.

The assumption of normal distribution was important, as it allowed the well-developed mathematics of normal distribution to be used. If the distribution proved not to be normal, errors would creep into the calculations, and the estimates of risk would be off – significantly so, under certain conditions. The breakdown of the assumption of normality was one of the factors that caused the risk models to fail so horribly during the credit crisis of 2008.

Thus, success in insurance, as well as in risk management, required making sure that the company had the scale of resources to live through the expected occasional deviations from the calculated averages, as well as sufficient diversity in the portfolio of risks to ensure that the distribution of results would come out as the laws of probability said it would. The actuarial portfolio model dominated all fields of risk management up until the 1970s.

The Black-Scholes-Merton Model

In the 1970s, risk management took on a totally new aspect as a result of the arrival of a breakthrough formula. In 1976, the research of three academics created a major paradigm shift in how risk was measured, thought about, and managed. Fischer Black, Myron Scholes, and Robert Merton developed what become known as the Black-Scholes-Merton (sometimes known as just Black-Scholes) financial option pricing model. The development of the model changed perceptions of risk almost overnight by introducing the idea that risk was not simply something to be avoided but instead was an element of business that could be exploited, leveraged, and traded. Risk became a commodity.

A financial option is a contract that allows the buyer the "option" to buy (or to sell) a security at a preset price and at a preset time. For example, consider the case of a purchasing manager for a trucking company who is concerned about fuel costs. To ensure that the cost of fuel does not rise above the cost implicit in customers' contracts, the purchasing manager can purchase an option on fuel. If the market price of fuel rises above the price stated in the contract, the manager will exercise the option and buy the fuel from the option seller at the specified price. Conversely, if the price of fuel stays below the price specified in the option, then the purchasing manager will simply buy fuel in the market in the usual way. The trucking company is thus "hedged" against rising fuel costs.

Financial options are available on a wide variety of securities and commodities. Options are available for commodities such as gold, silver, oil, or wheat, and for financial instruments such as stocks and interest rates. Newer option types are available as a hedge against such things as the weather (based on averages of temperature or precipitation) and even against catastrophic weather events such as hurricanes, earthquakes, or tornadoes. Options are traded on a financial trading exchange, or more customized contracts are available from major international financial institutions.

As implied earlier, option-type contracts have existed since the earliest days of organized commerce. However, Black, Scholes, and Merton's work changed the game forever. Before Black, Scholes, and

Merton there was always an open question of how to price options accurately. The Black-Scholes-Merton model gave traders a seemingly scientific way to price risk and options objectively and accurately.

Unlike with insurance contracts, a financial trader could not rely on the law of large numbers or frequentist statistics as discussed in chapter 2. The specific risks of option contracts, the fact that financial and commodity markets are not subject to the same mathematics as accidents and natural death, and the fact that there is usually an imbalance between the number of people who want to buy options and the number of people who want to sell options, meant that actuarial type calculations were of limited use in determining a fair price.

Black, Scholes, and Merton first published their model in 1976 – conveniently, just a few years after options on stocks started to trade on the Chicago Board Options Exchange. The insight of Black, Scholes, and Merton allowed the creation of a hedge portfolio. If some practical and generally reasonable trading assumptions held – for example, if trading commissions were not significant, and you could always buy or sell the asset or security on which the option contract was based – then a trading strategy could be formulated that allowed you to buy or sell options with no risk whatsoever. Furthermore, the cost of the offsetting trading strategy could be determined in advance, and thus the price of the option could be determined with a high degree of precision.

The Black-Scholes-Merton formula provided not only a way to price options but also a mechanism for measuring and controlling risk. In essence, the formula provided a precise mathematical algorithm that allowed risk managers to measure their risks and then precisely hedge their risks, in much the same way that bookies hedge their bets by also betting in the opposite direction. For those who understood the extremely complicated mathematics, it was a godsend. In a matter of years, physicists and mathematicians become the darlings of Wall Street, and they continue to be so to this day because of the academic training that allows them to understand the sophisticated mathematics. Risk was seemingly tamed! Risk could supposedly be treated and managed as if it was a complicated entity.

The development of the option pricing formula led to a frenzy of academic and practical research that continues to this day. The world of derivatives, of which options are the building blocks, became a central part of finance, commerce, investments, and of course risk management. The amount, type, and size of products available for both speculation and risk management proliferated. The belief was that with enough mathematical talent and the concepts of the Black-Scholes-Merton model, risk could be harnessed, tamed, and even exploited. What no one suspected was that a Pandora's box had been opened.

The Early Use of the Formula

There are a couple of instructive back stories to the development of the Black-Scholes-Merton model. In a paper written in 1989, Fischer Black outlined one of the more interesting of these back stories.[2] Initially, the formula was not well received. Ironically, the academic community believed it to be too esoteric and of little practical use. When Fischer Black and Myron Scholes eventually got their paper published, it was in a lesser known academic journal, with the title "The Pricing Of Options and Contingent Liabilities"[3] (a title that had little to do with risk management or speculation), and the emphasis in the article was on pricing corporate bonds rather than options. This was a very inauspicious academic debut for an idea that was going to turn out to be so significant. This in itself probably says more about the complicated thinking of academics and experts than it does about the model itself.

The second little-known irony is the trading results that Black and Scholes obtained when they tried to profit by trading with their formula. Reasonably assuming that few of the floor traders in the financial markets had the necessary mathematical insight to understand, much less properly implement, their formula, Black and Scholes decided to become traders themselves. Their strategy was comparatively simple. They would buy options in the market that were underpriced according to their formula and sell options that were overpriced. Using their trading methodology they would manage the residual risk of their positions. It seemed like the perfect strategy – the financial equivalent of taking candy from a baby.

Surprisingly, the net result was that they did not do very well as traders. What the academics Black and Scholes learned is that the market does not always behave in a totally rational fashion that can be captured by the rules of mathematics. Market traders behaved as if they knew something else that was beyond the mathematics of the formula. It was as if there was something else that was critically important that the mathematics did not, and could not, detect. As mathematicians and academics, Black and Scholes did not have this key insight – an issue that we will return to later in this chapter.

Despite its authors' own poor personal trading results, the Black-Scholes-Merton formula became a hit among traders and risk managers. The formula became the benchmark for measuring and valuing risk, while the concepts embedded in the model became the basis for virtually all risk-management techniques. In 1998, Myron Scholes and Robert Merton were awarded the Nobel Prize in Economics for their development of the model. Unfortunately, Fischer Black had passed away in 1995, or he would most certainly have received the award as well. The use of the formula was ubiquitous by this time, and the teaching of it was, and remains, a standard feature of business school curricula. The veracity of the formula is now taken as a given and is not seriously challenged on either theoretical or practical grounds.

The Black-Scholes-Merton model is a perfect example of a complicated model. Given a set of inputs, the precise value of a financial asset such as an option can be determined. Furthermore, by applying a bit more calculus to their technique, the method's originators were able to derive hedging strategies to eliminate the risk that owning such an option might entail. The financial world finally had a clockwork formula. It is the closest thing that finance has to mathematics' Pythagorean theorem.

Long-Term Capital Management (LTCM)

The timing of the Nobel Prize was auspicious, as Myron Scholes and Robert Merton had recently become partners in a hedge fund started by Bob Meriwether, who was a well-known superstar bond trader at the prestigious Wall Street investment bank Salomon Brothers. The name of the hedge fund was Long-Term Capital Management, better known as LTCM. The key strategy of the LTCM fund was to use the risk-management insights of the Black-Scholes-Merton model to trade large arbitrage positions in the global markets. The risk-management principles of the formula would allow the fund to enter into huge positions while simultaneously managing the risk. Furthermore, the fund managers had the "dream team" of Scholes and Merton to guide them, along with several other prominent economists and traders.

Virtually from its creation, LTCM was very profitable – so profitable, in fact, that the fund leveraged itself up even more by returning a large part of investors' capital. Estimates have placed the leverage of the fund at close to thirty to one. In other words, for every dollar that the fund had to invest it actually invested thirty dollars. The fund managers' confidence in the validity and appropriateness of the Black-Scholes-Merton formula allowed them to take such outsized risks, and to earn correspondingly outsized returns.

In 1998, however, increased volatility started to become a fact of daily trading in the financial markets. There was an Asian currency crisis and collapse, and then Russia defaulted on some of its sovereign debt. The models at LTCM said that things would be okay, but they clearly were not. As chronicled in Roger Lowenstein's book *When Genius Failed*,[4] the fund began to lose money at a record pace. The models could not take into account that markets sometimes appear to act irrationally. The LTCM models could also not accurately take into account the actions that other competing traders would take that would work against LTCM. In essence, unwittingly, LTCM had created a complex network of traders who were mimicking their strategies.

To exacerbate the situation, the fund had very large trading positions with all of the major international banks, and these banks, in turn, had also used the Black-Scholes-Merton formula to hedge their own risks. Thus there was a significant possibility of contagion in the banking community. The collapse of LTCM would have been catastrophic, creating a ripple effect in the financial markets that in all probability would have become a financial tsunami. For this reason the Federal Reserve Bank of New York stepped in and organized a bailout of the fund.

With hindsight, many market commentators view the bailout of LTCM organized by the Federal Reserve as a trial run for the more widespread set of bailouts that were needed during the financial crisis of 2008.

Ironically, the crisis of 2008 was also caused by risk-management principles that had their origin in the Black-Scholes-Merton model, an outcome that will be discussed later in this chapter.

The ultimate irony, of course, is that the formula that was supposed to prevent and manage risk actually wound up creating an even bigger set of systemic risks. Does this mean that the formula is wrong? The answer is no. The formula actually is a feat of brilliant financial engineering. It also has been proven to work with a high degree of precision and reliability in a wide variety of applications and in many different types of financial markets. It is even widely used for business applications such as valuing acquisitions or valuing flexibility in contracts, like those awarded to professional athletes. There is, however, an Achilles heel to the formula and the corresponding hedging methodology. The Achilles heel is that implementation of the model requires that markets are stable with a known and constant volatility.

Volatility is how much a financial asset's price will move up and down over a given period. A financial asset that has large price moves – both up and down – will have a large volatility, while a different asset with smaller price moves will have a smaller volatility. Technically, an asset's volatility is usually measured by the standard deviation of the asset's return around its average return. Some financial assets have characteristically large volatility, while other financial assets typically have much lower volatility. The Black-Scholes-Merton model works well regardless of whether the underlying asset's volatility is large or small. The problem is when the volatility changes. The problem becomes particularly acute if the return on the asset "jumps," or, equivalently, if the price of the underlying asset jumps significantly in one big move. The Black-Scholes-Merton strategy is predicated on being able to both buy and sell the underlying asset at small increments as the price moves smoothly from one level to another. This ability to be able to constantly trade the underlying asset without significantly affecting its price is what traders call liquidity. This assumption and a key part of the underlying hedging algorithm are violated when the asset price jumps.

Most of the time asset prices behave in a way that allows traders and hedgers to utilize successfully the Black-Scholes-Merton model.

However, as Black and Scholes and then later Scholes and Merton found out, the formula will not always be perfect. When a significant event happens in the markets, such as the Russian debt default, market prices will react quickly and significantly, causing the jumps and changes in volatility that violate the underlying assumptions. The model falls apart, and can in fact make the hedging outcomes worse than they would have been without any hedging whatsoever.

The Black-Scholes-Merton formula is an ingenious formula. It is a great work of creativity, mathematical genius, and paradigm-shifting insight into financial markets and risk. It truly is a formula that is worthy of a Nobel Prize. It is also a very complicated formula, in both our scientific sense of the word and in the lay person's sense of complicated. It utilizes a branch of mathematics known as stochastic calculus that is not widely known except by those who have studied advanced mathematics or physics. At the heart of Black-Scholes-Merton is the equation that also describes how heat moves through a metal bar. The heat-diffusion equation from physics is well studied and is based on how atoms behave in a piece of metal. However, the precision and uniformity, governed by the laws of physics, that dictate the characteristics of atoms in a metal bar are not present in the financial markets. Financial prices do not have such static underlying laws. Participants in any type of market, business or financial, have wildly different opinions about how the economic future will unfold. Therefore, individually and in the aggregate, their behavior lacks the predictability that characterizes the behavior of atoms in a piece of metal.

Unfortunately, because of the success of the model and its related risk-management insights, traders, regulators, investment managers, and corporate treasurers routinely ignore its weaknesses. In fact, they want to believe and trust in the formula so much that few traders or managers take the time and effort necessary to fully understand the mathematics and concepts underlying the formula. The model is treated as an infallible black-box calculator – a clear indication of complicated thinking. This unwarranted level of blind faith in the formula results in hubris and, too frequently, catastrophic results, as LTCM found out.

Complexity prevents the markets from having stable volatility and jump-free price movements. With complexity you get unpredictable jumps in prices or phase shifts that render the Black-Scholes-Merton algorithm impotent. However, the success of the formula has led to an industry of researchers and traders who understand the mathematics but do not understand and appreciate how the underlying markets work. This is why, when Black, Scholes, and Merton first started to trade with their formula, they suffered losses. In Fischer Black's own words, "the market knew something that our formula didn't know."[5] What the market knew that the formula didn't know was the collective adaptive wisdom of the markets. The markets understand that wild, unpredictable jumps can and will take place and accounts for them accordingly, perhaps with less precision, mathematical rigor, or consistency than the application of a complicated formula would have, but in a way that is more robust and flexible. The market, and more specifically the uninformed traders that Black and Scholes set out to exploit, did not completely understand the complicated mathematics of the Black-Scholes model, but they did intuitively understand that the markets were complex. Although it is doubtful that any of the traders had studied the science of complexity, the collective wisdom of the group acted as if they had mastered complexity. In other words, a leaderless group of relatively uninformed traders collectively acted in a superior fashion to and defeated a Nobel Prize–winning complicated formula. It is a classic case of complexity thinking trumping complicated thinking.

Despite its proven shortcomings, the Black-Scholes-Merton option pricing model introduced an industry of modeling and quantitative risk management and entrenched complicated thinking into financial and risk management. The demand for physicists and mathematicians rapidly grew after it became apparent that the Black-Scholes-Merton model held out the promise of the master key to risk management. That rush continues unabated to this day, only now the regulators, rating agencies, institutional investors, day traders, and even lay investors have joined the party. The rise in popularity of universities offering courses and programs in financial engineering is testament to this. The fact that the older, more experienced traders, with their relative lack of sophistication, tend to do better than their more sophisticated quantitative cousins does not seem to faze anyone – at least not until a Long-Term Capital Management-type financial debacle results.

I do not mean to imply that the Black-Scholes-Merton model is fundamentally flawed or unworkable. In fact, the model is indeed very useful and insightful. However, the model needs to be utilized with an appreciation that it only works when things are stable. The model's effective use requires the humility that comes from an appreciation that the markets are complex systems. In a complex world, any complicated model is at best an approximation of reality, and at times will be a gross misrepresentation of it. Blindly following a complicated model to operate within what is ultimately a complex system will eventually lead to surprising and, based on Murphy's Law, generally unwanted results.

The Psychology of Risk

Libraries contain a multitude of books and articles that describe the psychology of risk.[6] Although the adage that you must take risk to reap rewards is well known, the basic fact remains that we all want to avoid downside risk as much as possible in all aspects of our lives. Our risk preferences are what researchers call asymmetrically risk averse. Most of us are willing to give up more than a dollar of potential gain to avoid the potential loss of a dollar. In other words, good risk, unit for unit, gives us less pleasure than the pain caused by a unit of bad risk.

This asymmetry in risk preferences creates some seemingly irrational and inconsistent choices that we make in both our daily lives and as managers. As I mentioned in chapter 2, Daniel Kahneman and Amos Tversky were among the first researchers to demonstrate, through a series of innovative studies, that individuals make choices based on the asymmetry between potential gains and losses. They called the phenomenon "prospect theory," and it has been used to describe a wide set of behaviors that are commonly seen in risk management.

One particular behavior that Kahneman and Tversky noted was that an individual's response to a risky choice could be altered by the format or context of the questioning, an effect that they called framing. For instance, when they asked a series of doctors whether or not they would undertake a particular risky procedure on a patient, they got different answers depending on how the question was framed. Take the question, "Would you recommend this drug if it had a ninety percent chance of curing a terrible illness, but the rest of the time its side effects would be fatal?" An alternative version would be, "Would you recommend this drug if ten percent of the time the side effects were fatal but the rest of the time it cured this terrible illness?" Seen together like this, the two questions pose situations that are mathematically identical. However, Kahneman and Tversky noted that the percentage of doctors choosing to recommend the hypothetical drug depended on which version of the question was asked.

Of any particular group, one would expect medical doctors, who are among the most highly trained in rational thinking, to give the most consistent responses. However, the results from asking doctors were no different from those obtained in testing with random samples of people. The responses were similar – people will respond to a risky decision in different ways based on how a question or situation is framed.

It should be obvious that this creates significant difficulties for modelers of any situation that involves calculating how individuals make decisions. The fact that people make decisions asymmetrically when it comes to good risk and bad risk means that it is also not reasonable to rely on the statistics that permeate current risk modeling. A further complication, as Kahneman and Tversky show, is the fact that decisions are also made based on context. The predominant assumption in risk modeling is that outcomes are normally distributed. In other words, a plot of the frequency of outcomes on the y-axis, with the x-axis being the range of possible outcomes, will produce a graph that looks like the familiar bell curve. A key feature of the bell curve is that it is symmetrical around the average. Things are just as likely to turn out above average as they are to turn out below average. This is inconsistent with how individuals actually make decisions, as is convincingly demonstrated by Kahneman and Tversky.

The fact that individuals interpret risk asymmetrically creates a modeling challenge. While the differences for small deviations around the average may be small, the effects at either extreme of the distribution can be significant, and even paradigm shifting.

Of course, the risk modelers understand this to a certain extent as well. Thus, the current quest in risk mathematics is to develop a formula, or a series of formulas, to model what are known as Black Swans

or tail risks. Black Swans are those rare events that have a dispropor-
tionate effect on outcomes.[7] For instance, a major earthquake is a rare
event, but it has significant effects that can change conditions in an
entire region. Likewise, winning a large lottery prize can also be considered to be a Black Swan effect, although this time it is a good Black
Swan effect. The result, however, is the same. The life of a person who
wins a large lottery is changed in unpredictable ways forever after,
although unfortunately not always in the idyllic ways advertised by
the lottery organizers.

In short, using a complicated style of modeling for risk management
can be extremely challenging even before the effects of complexity are
taken into account. We have only discussed two out of several possible aspects of individual decision making in risky situations. The challenges for complicated modeling continue to build when we consider
the actions of groups of individuals.

Related but different effects are found when we consider how
groups make decisions. The first is known as confirmation bias. The
term "confirmation bias" describes the fact that, consciously or unconsciously, we tend to seek out information that supports our initial
thoughts or bias while simultaneously ignoring information that goes
against our view. Confirmation bias tends to quickly reinforce whatever views we started with, despite blatant signs that our decision is
flawed in some way.

A clear example of confirmation bias is the way in which political
groups divide along clearly partisan lines. The widespread influence
of media such as blog groups as well as the round-the-clock news cycle
help to perpetuate and reinforce the effects of confirmation bias, making them even stronger and harder to counteract.

A similar group effect is the phenomenon known as groupthink,
where people working in groups have an inherent urge to come to
some sort of consensus. Groupthink frequently leads to suboptimal
compromises and outcomes. As with confirmation bias, important data
or ideas are likely to be underappreciated or even ignored. In real time,
"in the moment," the decisions will be believed to be rational and the
best possible choices, but with more objective hindsight the same decisions will likely be roundly criticized and seen as weak and inefficient.

A further aspect of the psychology of risk is the phenomenon known as risk homeostasis.[8] Risk homeostasis states that individuals will always act in ways such that their overall exposure to risk remains relatively constant. For instance, if you are riding your bicycle and are wearing a helmet you are likely to take more chances than you would if you were bicycling without a helmet. The principle is that if you are wearing a helmet, you feel safer from risk, and thus take actions that actually keep your overall level of risk at the same level. The implementation of a risk mitigant (the helmet) may actually increase risk by creating overconfidence that compels an individual to act differently than they would have done without the risk mitigant.

Organizations are not immune from risk homeostasis. Bankers Trust was one of the premier financial firms of the 1990s. It was also the firm that originated advanced risk-management techniques as an integral part of its strategy. In fact, many of the current best practices in financial risk management were originally developed at Bankers Trust. Ironically, Bankers Trust was acquired by Deutsche Bank in 1998 in large part due to its failures in the management of risk. While Bankers Trust had a strong system for the management of financial risk, it ignored reputational risk, and a series of scandals involving its clients played a large part in the firm's demise. The confidence that Bankers Trust had in its complicated system for managing financial risk led the company to ignore the more complex people-based risks. The expertise that Bankers Trust had in modeling allowed them to take advantage of some of their less sophisticated clients. One of its traders was recorded bragging about how he was going to "rip off" one of Bankers Trust's clients in a financial transaction. The lawyers for one of the clients, Procter and Gamble, gained access to the tapes and successfully sued Bankers Trust for damages. The reputational damage to Bankers Trust essentially ended its dominance, and the company ceased to operate as a separate entity. Bankers Trust essentially mastered the complicated parts of risk management. Where it failed was in understanding and managing the more nuanced complex aspects of risk management.

The psychology of risk is critically important, but as phenomena such as confirmation bias and groupthink illustrate, the sociology of risk may be as important if not more important. Understanding the psychology of risk, which is how and why individuals make inconsistent and irrational choices concerning risk, is just one aspect of understanding the complexity of risk. Furthermore, decisions made as part of a group, such as an organization or a trading market, create a sociology of risk that in turn introduces another source of complexity.

The psychology of risk highlights decisions and traits of the market that appear to be irrational or inconsistent. The decisions of a crowd, or sociological risk, may even lead to paradigm shifts, as happened when clients of Bankers Trust refused en masse to deal with the the company after the Procter and Gamble scandal. These traits of players in the market are real and are not ever likely to change. That is why it is so important to realize that risk management is not complicated; it's complex.

Decision Making and Regulation under Uncertainty

Riccardo Rebonato's very insightful study of risk management, *Plight of the Fortune Tellers: Why We Need to Manage Financial Risk Differently,* outlines one of the fundamental truths about current risk management practice and the quest to live in a complicated framework. As Rebonato writes, "Fate has all but disappeared from our conceptualization of risk, and indeed, almost from everyday language. In sum there has been a general shift in attitude towards ascribing a responsibility or a cause of negative outcomes from Fate to ourselves."[9]

Risk management is the art of decision making under uncertainty. However, it is quite natural to dislike uncertainty. Uncertainty implies the unknown and, given that most people are risk averse, they tend to expect the worst, or at least attach more weight to the potential loss from uncertain outcomes than to the potential gains. This, of course, is consistent with Kahneman and Tversky's prospect theory, as discussed earlier.

In the quest to shed uncertainty, individuals, risk managers, and organizations tend to turn to complicated thinking practices such as the Black-Scholes-Merton model. Such formulas and scientific approaches certainly give the illusion of providing certainty and understanding. In addition, there is some measure of satisfaction in the mere fact that action can be taken based on calculable results. However, it is paradoxical that the field of decision making under uncertainty is predicated on the certainty of science and complicated thinking.

Complicated thinking practices are also favored by regulators and politicians,with the result that most regulation is geared toward preventing potentially adverse outcomes rather than trying to exploit uncertain positive outcomes. This skewdness of incentives, coupled with the desire by regulators and politicians to be viewed as implementing constructive actions that are the product of diligent thought and optimal choices, leads to many unintended consequences that, with hindsight, may appear to be of doubtful value at best and counterproductive at worst.

In an opinion piece in the *Wall Street Journal*, Kip Hawley, a former head of the Transportation Security Administration, outlined a critical analysis of the airport security measures that were implemented as the aftermath of 9/11.[10] In his article, Mr. Hawley stresses that "the TSA's job is to manage risk, not to enforce regulations. Terrorists are adaptive, and we need to be adaptive too. Regulations are always playing catch-up, because terrorists design their plots around the loopholes." This statement almost perfectly sums up the argument for why regulation and risk management need to abandon complicated thinking and adopt the flexibility and principles of complexity thinking. Terrorists, like financial traders or business competitors, are adaptive and complex in their responses. To successfully compete against them requires complexity rather than rigid rules and regulations.

The security practices at airports have caused incalculable inconvenience to the traveling public and have significantly changed business and leisure travel. The direct costs in terms of delays and time spent waiting in line are enormous. The hidden costs of the frustration and stress that security measures have caused are perhaps even more significant. While no one wants a terrorist act to occur, the unintended costs of managing the risks posed by terrorists cannot be allowed to become more significant than the cost of the risks they are trying to prevent.

In his article, Mr. Hawley argues that the TSA mandate is to "prevent a catastrophic attack on the transportation system, not to ensure that every single passenger can avoid harm while traveling." He further argues that "TSA's leaders should have more discretion to interact with passengers and to work in looser teams throughout airports. And TSA's leaders must be prepared to support initiative even when officers make mistakes." This is complexity thinking, from a person who is trying to buck the entrenched complicated thinking trend that is inherent in regulation.

Enterprise Risk Management

Enterprise Risk Management, commonly called ERM, is a specialty field of risk management that attempts to take a holistic view of the management of risk in an organization. ERM was first popularized by the Commission of Sponsoring Organizations of the Treadway Commission, more commonly known as COSO. COSO created a framework that explicitly acknowledged that risks are connected and correlated throughout an organization. After the accounting scandals and the bankruptcies of Enron and WorldCom in particular, the business community, and related regulatory agencies, clamored for improved risk-management practices. COSO provided one of the first comprehensive risk frameworks, which quickly came to be seen as epitomizing best risk-management practice for large organizations.[11]

One of the specific take-aways from COSO and subsequent risk-management frameworks is that risk management cannot be done in functional silos within an enterprise but instead must be a coordinated effort across organizational lines. In addition, the correlations between risks in different parts of an enterprise must be recognized, accounted for, and appropriately managed. Both COSO and later frameworks such as ISO 31000 specify that risks should be (a) identified, (b) assessed as to their potential impact, and (c) appropriately responded to, all couched in an atmosphere of ongoing monitoring and communication.

The two key steps in the framework are (a) the identification of risk and (c) ongoing communication and monitoring. As risk is part of an ongoing complex adaptive system, it is necessary to monitor it continually. Both good risks and bad risks, and their level of seriousness, will change dynamically over time. Thus, without continuous communication and monitoring, the organization will be dealing with risks that are no longer relevant, while missing new or emerging risks that need to be mitigated or exploited.

Risk management involves taking action to maximize the probability and magnitude of good risk events while simultaneously taking action to decrease the probability and severity of bad risks. With this definition, the importance of creatively identifying potential risks, both good and bad, becomes a central component of what I call Nason's First Law of Risk Management, which states that "recognizing that a potential for risk exists automatically increases the probability and magnitude of its occurring if it is a good risk, while simultaneously decreasing the probability and severity of its occurring if it is a bad risk."

It is a simple heuristic but generally effective and consistent with complexity. Complicated thinking implies that you can examine a situation and isolate its parts. Complicated thinking also implies that you can focus on the downside risk only, manage it in isolation, and thus mitigate your risks. The complexity view of things recognizes that there are both an upside and a downside component to risk. Managing one aspect affects all other aspects. To deal with complexity, risk management needs to take a holistic approach. Risk is not confined within separate independent boxes. Everything affects everything else, in often unpredictable ways.

As an admittedly trivial example of Nason's First Law of Risk Management, consider the risk of being appropriately dressed for the weather. The weather is notoriously unpredictable. However, if you recognize that the weather may change and carry both an umbrella and a sun visor, you will be much better positioned than people who gave no thought whatever to the weather when they left their house for their day's activities. Street vendors in major cities like New York understand the interconnected sides of risk management. As the weather changes, their goods offered for sale also change with a timeliness that is envied by even the most sophisticated companies with advanced supply-chain management systems. The street vendors build flexibility and adaptability into their business model. They do not do extensive forecasting and planning. Instead, they know the weather will change and that, as it changes, the needs for goods will change. This common but trivial example demonstrates that it's not complicated in any sense of the word.

The 2008 Financial Crisis: A Case Study of Complicated Thinking

A lot of books, articles, movies, and documentaries have tried to explain the financial crisis of 2008. Almost a decade later, its economic effects are still being felt on a global basis. What has become clear from all of the words written by the various pundits is that there was no single cause of the crisis but instead a confluence of catalysts that created the economic storm. Many of the contributing factors were the product of good intentions that had bad unintended consequences. The financial crisis is a classic case of the result of applying complicated thinking in risk management and regulation to our complex financial markets. It is a consequence of assuming that risks can be "solved" and "regulated" in isolation. It is a consequence of our not realizing the importance of the interconnectedness and the feedback loops that exist within the infrastructure of modern global markets. The crisis is a textbook example of emergence in action. Above all, the financial crisis of 2008 demonstrates that regulation and risk management are not complicated, they're complex.

Previous commentators have looked at and debated the importance of the various factors that either led to or helped prolong the crisis. Pundits have argued that if this regulation or that regulation had been changed then things would have been different. Of course, many commentators also point to the greed of bankers and investors as the primary culprit. Complicated thinking will look for a single cause or a finite set of causes. Complexity thinking looks at the system as a whole, including the causes and their interconnectedness. It is a different mindset that leads to a very different set of conclusions. With a complexity framework, it can be argued that it was regulation and the attempt to control markets with rational complicated thinking that actually caused the crisis – the very thing that these measures were intended to prevent.

One of the precipitating factors was low interest rates. No doubt, Alan Greenspan will continue to be pilloried in the history books for keeping rates artificially low for too long and in the process creating a housing bubble. It is ironic that Greenspan was hailed as the financial savior of the world while he was doing so – as long as the U.S. economy was booming.

Besides the housing bubble there were several other unintended consequences of low interest rates. The first was a dramatic fall in yields for investors, particularly institutional investors such as pension funds and endowment funds, which have contractual duties to invest prudently while earning acceptable yields for their constituents. These institutional investors were not a group of overzealous, greedy, hedge-fund types; they were earnestly trying to allow all of us to afford food, heat, and shelter in our old age through the payouts of our pensions. The low yields on traditional assets forced them to look elsewhere for acceptable returns. Regulation in terms of mandatory minimum returns and the types of instruments they were required to invest in left these institutional investors few alternatives in such a low-interest-rate environment. The demand for new investment products with the possibility of higher returns grew, and the investment bankers were only too happy to provide such products.

A second factor was "mark to market" accounting, which was a response to regulation that was intended to improve transparency in analyzing the financial statements of financial institutions. Mark to market (MTM) accounting requires banks and other financial institutions to periodically update the value of their assets (investments, trading positions, etc.) with current market values rather than the historical values of purchase. This is generally a good practice, but it assumes that the "animal spirits" of the market are always rationally and correctly pricing such assets. The low interest rates made investors overly confident, and thus prices on many assets were irrationally (with hindsight) pushed to bubble levels. In an MTM framework, this implies that banks had overvalued assets on their balance sheets, which in turn encouraged them to invest in more assets. On the downside, investors tend to panic and trade to prices that are artificially low. When downturns occur, it forces banks to devalue or unload their assets, which leads to accelerating feedback loops that erode the accounting value of investment assets and in turn destroy investors' confidence in the financial health of the banks and other entities such as pension funds that are subject to MTM accounting.

The push by political forces to increase home loans to the economically disadvantaged was another noble initiative with unintended negative consequences. Politicians pushed legislation that forced banks to make loans that, under prudent lending standards, would never be made; thus the creation of the sub-prime mortgage market. Bankers have faced a lot of ridicule in the popular press for making these loans, but in a sense their hands were forced by legislation. Even the most brain dead and greediest of bankers knew that a large proportion of these loans were going to go bust; the sole issue was how many of them and how fast. In a low-interest-rate environment, housing values steadily and almost predictably increase. The early experience of sub-prime mortgages in this environment gave results for the mathematical models that default rates on sub-prime mortgages would be minimal at best. In a worst-case scenario, sub-prime borrowers would be able to sell their home, and probably at a profit. The downside risk of these mortgages thus seemed limited, and as a result the sub-prime mortgage market grew rapidly.

The credit derivative and securitization markets came to the rescue of the bankers with the creation of Collateralized Debt Obligations (CDOs). Credit derivatives, securitization, and CDOs all have the feature that they allow banks to reduce the amount of credit risk they own by selling the risk to other investors – such as beleaguered pension fund managers who are concerned about how they will create enough value for retirees to survive their old age in comfort. CDOs and securitization techniques also helped to keep mortgage rates low, and provided new funding as global investors helped Americans get into new homes at ever-lower mortgage rates, with ever more cleverly constructed mortgage structures. In similar fashion, credit derivatives provided large pools of low-cost financing, which enabled corporations to expand. Credit derivatives even gave bankers a way to spread the risk of the sub-prime mortgages to others. By using credit derivatives, bankers could create investment assets with higher yields and supposedly lower risk (or at least that is what the models said). What perfect timing for those investors desperately searching for yield!

Credit derivatives spawned new research into quantitative credit-risk modeling. Banks clamored for newly minted PhDs in finance and physics to develop models that used esoteric concepts and mathematical tools such as "Extreme Value Theory" and "Gaussian copulas."[12] New global banking standards, intended to ensure the stability of the global banking system, encouraged this research. Under international banking guidelines known as Basel II, banks were incentivized to keep their ratio of credit risk due to loans outstanding divided by the amount of equity invested in the bank below a threshold level. The use of credit derivatives was encouraged by the regulators, as it reduced the credit risk that banks were exposed to and kept their Basel II ratios within compliance levels. The greater use of credit derivatives meant that banks were seemingly less risky and thus able to extend even more credit to both home owners and corporations.

This insight about credit derivatives led to the development of very elegant models for precisely measuring and pricing credit risk and to ever-more-sophisticated credit derivative structures and CDOs. The models, however, relied on some rather dubious assumptions and on precision in variables such as default rates and correlations. Initially, the models worked spectacularly well and become well accepted – even though hardly anyone over the age of thirty understood them (i.e., hardly anyone with meaningful banking experience or investment management experience).

These well-intended regulations led to a falsely benign credit situation. Funding was easy to procure at very attractive rates. Default rates were low, home ownership was at record high levels, and consumer and manufacturing confidence were high. Then the winds of fortune started to shift subtly, and the unintended consequences, patiently waiting their turn in the background, took their place at the front of the stage and began to emerge.

To begin, default rates started to creep upwards, exposing weaknesses in the models used to value credit derivatives and CDOs. Investment managers and bankers started to see the value of their assets dip slightly. They asked their "quants" for an explanation and, not getting a satisfactory (that is understandable) answer, decided to sell. The problem was that few market participants (or regulators or bank managers) understood what Gaussian copulas were or any of the other aspects of the mathematics behind the instruments, or even the mathematics behind the regulation, accounting, and bank financial ratios that depended on them. The complicated-thinking financial engineers who created the products understood the mathematics of what they were doing, but they did not understand or appreciate the nuances of the complexity of the financial markets and the complexity of the mindsets of investors and home owners. Conversely, those bankers and investors with extensive experience may have had an intuitive appreciation for the complexity of the markets, but they did not fully appreciate or understand the sophistication of the new investment mathematics.

When investors and banks started to exit and sell these sophisticated financial assets, it pushed prices down farther, which, because of the mark to market accounting regulations, damaged the balance sheets of the banks. Investors (and banks themselves) lost confidence in the banks, and funding for banks dried up as their MTM accounting led to ever-weaker-looking balance sheets. As funding for banks dried up, banks asked each other for more collateral in their dealings and started to sell assets. This led to a further decline in asset values and, in turn, higher interest rates, which meant that default rates started to increase. As default rates increased, the models and the associated assumptions used to price the assets began to fall apart, which led to more selling, which led to a further decline in values, which in turn led to an ongoing downward spiral and crash.

There are a few takeaways from this debacle. First off, it is incumbent on all (investors, regulators, politicians, and the general public) to think about the financial markets as an interconnected complex system. Ignoring this fact will almost inevitably lead to practices and regulations with unintended consequences. Practices that on the surface look great and seem perfectly rational in isolation may have other connections and relationships that undo their original effectiveness. Second, complicated models are not reality, and it is wise not to become slaves to them. Models are very useful, and indeed necessary, but they will never replace thinking and wisdom gained through experience. Risk management and regulation, particularly in the world of finance, are more like art and sociology than science and mathematics.

Many commentors have looked for the "cause" of the crisis. There was no "cause" as much as there was a confluence of events that came together to produce a series of interrelated and unintended consequences. The financial crisis was not so much a product of a single cause or set of causes but instead was a product of a complex situation from which emerged a financial meltdown. Ultimately, understanding the crisis comes down to recognizing that it's not complicated, it's complex.

Conclusions

The complex nature of risk teaches us that risk management is more than just auditing and applying checklists. Audits and checklists are appropriate risk-management tools when the risk is simple or complicated in nature. However, with the inherent connectedness and globalization of business today, important risk issues are almost always complex. Risk management is by necessity an iterative and emergent process. Risk management within the context of complexity requires the same traits of complexity thinking as other areas of business do. Risk managers need to learn to recognize the emergent properties of risks. They need to expect phase shifts, paradigm shifts, ambiguity, and nonlinear behavior in the risks they are or will be faced with. Complex risks must be "managed," not "solved." Finally, it is important to realize that we are all managing risk.

In this chapter we have examined the development of ideas about risk and risk management through various stages. What began as an actuarial exercise in probability changed fundamentally with the development of the Black-Scholes-Merton model. Currently we are living in the age where a variety of stakeholders expect risk management – the practice of making decisions under uncertainty – to be a science with all of the control and predictability that is traditionally associated with the physical sciences. This mode of complicated thinking is, however, quite poorly aligned with the reality of making business decisions in an increasingly complex world. An adherence to complicated thinking leads to unintended consequences, risk homeostasis, inefficiencies, and ineffective solutions and practices.

Managers need to embrace complexity thinking in their risk-management techniques, practices, and strategies. Perhaps it is best to remember the adage of seasoned financial risk traders who claim that "the only perfect hedge is in a Japanese Garden."

NINE

THE COMPLEX FUTURE

The Waning Complicated Age

Before the steam engine came into prominence, muscle and craftsmanship were the necessary requirements for a business venture to be successful. The steam engine facilitated the industrial age, as technical and engineering skill replaced raw muscle as the dominant factor of production. Muscle became a commodity. A machine could do the work of the muscle of many men, or even many teams of oxen, although craftsmanship was still necessary. Scientific management in terms of maximizing the interface between the human function and the engineering process started to play a major role in the first half of the twentieth century. The use of animals ceased to be a factor of production as tractors, trains, buses, and cars replaced the workhorse.

The end of the Second World War brought the rise of the consumer age and the ascendancy of marketing. With the rapid increase of the role of science and engineering, a plethora of new products became possible and affordable. There was increased emphasis on creating efficiencies in product development, marketing, and distribution. As machines and then robots were able to accomplish more and do delicate tasks more capably, the role of the human as a doer became less. But there was still a need for management. The "organization man" as manager was created and rose to prominence. This brought us to the current age of the complicated thinking manager – the professional manager.

In each era, the main components of success were replaced by new components, as developments in the business environment and new ideas and technologies emerged. We are currently in the age of the professional manager, where technical skills combined with managerial skills are needed for success. Slowly, however, this is giving way to the next era in business management.

In the current "age of the professional manager," a large number of professional, white-collar managers are engaged in managing a workforce of blue-collar workers. There is a dichotomy between those who do the work and those who manage the work. Ironically, those who manage the work likely do not have the trade skills to do the work of the workers they manage. This incongruity has been dramatized in the popular television series *Undercover Boss*, a reality show in which a senior manager of an organization takes on the role of a new employee of the company. The premise of the show is that the senior manager gets to experience what it is like to be one of the front-line employees who actually do the work. Generally, the "boss" does not perform the tasks of the front-line workers very competently.

More and more, however, just as manual work is being outsourced to workers in other countries, offshoring and the rise of the freelance professional are making many management roles redundant. The professional workforce is changing, and white-collar middle managers' jobs are threatened. Just as muscle became a commodity, and then engineering capabilities became a commodity, now the complicated-thinking professional manager is also in danger of becoming a commodity. Our new hyper-connected world, which has the scope to become even more connected, is making new demands on managerial professionals. Instead of the age of the knowledge worker, it is becoming the age of the creative worker, the flexible worker, the complexity worker. Complexity in business is crowding out the complicated thinker and creating new opportunities for the complexity thinker and for complexity-oriented companies and organizations. The age of the command-and-control manager is giving way to the risk-tolerant, try-learn-adapt manager. Knowledge is a commodity. The only sustainable competitive advantage belongs to those who are able to deal with complexity.

Complexity Is Increasing

Although we cannot predict the future, it appears reasonably certain that the context of business will become more complex. There are at least seven paradigm shifts that are not so subtly changing the business environment and causing an increase in complexity. These seven shifts are (1) globalization, (2) the Internet, (3) social media, (4) the new dominance of ideas and experiences over objects and services as means for creating profits, (5) the recognition that ideas and experiences are more scalable than products, (6) the increasing importance of big data, and (7) the role of complex social issues as drivers of the global political agenda.

Several of these factors have always been important to some extent, but now the nature of their importance is changing. Furthermore, the changes they precipitate are occurring more rapidly and becoming more significant on a global basis. The factors are all in some sense interrelated and mutually reinforcing. As such, these factors cannot be isolated and dealt with individually. These factors are complex by themselves, but also act as a complex system together. For instance, globalization drives the Internet, and the Internet drives globalization. Both impact social media, which in turn reinforce the importance of globalization and the Internet. These factors create a series of complex feedback loops among themselves.

The paradigm has shifted based on complexity. It has not been a linear change, nor will it start to become linear anytime soon. The world is not becoming more complicated, it is becoming more complex.

Globalization

Globalization has always been an important component of business and the overall economic environment. In large part, globalization led to the rise and dominance of the British Empire during the nineteenth century. The superior naval infrastructure of Britain provided it with a strong competitive advantage in opening and sustaining trade routes from east to west and north to south. The modern container ship, the availability of relatively inexpensive air travel, and companies that supply global logistics services have made the era of sailing vessels seem quaint and have also completely changed the meaning and dynamics of globalization.

The era when a company, much less a nation, had a competitive advantage through global connections and control of a supply route is quickly coming to a close. While knowledge of local markets is still important, its influence as the basis for sustainable competitive advantage is continually shrinking.

The world is now much more connected. The Internet and the different forms of communication it provides have contracted distances and changed the relevance of geography, so much so that, if it were not for regulations imposed for internal political purposes, trade would be virtually seamless around the world. Even then, there is a concerted effort by the governments of most developed and many developing countries to increase business efficiency and trade through trading blocs and trading agreements. The North American Free Trade Agreement (NAFTA) and the European Economic Community (EEC) are two prominent examples among many.

With greater globalization there is greater connectivity, which acts as a catalyst for complexity. Consumer trends and ideas that start in one part of the world are quickly communicated and copied across borders. More importantly, there is a greater and faster spread of ideas.

The rise of globalization diminishes the scale advantages of large corporations. It is as easy for a small manufacturer in India to bid for a contract in Brazil or North America as it is for a manufacturer whose home base is in those countries. Geographical distance becomes less of a barrier, and knowledge spreads cheaply and rapidly.

Globalization increases the speed and ease with which emergence can play a role. For example, the ubiquity of air travel has greatly increased the risk of a global pandemic. The Arab Spring that began as a small uprising precipitated by a single shop vendor setting himself on fire to protest government corruption in Egypt quickly spread through the Arab world and led to uprisings in over a dozen countries within a matter of months. The Occupy Wall Street movement quickly spread globally to more than 900 cities, as protesters, linked through social media, occupied their respective cities to protest growing inequality.

Both the Arab Spring protests and the Occupy movements had little in the way of formal leadership. The movements were essentially leaderless and grass-roots-driven and emerged organically as in a classic complex system. The fact that both movements crossed borders so quickly and seamlessly shows the power of complexity that is enabled by globalization. The leaderless nature of emergence also facilitates speedy global trends, since there is little or no need for formal and time-consuming coordination. Emergence can at times be astonishingly quick. The implications for corporations or managers that believe they are protected by borders and geography should be obvious.

The Internet

In less than twenty years – less than half the span of a typical working career – the Internet has given rise to a whole new set of industries and has significantly altered and even led to the demise of many others. Virtually no industry or profession has remained unaffected by the Internet.

Print publications, from newspapers to magazines and books, have been forever changed. Many once powerful and influential media outlets have become shells of their former selves or have ceased to exist altogether. The independent bookstore has almost become extinct. Even the major chains have not been immune, as evidenced by the demise of the once-mighty Borders bookstore chain. Electronic media have diminished the need for paper-based print. Retailers of all sorts have had to adapt or die, as a result of online shopping. Travel agents have to compete with Internet bookings and with social media in curating the desirability of hotels, airlines, and vacation and business destinations for consumers. Even the computer hardware and software industries are affected, as computing shifts to "the Cloud."

It is difficult to speculate how the Internet will continue to evolve and what the implications for business will be. It seems certain, however, that we are still in the early stages of the Internet era. The Internet is just starting to be ubiquitous on a global scale. As access to the Web becomes ever more widespread, there will continue to be changes in all aspects of life. The "Internet of things" is likely to produce some very surprising and unexpected consequences. Just as complexity and emergence produce surprises, the Internet is also likely to continue to alter the business landscape in dramatic and exciting ways. The Internet is a complexity machine. The Internet is also a complexity enabler and a complexity catalyst.

Social Media

Strongly related to the Internet is the influence of social media. The influence of social media changes how we think about companies and their products and services. The social media phenomenon has created an ever-evolving set of groups and associations that drive consumer, social, political, and lifestyle behavior. Social media outlets provide the connections between agents that allow complexity to thrive.

Until now the biggest driver of the smartphone industry has been social media rather than the music capabilities or Internet connectability that smartphones were initially developed for. Along with texting, the most used smartphone applications are social media apps such as Twitter, Facebook, LinkedIn, or Pinterest.

It could be claimed that the driving purpose of social media is to allow us both to be connected and to increase our connections. Having more "friends" or followers or associates "link in" with you is the objective. The quality of the connections is of secondary importance.

Bearing witness to the importance of creating connections is the fact that perhaps the greatest driver behind the rise of Facebook is the "Like" feature. Although few would be shallow enough to admit to it, the main reason to post to Facebook is to receive "Likes," which in a social media world are a form of self-validation. In the race to show one's stature in the social media world there is a built-in incentive to post things that are funny, interesting, creative, or attention grabbing in the hope of increasing one's Likes. Facebook Likes – or YouTube views, or Retweets – create a series of feedback loops and accelerate emergence. Social media users troll their applications looking both for what is currently popular and for ideas that are in the early stages of trending. The incentive is to catch an idea or a story early before it emerges fully. Being among the first to help something go viral is believed to validate a person as a trend creator, builds the person's credibility, and becomes the basis for a new type of social self-esteem.

CNN is one company that explicitly acknowledges the importance of social media. While as a news organization its traditional role is to curate and present the news, it also directly points out what is "trending" in the top line of its online newsfeed. The focus of the information has become not what you think is important, or even what is important, but instead what the "crowd" thinks is important. It is a democratic form of curation.

The rise of social media has created a new version of the "Keynesian Beauty Contest," a thought experiment developed by John Maynard Keynes to describe the actions of investors in the stock market. In a Keynesian Beauty Contest, the role of the judges is not to pick who they think the prettiest contestant is, but instead to pick who they think the other judges will pick as the prettiest contestant. Helping to create and support a social media trend has a similar focus on choosing what you think others will like rather what you believe is worth liking. This has some perverse and surprising implications for product marketing.

Ideas and Experiences, Not Things

Technology – such as smartphones, or Uber taxis, or even self-driving cars – is making this the age of ideas and experiences, not things. Increasingly, the products that are succeeding are ideas rather than physical objects. For instance, social media companies are among today's fastest-growing businesses. However, they do not manufacture any products or offer any services in the traditional sense. Instead they offer a way to connect. Products that get the most attention are apps that allow one to entertain oneself, connect, or do something more efficiently or quickly. The consumer is subtly moving away from possessions to experiences.

Even traditional products such as cars and refrigerators are moving in this direction. Google is already a leader in developing a driverless car, but the technology for collision avoidance is already included in some leading car manufacturers' offerings. Connected refrigerators can keep track of your refrigerator's inventory and create automated shopping lists. A wearable fitness device can track your physical activity as well as vital signs such as your heart rate and allow you to compete against your friends for the greatest amount of physical activity within a given period. The connectivity and automation become the selling points rather than the object itself.

New products such as Google Glass or smart watches are also best thought of as ideas and experiences rather than material objects. The selling feature behind both of them is that they offer the possibility of having a constantly connected view of the world. Traditionally, craftsmanship and style were the selling points for objects such as glasses and watches. At least at the current stage of development, the style of wearable tech is less important as a selling point than the experience it offers.

Another development still in its early stages is three-dimensional printing. As the availability of three-dimensional printing increases and its cost decreases, the value placed on ideas and concepts over things will also increase. The influence of offshoring on the diminishing role of manufacturing in Western economies may come to seem trivial compared to the potential transformational effect of three-dimensional printing. As the role of the manufacturer decreases, the importance of ideas and concepts as elements of value correspondingly increases. Blueprints will arise through the wisdom of crowds, enabled by social media rather than through the efforts of highly trained engineers and draftsmen.

The Age of Scalability

With the move toward businesses that are based more on ideas and experiences than on things, there is a related move to the scalability of whatever it is that a business is offering. The value of a new product now increasingly depends on whether it has the potential to "go viral" and scale indefinitely. Given the speed of globalization, the influence of the Internet and social media, and the ascendancy of ideas and experiences over physical products, the potential scalability of products becomes critical.

Perhaps no company has exemplified scalability as much as Amazon. Amazon's business model relies on scale. Amazon created scale by drastically undercutting the prices at which traditional booksellers could offer their products. The early days of Amazon were marked by steep losses. Furthermore, the more Amazon sold, the larger its losses. The joke was that "Amazon lost money on every book they sold, but made it up on volume." Currently, Amazon, although achieving tremendous sales growth, is still eking out a minuscule profit for a company of its size, and this is more than twenty years after going public.

Amazon appears to be on a quest to become the "everything store."[1] It is a pure scalability model. While economies of scale have always been an important competitive factor, the other factors of complexity are driving the importance of scalability to a new level. The search for scalability can be considered to be a proxy for trying to catch an emergent wave. It is the equivalent of breeding butterflies solely to see if a Butterfly Effect in commercial outcomes can be produced. It is seeding an idea in the hope that emergence carries it to profitability.

Big Data

The phenomenon of big data, in large part facilitated by the Internet and the prevalence of social media, is playing a two-part role in the evolution of complexity. First, the use of big data is translating the intuitions and hunches of managers into cold hard statistics. Second, it is modeling tendencies as probabilities. With these probabilities, managers can choose to consider as frequency distributions the random actions of consumers, or they can choose to treat them as non-random clues upon which to construct models of consumer behavior. In either scenario, the role of big data is to diminish the role of the complicated-thinking manager.

Objectifying intuition through the use of big data simplifies and hides what really makes us tick as consumers. It takes frequentist statistics to the maximum. It blends randomness into a series of averages and tendencies that intentionally hide a lot of the randomness and complexity of real life. For scale-oriented companies this is a very useful and efficient thing to do. For small and nimble companies it creates valuable niches to exploit in servicing the randomness or catering to the many who fall outside the averages.

What big data cannot do is imagine and create new trends or new paradigm shifts. Big data might be able to spot a trend but cannot create a trend. Furthermore big data can only say what is, not what is possible. This presents an interesting opportunity for the aspiring complexity thinker. At present there is demand for big data specialists – they are currently among the leaders of the pack in complicated thinking. However, as data are basically available for all, it is very difficult to build a competitive sustainable advantage on big data alone. This creates opportunity for someone with a complexity mindset.

The Age of Complex Problems

Many of the issues facing the world today are complex problems. Climate change, water scarcity, changing demographics, economic stagnation, and a shifting global power landscape are all issues that are complex in nature. These macro issues have the potential to dramatically alter political landscapes, consumer sentiment, and the future of the corporation as we know it.

Perhaps the complex problem that has received the most attention so far is climate change. The underlying science of climate change is in large part based in complexity theory. Most climatologists believe that the global climate is a complex system. The ambiguous nature of the underlying complex science underscores much of the political debate about whether climate change is occurring and what to do about it. Climate change is not only complex in its science, but also in its implications, which are long term, potentially catastrophic, almost completely unpredictable, and politically highly controversial. Climate change can be considered to be composed of a complex soup of issues, of which each of the constituent ingredients is itself complex in nature.

Climate change is an issue that has led to the emergence of new industries (related to alternative sources of energy, for example), new products (electric cars, energy-efficient green buildings), new activities (recycling), new political movements and parties, and changes in consumer attitudes (against large sport utility vehicles, for instance). Climate change is perhaps the current poster-child issue illustrating how the world is becoming more complex. Unfortunately, it appears that management of climate change is being driven by dogmatism, which of course is the antithesis of how one should manage a complex issue.

The availability of fresh water is another complex problem that in part may be linked to climate change. Fresh water is vital not only for drinking and personal use but also for a wide variety of industrial uses. The management and political issues surrounding something as basic as water are extremely complex. Although concern in developed countries has so far been relatively minor, it appears likely that fresh water will become an increasingly major issue in the relatively near future. Several commentators have already compared a potential water shortage with the oil crisis of the 1970s. As with climate change, the emergence of water as a global issue is also increasingly likely.

Demographics by themselves are not complex. By examining birth patterns and mortality rates, we can make quite accurate predictions about the relative sizes of different age groups quite far into the future. The complexity of demographics lies in the unknown implications and impact of the known coming changes in demographics. Most of the developed Western world is dealing with a rapidly aging population that is threatening to put a strain on pensions, elder care, and workforce availability and is already showing signs of changing the political landscape. Meanwhile parts of Asia and the Middle East have the opposite problem; with a disproportionately large number of people under the age of twenty-five, the challenge is to build economies fast enough to ensure meaningful employment for increasing numbers of people of working age. Demographics are also changing the global political sphere and have the potential to shift the balance of power between economies on a global scale. Complexity potentially offers insight into how developing powers such as China and India might play a role as developed economies, and how emergent economies such as those in Africa or the Middle East will evolve.

An additional complex factor is the assumption of continuous growth. Author and economist Jeff Rubin is just one commentator who has argued that the assumption of constant growth is a false one and that companies, industries, consumers, and governments need to be prepared for a world of no or even negative growth.[2] For certain, growth in North America has been stagnant coming out of the 2008 financial crisis.

Japan has gone almost twenty years with anemic growth by its historical standards. In large part, economic growth is (very simply) based on people making things and buying things. However, when ideas and concepts are the consumer goods, there is infinite scalability that can be achieved with little or no economic growth. For instance, for a car manufacturer to make an extra car for sale there needs to be a team of workers to manufacture the car. This is in contrast to a software vendor, who after the initial development stage, has virtually zero production costs and little value added for each additional unit sold.

Limited economic growth has several complex implications. There are political implications as politicians promise voters a complicated view that if elected they can "command and control" growth. There are global implications as centers of growth shift from country to country and from continent to continent. There are also individual and social implications as steady employment becomes a luxury in periods of non-growth.

The current crop of developed countries mainly rose to economic dominance in large part through their technical competence. Perhaps not tomorrow, or even in the next few years, but slowly and surely it is likely that the next societies to become economic powers will do so in large part through their ability to deal with complexity.

Similarly, the manager who relies solely on technical skills is giving way to the manager who can also manage complexity. Earlier it was conjectured that Steve Jobs might not have been nearly as successful working in a factory at the turn of the twentieth century as he was in developing Apple. Likewise, we can conduct an experiment to speculate how well Henry Ford would do in the current business climate. Would Ford's technical skill in engineering and developing the modern factory allow him to produce the next iPhone or Google or Facebook or Uber?

Adjusting to a More Complex Business World

As the world becomes more complex, complexity itself needs to emerge as a field of study, a topic for discussion, and a movement promoting the conscious utilization of complexity techniques. The change in attitudes from complicated thinking to complexity thinking will not happen overnight. The change itself will emerge in its own complex way. That, however, does not mean that there is nothing we can do proactively to facilitate change.

A key way to change mindsets is through education and raising awareness. It is my hope that this book is a positive step in that direction. Awareness by itself is a great complexity-management tool. Once a challenge or an opportunity has been identified, the history of business entrepreneurship has repeatedly shown that it is capable of developing and producing creative and effective solutions. The sole remaining issue is that the solution now needs to arise from complexity thinking rather than complicated thinking.

Shifting to a complexity mindset requires confidence in one's ability and in the benefit of taking chances and accepting risk. It requires an intellect that can repeatedly switch back and forth between complicated thinking and complexity thinking. It is not difficult to do, but it does require a dedicated and conscious effort.

The frameworks within which business is conducted, specifically the political and regulatory environments, also need to evolve. As the financial crisis of 2008 clearly showed, even the best-intentioned regulation will cause adverse unintended consequences if the regulation is constructed in a complicated construct of command and control. More flexible regulation that is based more on the "spirit of the law" rather than the "letter of the law" needs to be encouraged.

Political solutions, as well, need to be more flexible. The trend seems to be more toward right-versus-wrong policies, where in reality the better attitude to adopt might be one of "getting to maybe." Achieving change in the political sphere will be especially difficult, as politics is so closely intertwined with societal attitudes. Perhaps the increasing complexity of some of the issues mentioned earlier in this chapter will help the necessary changes to evolve.

The need for more complexity thinking in the political and societal spheres is a topic for a different book. However, it impacts greatly on business, as increased regulation devised with complicated thinking is doomed to failure in attempting to solve economic issues of a complex nature. Perhaps the change in societal attitudes will come about more easily given how events such as the Occupy and Arab Spring movements rose to prominence through complex leaderless emergence.

The Two Cultures

In 1956, the scientist and writer C.P. Snow wrote an article called "The Two Cultures."[3] The article (later followed by a series of speeches and books) lamented the fact that there was a distinct dichotomy between the world of the scientist and the world of the humanist, particularly in academia. Snow discusses how very few members from either culture can adequately discuss fields other than their own, and observes that members of both cultures appear to have a mutual distrust of and disdain for the other group. As one piece of anecdotal evidence, he points out that academic faculty from the two cultures rarely have lunch together.

Snow's point is not that one of the cultures is superior to the other but instead that the two cultures need one another. Furthermore, for cross-fertilization of ideas to occur, each of the cultures needs to make a conscious effort to understand the other.

In his articles, Snow largely puts the blame for the dichotomy on the academic institutions of the time. In particular, he highlights the differences between the German system, with its emphasis on technical and scientific knowledge, and the upper-class British system, with its emphasis on the humanities. Snow argues that the source of the problem and the solution to the problem lie in education.

What is currently developing in management is also a dichotomy between two cultures – the culture of the complicated thinker and the culture of the complexity thinker. A truly competent manager needs to understand and be proficient in both cultures – analogous to what Snow argued about science and the humanities in 1956.

While this book has focused on the importance of complexity, the intention has not been to dismiss complicated thinking. There is definitely a place for complicated thinking in business and in management, but it has to exist alongside complexity. Likewise, complexity-oriented management cannot succeed on its own without the appropriate use of complicated thinking.

What is happening, though, is the emergence of a relatively small set of complexity thinkers in business, generally concentrated in digital and social media companies, offset by a preponderance of complicated thinkers elsewhere. Furthermore, just as in C.P. Snow's example, the two sides do not appear to be talking to each other, and, even more worrying, are showing signs of mutual distrust and misunderstanding.

In the preface, I described a presentation on complexity in risk management that revealed a division of opinions in the audience. One side was arguing for even more complicated thinking approaches, while the other was arguing for more flexible, intuitive approaches. A heated discussion ensued, with both sides seemingly becoming more polarized and hardened in their positions. It was a case of two cultures clashing, when instead they should have been cooperating and learning from each other.

Snow argued that the source of the problem was in education. The modern professional manager is very likely to have a university education. Education, and business school education in particular, has shown that it is capable of producing complicated thinkers. Can it come up with ways to produce complexity thinkers? The next section introduces one attempt to do so.

An Unstructured Simulation

To change mindsets it is necessary to start with some form of education. The existing paradigm of educating based solely on complicated thinking principles and theories can be not only very limiting but also misleading. Complexity is a concept that may best be grasped through experience rather than taught. The subtleties of complexity certainly are not easily communicated through a traditional lecture format. New methods of getting students and managers to appreciate complexity are needed.

There are several problems with traditional business school pedagogy. The traditional lecture is fine for developing technical knowledge, but technical knowledge is only relevant to the complicated tasks a student may face as a future manager. This type of knowledge is becoming a commodity and increasingly is subject to offshoring and outsourcing to freelancers.

The Socratic case study method, where students are given a real-life business event to analyse, is an improvement on lectures, as students can read about and debate complex, real-world issues. However, a case study is static, backward looking, and does not always fully convey the sense of competition and the resultant adaptive complexity involved. A case study simply cannot convincingly convey the subtleties that lead to complexity and emergence.

To demonstrate the effect of competition, computer simulations have been developed specifically for business school use. While computer simulations introduce an element of competition, they do so in a very linear way. There is no room for innovation, and students often learn more about reverse engineering the algorithm that underlies the computer model than they do about business or true, emergent competition.

In an attempt to overcome the shortcomings of the traditional business school curriculum, my colleagues and I developed what we call an "Unstructured Simulation." The Unstructured Simulation is set up by first assigning students to teams. Each team is then told that they are playing a given role, such as a managerial team, the board of a company, a consulting company, a governmental agency, or perhaps a bank. The roles could be just about any organization or role that impacts an organization's decision making. The key is to include several roles that are competing directly against each other. The teams are given a very brief description of a situation and then left to act out their resulting roles over a two- to three-day period.

The first time we ran the situation at Dalhousie University with a cohort of MBA students, we had ten teams composed of four students each. One team was to play the role of a very powerful but also very publicity-averse private business owner of a large international chain of retail stores of which many were independently owned and operated by franchisees. This particular owner, whose name would not likely be recognized by the students, held all of the voting shares of the company. The chain was under severe competitive threat from Wal-Mart, Target, and several other large global retailers who were expanding their product lines. Another team was directed to play the role of the management of Wal-Mart. A third team was told they were to play the role of the board of the Franchisees' Association.

Seven groups were told that they were to play the role of investment bankers. At the beginning of the simulation, the roles of the groups were kept secret. None of the teams knew what the roles of the other groups were. The only information that the teams were given was the name of a certain individual (the name of the owner of the voting shares of the retail chain) and the fact that there was a rumor in the market that this individual was considering selling the shares. (They were also given the location of a breakout room that they could use for the three-day period of the simulation.) The Wal-Mart group, the Franchisee group, and the group playing the role of the voting shareholder were also told that they could, if they wished, engage the services of an investment bank to help them with whatever decisions they might want to make.

Initially, there was a great deal of confusion among the students. The students initially did not know who the individual was who was considering selling the shares, as the name was not familiar to them. Nor did they know what the immediate implications of the sale of the shares might be. In the simulation set-up, it was an intentional part of the design to create an initial sense of confusion and ambiguity. Real-life business situations rarely come with a specific problem statement, and the first objective was to get the students to ask some intelligent questions. In complex situations, the questions that are asked are generally more useful and valuable than any answers that might be forthcoming.

After the students got past the initial confusion and ambiguity caused by a lack of information and lack of structure, they quickly began to act, and a wonderful emergence soon developed. The investment banks figured out that if the shares were sold then the company would effectively be sold. It was thus an acquisition opportunity, and although there were no students with investment banking experience in the class, they recognized the opportunity to get at least a valuation assignment from the company in question.

It was at this stage that the competition aspect started to become significant. As the investment banking groups approached the company, they quickly learned that other groups were also playing the role of investment banks. Furthermore, the students quickly ascertained that there were more investment banks in the simulation than there were potential clients who would need investment banks. Knowing that their assessment (grade) in the simulation would be dependent on their response, the groups soon quickly intensified their competitive behavior.

After about a day, the shareholder group, the Wal-Mart group, and the Franchisee group had all secured the services of an investment bank. This was preceded by fierce competition among the investment banks. The students literally worked around the clock – just as they might if it were a real-life situation.

The four investment banks that were left out of securing a mandate were at this stage told to assume that they were acting on behalf of another company that might be interested. This meant that the students then had to consider what other companies or organizations might be interested in playing a role in the possible sale of the company. Each of the groups had to check with the facilitator to ensure that the organization they were choosing to represent was not already chosen. This was the only time in the entire simulation that the facilitator played a role other than observer.

The remaining two days were filled with offers and counteroffers. The students competed and tried to negotiate deals, just as they might if they were involved in a real business transaction. The simulation concluded with each of the groups making a final presentation and offer (pitch) to the shareholder group, and the shareholder group concluding with their own presentation outlining their decision about which offer, if any, they would accept.

When the idea for the Unstructured Simulation was first proposed in front of a faculty group, it met considerable ridicule. Most of the faculty members thought we had gone loco. There was a great deal of skepticism that any learning would take place, and doubt that, with such limited guidance, students would by themselves figure out what to do. It was felt that more information and more structure had to be given to the students. It was believed that there would be little to no learning under the proposed minimalist structure. The most common sentiment expressed was that all it would achieve was chaos and a wasted three days that would be better spent in the classroom. Admittedly, I too also believed that there was a very real possibility that the Unstructured

Simulation would be a waste of time and a negative learning experience. We successfully argued, however, that to make it possible for a genuinely emergent learning experience to occur, it was necessary to give the students very minimal guidance. The need for a learning experience that deliberately put the factors for complexity in place for the students to experience was worth the risk of a flop.

From the students' perspective, the Unstructured Simulation was rigorous, taxing, and a fantastic learning experience. For many of the students it was the first time they fully appreciated how the complex adaptive behavior of others made static business theory appear moot and impotent. The most common comment made when we collected feedback was that they had not realized how working under stressful and competitive conditions would make them and others act in ways that they did not expect. The second most common comment was that it was the most memorable and valuable learning experience they had had in all of their schooling. In informal follow-ups five years later the reaction is still much the same, although now they add that it has helped them to look at the real business situations they are facing in a more holistic way and with a complexity mindset. That is what they have found most useful.

When we set up the first Unstructured Simulation, we really had no idea what to expect. Admittedly, it had the potential for disaster. Maybe the students would choose not to compete. Perhaps the students would come to a "solution" almost immediately, rendering most of the scheduled three days a waste of time. There was also a risk that the situation would be so open-ended and ambiguous that the students would be stuck in a hopeless rut from the very beginning and that nothing would happen. We took a risk, and perhaps we got lucky that the learning activity was as exciting and stimulating as it turned out to be. Even after the very successful initial running of the Unstructured Simulation, there remained doubt among our faculty colleagues that it would be a good idea to try it again.

In further Unstructured Simulations that we have run with different cohorts of students the results have overall been very positive, although there have admittedly been a few less successful iterations. Each time we have run an Unstructured Simulation we have used a different business situation – for instance, using a consulting assignment rather than an investment banking assignment. While the results have overall been positive, the main difficulty is that students have gained institutional knowledge about the exercise from their peers. This has reduced the ambiguity of the exercise, and as a result the competition and the emergence that occur take on a slightly different character. The main challenge for us as facilitators is to convince the students that there is no "right" way for them to "perform" in the simulation. It seems the students have an entrenched mindset of searching for a complicated solution when none exists. The students who go into the simulation with a flexible mindset not only tend to do better; they also report more positive learning outcomes.

Skepticism about the value of the Unstructured Simulation remains widespread. After presenting the concept and outcomes of the Unstructured Simulation at several academic conferences, I have noticed that academics are reluctant to believe that such an exercise would work at their institution. In part, this reaction shows the depth to which complicated thinking is the default paradigm for business education and thus illustrates the need for more ideas like the Unstructured Simulation to advance complexity thinking.

Final Thoughts

The aim of this book has been to present the science of complexity in a way that is of use to the business practitioner. A second objective has been to start a conversation about the differences between complicated thinking and complexity thinking. It is hoped that you, the reader, have come away with an appreciation of these differences and of how complexity plays a significant role in your success as a manager and, ultimately, in the success of your organization.

Complexity is a real phenomenon, despite the fact that it perhaps cannot yet be accurately or unambiguously defined. It is playing an ever-increasing role in all parts of modern life, but especially in business, which by its very nature is a competitive and adaptive endeavor.

Complexity is still a developing field. It is much more advanced in some disciplines than in others – for example, in the natural sciences as well as in computing and mathematics. It is hoped that in some small way this book will act as a catalyst to advance the understanding of how to manage complexity in business.

The operating paradigm of the learned in business is that of the complicated thinker. Conversely, the operating paradigm of the learner is complexity. It remains to be seen if you the reader will stick with the traditional reductionist "command-and-control" complicated paradigm or evolve to adopt a complexity-thinking paradigm. The choice is yours. It's not complicated.

NOTES

Preface

1 The name of the student has been changed.

Chapter One

1 It is assumed for this example that this is not a low-level sales call for a product or service, such as a magazine subscription, that could be outsourced to a call center.
2 For some very readable books on complexity, see: Melanie Mitchell, *Complexity: A Guided Tour* (New York: Oxford University Press, 2009); M. Mitchell Waldorp, *Complexity: The Emerging Science at the Edge of Order and Chaos* (New York: Simon and Schuster, 1992); John H. Miller and Scott E. Page, *Complex Adaptive Systems: An Introduction to Computational Models of Social Life* (Princeton, NJ: Princeton University Press, 2009). Interested readers may also want to review the variety of materials and courses available on complexity at the Santa Fe Institute's website: https://www.complexityexplorer.org/.
3 For an interesting look at how computers and robots are fundamentally changing the role of humans in the workplace, see Geoff Colvin, *Humans Are Underrated: What High Achievers Know That Brilliant Machines Never Will* (New York: Penguin Random House, 2015).
4 Perhaps one of the best and most beautiful natural examples of emergence is a murmuration of starlings as they move in unpredictable formations in the sky. The reader may wish to do an Internet search on a murmuration of starlings to view one of the many videos of this remarkable phenomenon posted there.

5 You may have had a chance, as previously mentioned, to view a video of a murmuration of starlings. It is a truly dramatic illustration of complexity and emergence in the natural world.

6 Kurt Vonnegut, Jr., *Player Piano* (New York: Charles Scribner's Sons, 1952).

7 The documentary *Colors of Infinity* by Arthur C. Clarke is an excellent introduction to Mandelbrot diagrams and can be viewed at: https://www.youtube.com/watch?v=pJA8mayMKvY.

8 Scott Page, *Understanding Complexity*. The Great Courses DVD: http://www.thegreatcourses.com/courses/understanding-complexity.html.

Chapter Two

This chapter is based in part on the academic paper R. Nason, "Business School Myths," *Journal of Higher Education Theory and Practice,* 11, 4 (2011): 23.

1 D. Kahneman and A. Tversky, "Prospect Theory: An Analysis of Decision under Risk," *Econometrica*, 47, 2 (1979): 263.

2 It may be hard to realize this if the size of the bet is just one dollar. Ask yourself if you would take the bet if the outcome was that you could win – or lose – a million dollars.

3 S.E. Asch, "Effects of Group Pressure on the Modification and Distortion of Judgements," in H. Guetzkow (ed.), *Groups, Leadership and Men,* 177–90 (Pittsburgh, PA: Carnegie Press, 1951).

4 In chapter 6 we will see that even this assumption is highly questionable when the experience of the developers of the Black-Scholes Option Pricing Formula is discussed.

5 For example, see Geoff Colvin, *Humans Are Underrated: What High Achievers Know That Brilliant Machines Never Will* (New York: Penguin Random House, 2015).

6 See http://www.goodreads.com/quotes/10562-in-times-of-change-learners-inherit-the-earth-while-the.

7 Vanessa Lu, *Toronto Star*, 7 April 2014. Available at: https://www.thestar.com/business/2014/04/07/why_ups_said_no_to_left_turns.html.

8 H. Mintzberg, *The Fall and Rise of Strategic Planning* (New York: Free Press, 1994).

9 R. Rebonato, *Plight of the Fortune Tellers: Why We Need to Manage Financial Risk Differently* (Princeton, NJ: Princeton University Press, 2007).

10 Philip Tetlock and Dan Gardner, *Superforecasting: The Art and Science of Prediction* (New York: Broadway Books/Crown Publishing/ Penguin Random House, 2015).

11 James Surowiecki, *The Wisdom of Crowds* (New York: Doubleday, 2004).

Chapter Three

1 The Heisenberg Uncertainty Principle states that one cannot simultaneously know the position and momentum of a particle to an arbitrary degree of accuracy. The Uncertainty Principle helped to usher in the quantum age and the use of probability to measure certain aspects of subatomic particles versus absolute measurements. The Heisenberg Uncertainty Principle also confirmed that Laplace's belief that one could theoretically know the position and momentum of every particle in the world was not even conceptually possible.

2 Later, in chapter 5, I will discuss how Robert McNamara dramatically changed his views on scientific management and policy analysis, as described in the 2003 documentary *The Fog of War: Eleven Lessons from the Life of Robert S. McNamara.*

3 Tom Wolfe, *The Bonfire of the Vanities* (New York: Farrar Straus Giroux, 1987).

4 Christina Desmarais, "Your Employees Like Hierarchy (No, Really)," Inc.com, 16 August 2012. Available at: http://www.inc.com/christina-desmarais/your-employees-like-hierarchy-no-really.html.

5 P.R. Clance and S.A. Imes, "The Imposter Phenomenon in High Achieving Women: Dynamics and Therapeutic Intervention," *Psychotherapy: Theory, Research and Practice,* 15, 3 (1978): 241–7.

6 Sir Ken Robinson's TED talk can be found at: http://www.ted.com/talks/ken_robinson_says_schools_kill_creativity.

7 For a variety of tasks that were formerly done by professionals but are now done by computers or robots, see Geoff Colvin, *Humans Are Underrated: What High Achievers Know That Brilliant Machines Never Will* (New York: Portfolio/Penguin, 2015).

Chapter Four

1 M. Granovetter, "The Strength of Weak Ties," *American Journal of Sociology*, 78, 6 (1973): 1360–80.

2 Merriam Webster Online Dictionary: http://www.merriam-webster.com/dictionary/emergence.

3 Scott Page, "Understanding Complexity," The Great Courses DVD: http://www.thegreatcourses.com/courses/understanding-complexity.html.

4 May has also written about the role of complexity in business and economics. A particularly interesting and accessible article is Robert M. May, Simon A. Levin, and George Sugihara, "Ecology for Bankers," *Nature*, 451 (21 February 2008).

5 As quoted in Thomas Oliver, *The Real Coke, The Real Story* (New York: Penguin Books, 1986).

Chapter Five

1 Atul Gawande, *The Checklist Manifesto: How to Get Things Right* (New York: Holt, 2009).
2 Ironically, in a game with two perfect tic-tac-toe players, it can be shown that the game will always end in a draw.
3 Eric Ries, *The Lean Start-Up: How Today's Entrepreneurs Use Continuous Innovation to Create Radically Successful Businesses* (New York: Crown Business, 2011).
4 See https://twitter.com/jseelybrown/status/1898163139.
5 For more on the important role that Walther Mayer played in developing the mathematical underpinnings of Einstein's theories, see W. Isaacson, *Einstein: His Life and Universe* (New York: Simon & Schuster, 2007).
6 For instance, see the STEM to STEAM website: http://stemtosteam.org/.
7 Henry Mintzberg, *Managers Not MBAs: A Hard Look at the Soft Practice of Managing and Management Development* (Oakland, CA: Berrett-Koehler, 2005).
8 See http://www.goodreads.com/quotes/10562-in-times-of-change-learners-inherit-the-earth-while-the: accessed 15 December 2016.
9 Rita McGrath, "Management's Three Eras: A Brief History," *Harvard Business Review*, 30 July 2014.
10 Daniel H. Pink, *A Whole New Mind: Why Right-Brainers Will Rule the Future* (New York: Riverhead Books, 2005).

Chapter Six

1 M.E. Porter, "How Competitive Forces Shape Strategy," *Harvard Business Review* (March–April 1979): 137.
2 https://www.brainyquote.com/quotes/quotes/d/dwightdei164720.html: retrieved 15 December 2016.
3 https://www.brainyquote.com/quotes/quotes/h/hochiminh347067.html: retrieved 15 December 2016.
4 Robert S. McNamara, with Brian VanDeMark, *In Retrospect: The Tragedy and Lessons of Vietnam* (New York: Vintage Books, 1966).
5 One clip in the documentary *The Fog of War* records a reporter questioning McNamara on camera and asking him how he felt about being called "an IBM machine with legs."
6 *The Fog of War: Eleven Lessons from the Life of Robert S. McNamara* (2003). Distributed by Sony Pictures Classics.
7 Michael Porter, *Competitive Strategy* (New York: Free Press, 1980).
8 M.E. Porter, *The Competitive Advantage of Nations* (New York: Free Press, 1990).

9 David K. Foot and Daniel Stoffman, *Boom, Bust and Echo: Profiting from the Demographic Shift in the 21st Century* (Toronto: Stoddart, 2001).

10 Peter Schwartz, *The Art of the Long View: Planning for the Future in an Uncertain World* (New York: Doubleday Business, 1991).

11 Henry Mintzberg, "The Fall and Rise of Strategic Planning," *Harvard Business Review* (January–February 1994): 107–14.

12 Ibid., 107.

Chapter Seven

1 Gary E. Porter and Jack W. Trifts, "The Career Paths of Mutual Fund Managers: The Role of Merit," *Financial Analysts Journal* (July/August 2014): 55–71.

2 M. Mitchell Waldrop, *Complexity: The Emerging Science at the Edge of Order and Chaos* (New York: Simon and Schuster, 1992).

3 From the CRISIS homepage: http://www.crisis-economics.eu/.

4 The "burn rate" of a company is how fast it is going through its investment capital in developing a new product or service.

5 Facebook news release, "Facebook to Acquire WhatsApp," 19 February 2014. Available at: http://newsroom.fb.com/news/2014/02/facebook-to-acquire-whatsapp/.

Chapter Eight

1 Peter L. Bernstein, *Against the Gods: The Remarkable Story of Risk* (New York: Wiley, 1996).

2 F. Black, "How We Came Up with the Option Formula," *Journal of Portfolio Management*, 15, 2 (1989).

3 F. Black and M. Scholes, "The Pricing of Options and Corporate Liabilities," *Journal of Political Economy*, 81, 3 (1976).

4 R. Lowenstein, *When Genius Failed: The Rise and Fall of Long-Term Capital Management* (New York: Random House, 2000).

5 Black, "How We Came up with the Option Formula."

6 A particularly interesting and readable survey of the psychology of risk is given by Dan Gardner in his book *Risk: The Science and Politics of Fear* (Toronto: McClelland and Stewart, 2008).

7 For a very readable account of Black Swan effects see Nassim N. Taleb, *The Black Swan: The Impact of the Highly Improbable*, 2nd ed. (New York: Random House, 2010).

8 R. Nason, "Is Your Risk System Too Good?," *RMA Journal* (October 2009).

 9 R. Rebonato, *Plight of the Fortune Tellers: Why We Need to Manage Financial Risk Differently* (Princeton, NJ: Princeton University Press, 2007).
10 K. Hawley, "Why Airport Security Is Broken – And How to Fix It," *Wall Street Journal*, 14 April 2012.
11 The full COSO Enterprise Risk Management Framework is available on the COSO website at www.coso.org.
12 For a readable explanation of Gaussian copulas and their role in the financial crisis, see Felix Salmon, "Recipe for Disaster: The Formula That Killed Wall Street," *Wired*, 23 February 2009.

Chapter Nine

1 Brad Stone, *The Everything Store: Jeff Bezos and the Age of Amazon* (New York: Little, Brownzx /Back Bay Books, 2013).
2 Jeff Rubin, *The End of Growth* (New York: Random House, 2012).
3 C.P. Snow, "The Two Cultures," *New Statesman*, 6 October 1956.

INDEX